21 Days with Braco

21 Days with Braco

ANGELIKA WHITECLIFF

AWAKENING WITHIN
Kealakekua, Hawaii, USA

21 Days with Braco

Published by Awakening Within
PO Box 2013
Kealakekua, HI 96750
USA

ISBN: 978-0-9842970-0-9

Library of Congress Control Number: 2009910838

Printed in the USA

Cover Design, Sareighn

Publisher's Website: www.AwakeningWithin.us

For Braco

You gave me back my dearest hopes and dreams, and the strength to fulfill them.

The author wishes to thank Dr. Michael Salla, her partner in life whose love and support was a beacon of light from the first time they met, and who edited this book with confidence and belief in its success. She also wishes to thank Charlene Nevill for her conviction and confidence that a book was meant to be written, Monica Robles for her friendship and love through the years, and Mrs. Elrick, her high school English teacher who first encouraged her to become a writer.

CONTENTS

PROLOGUE

Through the eons, great struggles, strife and chaos within countries and civilizations have driven the people to cry out, into the very depths of the collective psyche for a solution. And so great leaders, teachers and unifiers emerged to answer that call; created and forged by the common need led by the greater destiny of an age. In the present, an awakening is taking place within us on a vast scale, an unprecedented call to a more spiritually connected life, a reconnection back to nature, our hearts and each other across the globe as one human family. In the United States, the self-help movement, alternative healing, environmental activism, new energy research and a call for peace is rising in strength.

Our collective minds and hearts are calling out for help and action to survive the ills we have inflicted upon each other and our natural world. And the numbers are growing of people interested in rising to the challenge of righting the imbalances before it is too late. We are in an age of awakening and transformation, this is our current destiny, and our stalwart calls together stem from our intuitive inspirations generated here. The boundaries our minds so easily place have shackled us, and now it is our hearts and intuition that break us free of such confinement. For our hearts and spirits know our deepest wishes and incorruptibly hold steadfast in a greater understanding that all things are possible, even beyond the ideas of our minds.

Hope is calling out from our unbounded hearts for a miracle to change things for the better, for a new strength and clarity than can give us the ability to help ourselves - back into balance with all things. And the uniquely made solution delivered in answer to this sincere call comes back to us from that greater source that is 'All'.

Beyond body, mind and spirit, it can deliver the gift satisfying the collective need in the most unexpected of ways.

I have met a man from Croatia who has been helping the people of the Balkans, and many countries in Europe for the last 14 years, who I believe has a monumental role to play in this world. In fact, he not only represents a tremendous opportunity to the people, but that precise solution called for by the collective masses wishing for a dramatic change toward more happiness, peace and balance in our world. His name is simply Braco, and in his native tongue this means 'little brother'. He is normal like us, one of us, but he has manifested an exceptional gift through his gentle gaze alone that represents a key. A key that awakens, transforms and heals not only the ills of a body, but of lives - which have been disconnected from that inner illumination of strength, determination and purpose.

Braco is a great catalyst and the gift of energy that comes through his gaze can spontaneously reconnect people back to themselves, to source, to that inner illumination, to wellness. This is what makes all things possible, that special knowing within that can unlock the shackles of the mind and conventional limitations that stop us from healing our bodies and our lives. There have been saints, sages, yogis, prophets and healers through the ages who have performed healing miracles. Braco too has to his credit meter tall stacks of verified cases of miraculous healings from incurable diseases, illnesses and injuries from those who have come to attend his gazing sessions for the public. But Braco does not fit into any of these categories, he is a man who lives with a sincere love of nature and the people, a normal family man who has devoted his life to a mission to better peoples lives.

Healer is the term often associated with Braco, but his ability to heal not only the body, but also a person's life difficulties raises him beyond this classification. Never would Braco call himself a healer, but for a different reason. He is not here to heal the people, he instead has chosen to serve without restraint that which we can only call the divine will. It alone gives the gift through him and decides what form it will take in a person's life. And it answers the call of the wishes of our hearts, not our minds. No part of him is withheld from this service and perhaps this is why he has been chosen to deliver this gift to humanity. The responsibility of such a commitment is immeasurable.

Not all who come to Braco are healed and this is because we all have the free will to deny entrance to our hearts and wishes. We can close ourselves to our world and possibilities, blocking our own heart's expression - this is our great choice in the world. But for most a feeling of positive, good energy and something more takes place in his gazing sessions. An inner light is turned back on and the impossible or insurmountable fades, answers to challenges arise within as we find our own solutions, and so bodies heal, sometimes miraculously and instantaneously. Many times people feel compelled to come back and it takes a few sessions before the healing takes place, but that is because of the individual, not the energy, or this would be true for all. Our hearts only need to be open to accept that a gift without a price can be real.

For the last 14 years, Braco has worked solely in the Balkans and parts of Europe, and hundreds of thousands of people have come to visit him each year to experience the power of his gaze. This has happened by word of mouth, Braco does not give interviews to press, speak in public or advertise. A foundation for his work has been laid in his homeland and he is loved, honored and respected as he works tirelessly to see all who visit. Yet Eastern and parts of Western Europe still hold dear certain traditional values that border on tribalism. There is still much jealousy against those who rise up and succeed within a community.

This is different in America, which honors and respects individuals who achieve. European mindset is also very linear and oriented around the conventionally scientific. It tends to define according to social normality and conventions. Yet it will accept the idea of a saint or savior because the church traditions are inextricable interwoven and cast here. These factors confine him. The phenomenon of Braco's gaze cannot at this infancy of our sciences be explained by the standard knowledge or linear thought. He is not a saint saving the people. Outside these governing parameters, Braco needs a different fertile soil to grow the gift and his legacy within.

Even he himself knows soon he must leave the Balkans and Europe to find a new home to reach to the world.

I believe Braco must come to the United States to fulfill his expansive mission. He will be tried and tested as all are here, but his results will be his measure, and through this he will be recognized for his contribution to the upliftment of the people. American consciousness is ready to awaken and transform, to heal and help the world by its own example. Our people are searching for new ways to be self-empowered, and value those who conquer their challenges to make good in the world. It is the land of opportunity, the land where you make it by your own hand and hard work. Even if someone succeeds and then falls because of their shortcomings, we will forgive them if they take responsibility and applaud them when they rise high again with newfound humility.

America is the new world, the hope, and the people value and treasure ingenuity and endless possibilities. We help ourselves. This is why I believe Braco must make his way here now, the time and consciousness is ripe, for something greater in this world to unfold, for a solution to rise to the surface and be seen by all. Together more and more people look for positive change and seek a deeper inner connection to help in their own ways to better their communities, the nation and the world. I have seen a possibility that awes me, and my wish is that this book can offer a glimpse of a solution before us now that can lead to a future for us and our children to live in a world of balance and joy because we are empowered to make this a reality.

Destiny is calling. To reach it, we must reconnect to nature, become child-like again in our spontaneity and love of simple pleasures, simplify our lives and reorganize our values to step away from our consumer driven ways to embrace an integrity of connection to the spirit within; to family, communities and our world. I have met a man whose loving gaze can bring alive the very qualities that difficulties and challenges can strip away, who can catalyze healing and a sense of wholeness in an individual that does not diminish with time. Destiny is calling, and it is offering us opportunity, a gift to have back our happiness and strength, and it has come in the most unexpected of ways.

Braco

Ivica Prokic

Angelika Whitecliff

INTRODUCTION

"He who would save the world must be one with the world" – *Sri Aurobindo*

Why do we allow our hopes and finest dreams to be striped from our grasp as life moves forward with our destiny to fulfill? As children no mountain is too high to climb, for no limit to our possibilities yet wounds us into believing we are somehow not worthy enough to have satisfied our sweet, innocent wishes. Yet our chaotic world soon crashes in upon our joy and can dampen our enthusiasm with problems and challenges that take our breath away. Our civilization does not teach us how to harmonize with nature, how to treat each other as beloved brethren seeking a common happiness. Instead isolation and distractions fill us with a self-regulated weakness that slowly or quickly can drain our best away.

What seems to be lost, however, only has faded into slumber awaiting the promise of a new sunrise. The time of darkness, like the night, is only temporary because the sun can never be held back from a new day, a new hope and a new possibility to nourish a breakthrough, even permeating hardened ground that contains our seedling essence striving to burst forth into the fulfillment of our divinely crafted form. No matter how broken or damaged the soil around us, we are indestructible seedlings that ever contain the template and capacity to come fully to bloom.

I have witnessed a new possibility on this planet in a way completely unexpected, through a man whose gaze reflects this awakening glory of our sun's light . . .

Twenty-one days in the company of Braco, a man from Croatia with a gift of energy that heals and defies scientific understanding and human comprehension at this time, has shown me an opportunity for humankind that is nothing less than divinely magnificent. The question is only if we are ready as a species to accept this gift that is offered to us now that spans beyond our conventionally accepted normality. Are we ready to open our hearts without the boundaries our minds so easily impose to become childlike again in our ability to receive nourishment freely offered as our birthright? This is our great challenge today as we stand at the precipice of the destruction of our world, rendered by our own hands through our fears and manmade contrivances that place us out of balance with the natural world.

Meeting Braco

I first heard about Braco in January 2009 when my friend and colleague, Italian photojournalist and Exopolitical researcher, Paola Harris, sent me an email to let me know that a very special person was coming to a prestigious UFO/paranormal conference in the Las Vegas area that February for his first visit to the United States. She wrote:

> "I 'd like you to see Braco from Croatia (Zagreb). He heals with a glance. He had over 10,000 people see him in Switzerland. A professor speaks for him although he speaks English well. Drago Plecko, the professor, knew Andrija Puharich, MD (Croatian also) who discovered Uri Geller.
>
> Braco does not talk but he has a particular vibration.
>
> It will be interesting for you." – Paola (January 26, 2009)

Along with this short note she attached a picture of Braco. When I saw his photo, something lit up inside of me. An excitement instantly made my heart happy and I could not stop staring at him. Recognition of something profound took place in my spirit although my mind could not grasp beyond a desire to meet this man. I decided that day to book an airline ticket to fly from my home in Hawaii to Laughlin, Nevada for this one-week conference event. My only motivation was a strong feeling I had that Braco was somehow completely unique.

Next I began my research to learn more about this healer who came from the region formerly known as Yugoslavia, an area from which many exceptional healers had emerged through the centuries. Without explanation, the abilities displayed by certain healers out of Russia and Eastern Europe were incredibly dramatic. Braco came from perhaps one of the most strife-ridden places on the planet like a balancing beacon of light into a stronghold of racial and religious violence.

I discovered a website about Braco and read every page, watched a You Tube video about him online and read all the personal accounts I could find in which people reported the stories of their own healing experiences. Over 220,000 people had come in 2008 alone to see Braco either at his Center, Srebrnjak 1, in the city of Zagreb, or to a tour event in Germany, Austria, Switzerland and other Balkan countries. Numerous people wrote of experiencing not only miraculous cures from serious illnesses and injuries, but also of their lives improving in all ways imaginable.

My enthusiasm continued to build as I validated my own initial reaction and confirmed the potency of the gift this man was bringing to the people. At the conference registrations desk, there was a sign-up sheet for Braco's healing sessions limited to fifty people each day. I was the first person to signed up for all seven days, determined to experience to its fullest whatever was present here.

My first encounter with Braco's gift of healing energy did what I had imagined to be impossible. It gave me back my abandoned dreams, hopes and finest aspirations for this life and something much more - the very strength to make such things a reality. I felt an energy pouring down on my head and in my hands and this was very tangible. More fascinating, I instantly recognized a profound shift within myself that gave me room to breath a fresh breath of life.

In my travels around the world over the last twenty years, visiting with healers, shaman and spiritual leaders across the United States, Europe, Japan, Mexico, South America and the Philippines to explore and promote the work of a transformation in consciousness, I had never encountered an individual with such power. Many good healers could help people with different levels of problems, yet Braco had delivered a light into my spirit that opened the door to a wholeness I found completely astonishing. My experience was like flying, soaring to the heights with uncontained joy.

A light entered me in Braco's presence that filled me with a new foundation that could not be taken from me - of this I was absolutely certain. During his gazing sessions, I felt everything changed for the better in my life and in the next five months until an unexpected gift brought me back to see him again, I found my new strength no longer allowed life's challenges to rob me of my natural happiness. Something was now alive in me that I had never experienced before that helped me to face everything with a new empowerment and a greater certainty.

He did this so simply, so gracefully. Braco never spoke nor laid his hands upon anyone to help them. Silently, peacefully, he gazed softly before groups for the duration of five to ten minutes while people stood in front of him. No religious or spiritual belief was encouraged or required. One did not need to accept nor understand the power behind Braco's gaze, nor would he ever ask anyone to revere or worship his unique ability. He would not allow himself to become anyone's guru. His gift could work despite even doubts, yet an open heart could enhance it - a willingness to feel, to be receptive to new possibilities.

I received more than my mind conceived to ask for in my first gazing session with Braco. In hindsight, I expected something quite small, relative to what my mind thought was within reach, but my heart innocently wished for more and it was granted. The human will meant nothing to that unnamable *Source* behind his gaze for our wills were governed by our naïve and chaotic minds. It was the innocent, childlike wish that meant everything and opened the doorway to all possibilities. The word 'wish' was one that would come up often in future conversations.

After the second session with Braco and each day after, I felt that energy grow within me to take on a vibrant life of its own to help me in all ways. My friend Paola introduced me to Braco after that first morning and I saw a possibility and jumped. I asked Braco if he would come to a conference in Hawaii that I would arrange according to his schedule of availability. In those moments of our meeting, I was inspired and instantly decided to do my fourth *Earth Transformation Conference* event, which I had co-organized with the help of my partner, Michael Salla, in previous years. It offered an education to improve people's lives, and now I saw a truly awesome potential to bring his energy not only to my beloved home, but to share it with the many who would come from far and wide.

Hawaii was like a siren's song, a destination of such beauty and attraction that few turned down its melody of invitation. And when Braco told me of his love of the ocean and all the creatures of the sea, I knew my location was an added sweet enticement. I spoke to him of our ways that honor nature and trips to swim with wild dolphin pods off the shores of our coast. The Big Island was also located at a 19.5 latitude on the globe, a power spot of great significance that had birthed the spirit of Aloha, the spirit of love, governing our shores.

To my surprise, Braco told me he would check with his staff on dates for his availability, probably in January 2010, and get back to me. Later I heard that Braco was booked four years in advance and he was rearranging some plans to come to Hawaii. By the next day he gave me dates for January and now all I had to do was to build another conference, this time interweaving a healing theme that I knew would offer more than ever before. Without looking back, I plunged forward and thought I would not see Braco again until almost one year later in the beginning of the next year.

Yet that active light within me had other plans in store. Soon after Laughlin, my partner was invited to give a lecture on Exopolitics at a conference in Barcelona, Spain that July. Two months before this departure, I had the wish to once again see Braco and hoped that while in Spain, Braco would be on tour in a nearby country so I could attend a gazing session again. In the end this did not work out, but I continued to hope for an opportunity. And then in June I received an email unexpectedly that Braco wished to speak over the phone with me.

At a prearranged time Braco called and he immediately invited me to come to Croatia to visit his Center, Srebrnjak 1, and to join him on tour so that I could see how such events were set up, and perhaps learn how to present him to audiences at events. It was also an opportunity for me to write articles about his work for my online newspaper column with the *Examiner,* and to begin to tell the American people about this type of transformative work. This invitation was simple and generous. He wanted to know if I could come right away and because of my travel to Barcelona, he spontaneously decided I would be with him for a total of twenty-one days so that I could then go directly to my other event afterwards and meet my partner.

At the time, Braco's invitation was a complete surprise, yet I did not need to give it a moment's thought; I knew with a certainty that it was the opportunity of a lifetime and my *yes* was without pause. Afterwards, my mind was reeling with all the things I had to do to prepare to leave my office for a total of one month with my Barcelona excursion included, but I would have moved a mountain and felt the strength to do so. Since I had met Braco, I had told all my dearest friends that I had met a man who embodied something great for this world. When I talked about him, my enthusiasm was without end.

In a week and a half I was on a plane to Croatia to travel to the other side of the globe from my home. I would later learn that Braco lived with a rare spontaneity in all things and his ability to move quickly with an inspiration and opportunity was without hesitation. He sent my air ticket to Europe and my connections to his tour destinations. As my host, he would look after me with a splendid generosity and care that was beyond all expectations. Excited by the idea that no one before had spent so long a period of time in his company like this, he was certain it would be a worthy venture.

Impressively, I would not only have my wish to attend Braco's gazing session again, but I would be at his side for three weeks. So begins the real story . . .

About this Book

Braco himself gave me only one constraint for this book. I was told that I would not be able to quote him directly. Instead, this story is meant to be an introduction to life as Braco lives it, with stories about him and interviews from his parents, best friends and those who have worked for years at his Center, Srebrnjak 1. My travels with Braco allowed me the opportunity to see sides of him never yet written about. Conveyed are my direct experiences and observations of Braco after working side-by-side, from early morning until days end, often with only a few hours sleep due to the demanding travel schedule for the gazing sessions in multiple countries.

A special doorway was opened for me so that in the end, I could share the story of the real man behind the miracles, and I hoped that it would help others to understand why he is the one who must carry this great gift and responsibility. Along the way, I spoke with people who came for Braco's gazing sessions from many countries and from all circumstances of life. I encountered the boundless nature of this energy he shared so completely. An energy that created healing miracles for people not only with severe illnesses of the body, but with the deepest problems and challenges of life that render an individual helpless in relationships, work, money, family and all the difficulties a life may bring.

All these factors demonstrate the foundation and background of an unusual man, and this book is written to bridge the way for Braco and his work to be understood by a new audience. In a profound way, I myself am still working to penetrate the mysteries of this special man who represents a step forward for humanity. He is a peaceful man who lives by example, not by mere words and intellectual concepts. An intimate love of nature and the simple joys of life, friends and family infuse him with a vibrancy of being that stand him apart from the confusions of the modern psyche and mode of living.

Braco's gift is one that I do not believe can ever be taught to others. This is because this is a gift to the world from the divine *Source*, and only it can choose the perfect vessel for such an expression of energy. It is a gift so precious and rare that it cannot be held without perfect balance and if the balance if ever lost, so is the gift. Therefore the responsibility is beyond comprehension, and must be served with an entirety of spirit and service that is just as rare and precious.

To possess this gift is to serve life itself without personal concern or conceit. Perhaps in concept we are all capable of aspiring to this service, but in actuality few can achieve within this lifetime such heights because the work demands absolutely everything without reserve. Fortunately, we do not need to take such a labor upon ourselves. The gift is here and freely offered to all who will come to only experience its possibilities. This is exquisitely and precisely enough to create the transformation we all innocently wish so dearly for in our hearts together.

Part One

Braco & Ivica

Viktor, Josip (Braco) and Ivanka Grbavac

Braco at Age 9   *Braco at Age 32*

Braco Parents: Ivanka & Viktor

Braco & Angelika, Island of Trogir   *Braco's Friend Ivan*

Braco's friend Nikica with Viktor, Island of Trogir

Franka and Mate, proprietors of the Hotel Pasike Restaurant, with Braco – Island of Trogir

Braco reading his father's story for this book

Anya, Angelika, Braco, Dragana & Marjana in Ljubliana, Slovenia

Braco, Adriatic Coast

Chapter One

Day 1 – Monday, June 29, 2009

Reunion with Braco

Adventures of travel and new destinations had always fed my spirit and a childlike fearlessness within awaited new sensations and experiences. Exotic languages and cultures were marvels, so I embraced what was before me without hesitation over unknowns. Eastern Europe and the Balkans were an enigma to me, and the bitter past conflict between Serbia and my destination of Croatia an unseen shadow. As an American researcher, all I could think about was entering Braco's mysterious world. I would have ventured into any alien territory for this experience, and fortunately fate arranged magnanimously something exceptional.

As I flew for more than twenty hours with many plane changes from Hawaii to my destination, I thought about something Drago Plecko, the paranormal researcher who gave a presentation on Braco at the Laughlin conference, had told me. He stated that Braco's mentor, Ivica of Serbia, had prophesied well over a decade ago that Braco would not set foot on U.S. soil until a great change of consciousness had taken place in the American psyche. It was no coincidence to me that Braco came to the United States only one month after the newly elected President, Barack Obama, took office. This event heralded a new direction chosen by a constituency claiming a vibrant possibility for a better future. I wondered how far this change could go and its connection to my journey ahead? America had taken a step in readiness; perhaps it could support the gift Braco had to share.

I arrived at Zagreb airport without much sleep and no luggage to welcome me. A filmmaker, Sead, his female assistant, and Damir, a quite man with a sweet smile, met me outside of customs and a microphone and was immediately held to me with a video camera filming. I was asked to talk about my journey and impressions, which took me quite by surprise. Yet in the spirit of the moment I did my best to be composed despite my travel worn appearance, and made a short speech before asking for assistance with my errant baggage. With Kindness, Damir, Sead and his assistant were understanding and helped me to fill out a report, while promising all would be looked after. Together, we then embarked off to Srebrnjak 1, a place with a very special history I would later learn.

While driving I was told that a taped statement I had given about my experience in Braco's gazing sessions at the Laughlin conference had been put into Sead's newest film about Braco's visit to America. I was amazed and delighted to be already a part of my new world in this small way. Soon, I would be further startled when a few people would recognize me from this film that was already being marketed in DVD form. Here I would learn that all inspired projects moved quickly to fruition at Srebrnjak 1, guided by a tangible spontaneity.

Zagreb was a city of mild character, mixed architecture, and like most European cities, it boasted a great park that people actively used for walks, gatherings and events. Upon arrival to the Center, we first walked past the impressive, three-story building to a back garden of vibrant green bamboo. Oddly, it reminded me of the many bamboo forests of the Hawaiian Islands, and I found out that it was planted according to Braco's vision. Despite being told that he was crazy to place such flora in the regional climate, he had it planted. And it thrived, tall and lush, with a stone pathway that wound through the grove to a large bamboo gazebo. Here Braco was seated on a sea grass cushion, and the surroundings clearly portrayed his love of nature and simple beauty.

He rose with a warm smile when he saw me, and we embraced in a greeting of delight. I was made to feel completely welcomed by his open happiness and refreshments were brought. Standing before him, I enjoyed something I had experienced in his presence in Laughlin; I felt stronger to my very core. It was as if a light had been turned up inside of me suddenly, and I was more present. An energy that flowed through and around him awakened this unknown potential within me, and just being near him was enough. There was no denying this tangible effect and for the rest of the day, I would be active without any sign of jet lag. In fact, I rarely would experience tiredness at all during my stay despite a rigorous work schedule, and many conversations and gatherings that lasted late into the nights.

The day was almost hot in that morning hour, but he looked fresh and relaxed, with a wise innocence. Long brown hair framed his boyish face with premature, but fitting grey streaks at his temples, and I wondered if the grey was a sign of the responsibility he carried. Braco appeared part youth, part timeless man at his 42 years of age. Over the weeks ahead I would watch his face change dynamically to accentuate the diversity of his many character traits and inner spiritual expressions.

Braco's Beginning

In that first conversation, there was an effortless intimacy as Braco told me about his childhood and the beginnings of his work. Without hesitation, he was candid and forthright. I learned that he was born in November 1967, as the only child to loving parents with an extremely close bond to his father. As a boy he spent much time alone fishing and enjoying nature. He was normal in all ways and went to university to study economics, like his father, and earned a Masters degree in business finance at the age of 24. As is typical in European culture, he continued to live at home, spent most of his time in Zagreb and never left Croatia. His parents had a summer home in a seaside village on the Adriatic, and here he spent time as well. Those material things most people crave, including the sport cars and the comforts of a wealthy family, were all his.

He would work for the police ministry for a short time as an investigator of corruption, but soon left when he found the police to be as corrupt as those criminals he sought out. Next he started his own company and began to achieve success, but soon all was to change. His meeting with a healer and prophet from Serbia, Ivica Prokic, who was working and living in Zagreb, would change the course of his life permanently. Braco had never been interested in healing or spiritual subjects. Yet on a fancy, after reading a book by Ivica bought by his mother, he decided to accompany her for a visit to this healer.

He did not have an illness or issue to heal as a reason for going, only an excited curiosity, and he ended up sitting all day in the healer's home while Ivica saw the crowd of people, one-by-one, who had come with their many problems seeking help. Because he felt so peaceful just sitting there, Braco chose to miss a business appointment that afternoon, and continued to wait for his turn - he was last. Braco was 26 years old at this first meeting in the autumn of 1993 with the person who would become his mentor, his friend and to whom he would one day become successor. Because of Braco's closeness to his father, this new relationship and change of priorities caused many difficulties between them.

Braco's father, Viktor Grbavac, had a very strong reaction to Braco's interest in Ivica and hardships followed because of his fears. His son was walking away from him and all his material gains, and this to him was as abnormal as the new peaceful quiet his son had begun to exhibit at home. Viktor even asked his wife, Ivanka, what Ivica had done to their son? First hiding from his parents, even his girlfriend, his daily visits to Ivica after that first meeting, Braco clearly knew those closest to him would not understand his choices, but soon he shared the truth.

His mother was at first afraid because Braco was treading into unknown territory, and since he did not come home regularly as before, she was fearful for his future. However, she was not afraid of Ivica, she even liked the healer, but she saw she was losing her son and was very concerned. After about a week, Braco told his parents that he was leaving everything, including his business and them, to be with Ivica. Immediately his mother began crying and his father became angry. Braco had spent all his spare time with his father since boyhood, so they were both deeply shocked. Yet the young man soon turned away from the distress of his parents, because his love for Ivica quickly grew so strong that it superseded even that which he felt for his parents. Filled with worry, Viktor hired a detective agency to follow Braco, to find out what his son was doing. He would also blame his wife for a while for taking their son to Ivica in the first place.

It became apparent to me that Braco came to love Ivica as far more than a friend, but as someone who represented an authentic and rare light of hope in this world. The impression left was indelible. Ivica did not charge people money for his prophecy and healing work, he simply was there to help the people and that was that. He looked at all people as the same; whether poor, young or old, ugly or beautiful, and he treated them all as equals. This philosophy of giving all without hesitation or asking for something in return would deeply affect Braco. Initially, it did not impact him as a healer, because Braco never performed any healings while Ivica was alive. Yet there was a bond of spirit, which led this young man to find a new peace within himself and something much, much more.

Viktor had known his son's full attention and devoted love from childhood. Suddenly everything changed as Braco chose instead to spend all his time with Ivica. A powerful businessman and well respected in the community, Viktor was able to use his power, now in anger, to stop his son the only way he knew how - by having him conscripted into the army. This was during the war between Croatia and Serbia, and although Braco's education level would exempt him from combat, this was still a drastic and harsh action that could have led to a severe fate if the war had escalated and such rules changed.

In the army, Braco immediately refused gun-training exercises after only three or four days, because he abhorred them. This led to his imprisonment for refusing an order, and during this incarceration, he refused to eat. As a consequence, he was transferred to a hospital where he was fed intravenously. A hospital psychiatrist saw him there and the doctors gave him medication, which he flushed down the toilet after they left. When his parents visited him, they asked him why he would not eat since he had everything - a good education, a good job, money and a girlfriend? With serious resolution and heartfelt conviction, Braco made it clear that if he could not be with Ivica, he would rather die.

Braco immediately escaped out a hospital window and went to Ivica. The healer urged him to return to his own life because his father was crazed over the situation, and he himself had people to help. Braco agreed but felt that he was no longer responsible for his actions and had the thought of not wanting to live. Ivica sensed the depths of Braco's feelings and suddenly changed his mind, telling Braco to stay. Even though the healer worried greatly for Braco's life, now filled with unhappiness because of their meeting, he said that he would help his young friend.

Ivica told Braco to go back to the hospital because the police would be called, and he promised he would come that very night at 8 pm to visit. Braco agreed and then had the challenge of getting back into his room unnoticed, but it was too late. He arrived back to find police already present and angry. Yet Braco told them boldly that he had been with Ivica, and no one could stop him from going again. His father was there too, and a discussion ensued in which he finally relented in the face of his son's determination.

It was decided that Braco would only have to stay at the hospital a few more days to finish the appropriate paperwork, which would allow him to be legally discharged from the hospital and army service. At 18 year of age in Croatia, all men had to go into the army for one year. Braco had gone, but was diagnosed with hepatitis and sent home after three days. In one year he had to go back, but since he was in school, he was excused again. Fate had stepped in twice and Braco's feelings against guns and shooting people, and being taught to react this way, was not forced upon him.

That night, Ivica came as promised, and they took the elevator to different floors, searching for a quiet place to talk, and finally ended up in the morgue until the early morning hours. Soon after, Braco's father had a talk with Ivica, and said it was all right for his son to see him. Viktor thought the fascination would dwindle for his son. Then his father began to meet with Ivica regularly, and the healer came to Viktor and Ivanka's home. Ivica would tell Braco that his father failed to believe in their work, but he came because it was the only way to communicate with his son. The healer also said his father did what he did out of love and concern to protect his only offspring.

After Ivica died and Braco stepped forward to continue the work, his father thought people would stop coming. After a year, he still hoped that people would lessen and finally stop. Today, Braco's father believes even more than his mother in his work. Viktor could now deeply see and respect the changes that took place in Braco, and though he was still a little afraid, he had found respect. Overcoming his own ignorance and expectations for his son, Viktor finally was able to see something more within Braco's chosen life and work.

It was Ivica who gave the young man who gave up everything to be at his side his spiritual name, Braco, currently known solely to most. The day he proclaimed it he said all would use this new name, which in Croatian meant 'little brother'; except for his parents who would be the only ones to continue to use his birth name, Josip. Ivica stated many prophecies, and he had an acute accuracy for detail in foretelling past, present and future. He said that Braco would not only be his successor one day, but that multitudes would visit him at Srebrnjak 1, and after that the world would come in unending masses to see him.

Born in Serbia, Ivica would come to Croatia to do his prophetic healing because he understood that a prophet could never work in his birth land, and prosper there. The same holds true for Braco, and his real work begins once he leaves Croatia to live elsewhere in the world. In Laughlin, Braco spoke of a dream image he had of a place rich with nature, where people lived naturally, with homes of wood in lush foliage and a vast expanse of water. At the time, I informed him that perhaps it was Hawaii, my own beloved home, and because of the obvious similarities, I described it in detail with excitement.

The Center, Srebrnjak 1

That morning conversation included an animated chat about the beauties and uniqueness of Hawaii again, a place like no other on earth where people ate fresh fruits off the abundant mango, papaya and banana trees that were found everywhere. Braco's eyes lit up as I described the very spiritual and non-material attitudes of the people of my island home, and I wished again that his dream would match this reality when he finally came to visit. Prior to my coming, in our short phone conversation, he had told me I would deliver a message to the people in the Balkans to prepare them for his leaving of Europe. I did not fathom the role he wished me to play at the time, but I would soon walk into it full force in that first week.

Later, Ivica's story would unfold in greater detail in the weeks ahead and I would come to know this extraordinary man through his deeds and actions. A temperamental man who always stated things plainly and honestly, without the embellishments and niceties we often mask our words with in western society, Ivica was like a force of nature - wild, free-spirited and with a god-given power used wholeheartedly in the service to others. It seemed that Braco and Ivica were one soul in two bodies; now one seen and the other still vividly present, but unseen.

As we talked in the shade, one of the many staff members at Srebrnjak 1 came to let Braco know that a group of people was ready for his gazing session. When he was not touring other countries, Braco had four regularly scheduled days a week at his Center open to all who came to see him without charge. Sessions would occur all day long on the hour or half hour depending on the amount of people who came that day. Sometimes there were large buses that pulled up from other countries that had traveled all night. Branko, a trusted staff member and devoted friend, was the person responsible for all security. He was a retired police chief for all of Zagreb, and had once helped Ivica get out of prison during communist days when spiritual healing and prophecy were a state crime. Although he did not speak English, he seemed to understand some words and had been listening to part of our conversation. Now he rose to escort Braco and I from the bamboo garden into a room built especially to hold the energy of the work.

Braco never walked anywhere without at least one or two staff members at his side on tour or at Srebrnjak 1. His popularity and the high volume of people in constant flow around him made it essential to have this assistance at his side. Otherwise he could not move around freely without being mobbed or grabbed by the countless people who wanted to express their gratitude. In general, he did not talk to anyone but his staff. Long ago his words had been taken without permission and altered by the media that did not understand his method of helping the people, so Braco had decided to let his work alone speak for itself. Braco has never given an interview to the press or media, despite the advantages to doing so now.

The gazing room was like a sacred shrine, beautifully crafted, floor to ceiling, out of polished slabs of yellow onyx. This was Braco's vision and he spared no expense to have it built this way. It inspired awe to enter the giant, carved wood doors and walk into this chamber. We arrived at a back entrance while the crowd waited outside. Off to one side of the great room was an alcove for Braco to sit while the people entered, and it gave him privacy until it was time for him to step before the group onto the onyx stage that held a single platform at its center for him to stand upon, so all could see him well.

I was invited by a staff member to stand in the front row for my first gazing session. As the people walked in they carried flowers, all varieties in bouquets small and large. This was the tradition at Braco's sessions everywhere. People honored his love of nature with flowers; they were a sign of their love and respect. When someone arrived at Srebrnjak 1, they put their flowers on a special table, and when they left to go to a session, they were given a different bouquet so that no one was left empty handed. Surveying the crowd I saw people of all ages, many holding photographs of loved ones with problems. A special quality of Braco's gaze was that it affected people through their pictures as tangibly as if they were present.

Some people looked so happy to see Braco and others looked scarred or worried with the burden they brought through the door.

Once the crowd of about one hundred was ushered inside and skillfully directed into rows with the shortest people in front, the four or five staff members stepped to the sides to watch the group while another picked up a microphone and walked onto the stage. Because the energy of Braco's gaze affected some people strongly, this crew was necessary to assist people as needed, and I witnessed several who needed their strong arms at different times. A short introduction was given in Croatian and then music, always the same special instrumental song, was played. Once the music began, Braco emerged from the side and came onto the platform. His face was gentle and natural - then he lovingly and silently looked ahead slowly moving his gaze across the audience. I heard someone in tears behind me as I focused upon him with my full attention.

This was what I had been looking forward to for five months, this amazing gaze of liberation, peacefulness, strength, energy and so much more. It is what had given me myself back in a new fullness, rescuing parts I thought lost and surprising me with parts yet undiscovered. I felt peace and comfort, and also something indescribably dynamic and alive. If it was coming directly from him or if he was opening a doorway to the unseen and divinely inspired reality I did not know, but I could feel energy moving through me from the bottom of my feet to the top of my head. Soon I discovered each session could feel different, yet there was a constancy too in that illuminating force.

My mind quieted as I relaxed to fully feel all that I could feel in those five or six minutes. Sometimes a certainty would pop into my mind during gazing sessions, the solution to a problem or a knowingness that something had changed in my world for the better. Braco did not tell anyone their answers and solutions, yet so many would report knowing afterward what to do or what had changed spontaneously within them, either during or after a session. This was a source point, for me and for anyone who accepted such a possibility either consciously or unconsciously in their hearts. Fortunately, the heart could override even a stubborn mind here to drink of this energy of new beginnings. Some of Braco's greatest supporters were once complete skeptics who came expecting nothing or worse.

At the end of the music, Braco stayed a few moments more before leaving. The room was silent except for a few sobs of happiness, and I did not want to move or anyone to talk. There was such fullness in that last moment that I wanted to stretch it on and on, but another group would come soon and the staff had to finish with these people so they could go off to the next assembly. Again, the person who gave the initial presentation came forward and asked if anyone felt anything. There were smiles, nods and many who said 'yes', and then a few people, sometimes very emotive, shared what they experienced.

They spoke of feeling energy, seeing a white or golden aura around Braco and contentment inside. Then the host thanked the group and mentioned the next tour dates before the doors were opened to allow the crowd to depart. This took place in a timely manner due to the expert staff that graciously directed everyone with kindness and care. I waited until the last person was at the door before making my way to the alcove and Braco. A big smile lit my face and all I could say was 'thank you'. Branko, Braco's great protector, then escorted us back to the bamboo garden as we passed some of the people leaving and newly arriving.

A breakfast of fresh fruits and pastries was brought as well as a drink I would learn to love, strong Yugoslavian espresso. We chatted more and different people who worked at the Center came and went, partaking in an espresso and sometimes a snack before going off on their business. There was a solid sense of family amongst everyone who worked there and a special ease. Braco was soon called for another group and I was always left with someone to keep me company. Many sessions would follow and at some point I asked if I could attend another session, and Braco agreed without hesitation.

For my next time I was placed to the front side of the group so I could watch the people as well as turn to face Braco for the gazing session. Mostly individuals from the local community came that morning because the months of July and August were the holiday months when people across Europe enjoyed travel and vacations. It was customary in the Balkans and most of Europe to have four weeks as standard yearly vacation time unlike the meager one to two weeks in the United States. Therefore, fewer buses would arrive than was normal during other months. Yet to me they were coming in noteworthy numbers anyway.

Since many locals were present who had come before, some stared at me with a question evident in their eyes. I smiled back warmly but had little response at first - the majority of people in the Balkans did not smile and warmly greet strangers. They looked at one without changing expression, something I had to get used to as normal and not with any bile behind it. Yet I was told they would go out of their way for a stranger in need of help. Later, however, I would get many smiles as I was introduced to them as a visitor from the land of paradise who would bring Braco to a conference in the islands. That they approved of as long as I brought him back, and several wished me a good conference.

During that gazing session I felt like I was literally eating the energy. I had a feeling so special and so deep that it touched my soul, and I recognized I had waited my whole life to experience it and could not get enough. In those minutes, I was in heaven, and heaven was growing within me. Although spontaneous healings and life changes could happen in a split second, I also understood that I was literally taking that energy into me creating a storehouse of it. This feeling and energy had been so staunchly missing in the face of my own life depleting challenges and denials that I could have stood there for time immeasurable before being sated.

For some reason, I missed the next session when I was talking to someone while Braco was engaged with business for a short time. The timing was just off and it happened before I could think to tell someone that I wanted to go again. As I sat in the warm shade of the gazebo, I felt terrible with the loss of something precious. With all my heart I wished to not miss out on a single drink of nourishment from that spring which Braco offered.

When he returned to the bamboo garden, I asked Braco if I could please attend his next gazing session. I told him forthright how awful it felt to miss his last session. Then innocently, I told him it was my wish to attend all of them. Again, without hesitation he agreed. Only later would I find out that no one did this, that in fact as a rule people were required to come not more than once a day. Even staff members present in the onyx room looked only to the crowd to do their job of assisting in a quick moment, if needed by someone overcome by the energy. At the end of the day, others would relieve those who had worked in the gazing room so they could have their turn for a gazing session.

I was an experiment, but I was so grateful to Braco for his flexibility and desire to make me happy. He had a gift for seeing possibilities hanging invisible in the air, unobserved by the sleeping masses and yet completely real on the unseen planes of reality ready to manifest our future. Because of my discovery of normal procedures, I was wholeheartedly determined not to fall down no matter what I experienced in the energy and to meet and pass this test with grace. Braco offered a natural support that made me feel he assisted what I was capable of achieving. How refreshing that was for my spirit. It is how all of us could live, supportive and helping to open the way for each other. But most people were subject to jealousy and competition against others as if a win must mean a loss too. Win-win was the next evolution of thought and action.

Before long, it was time for lunch and I was given a tour of Srebrnjak 1. Ivica had lived and worked out of one of the apartments in this building. Braco would in time acquire the entire building and renovate it into the place I was shown today. Long ago he knew that after he completed Srebrnjak 1, where everything began, he would leave. Now it was close to finished, including the bamboo grove and garden, and change was immanent.

Three stories tall, the bottom floor housed the precious onyx room with a great golden sun as the centerpiece on stage. Here there was no furniture accept for two chairs and small table in the alcove for Braco to await his next group. A long staircase led to a large vestibule with many paintings of Braco and Ivica, and a large stained glass tribute to both men together adorned one wall with vibrant colors. People left their flowers here before entering another large room divided into two parts that acted as waiting areas. It was filled with chairs and people could relax in the calm atmosphere before their group was ready to be called.

From the waiting area, another door opened into a room crafted in fine woodwork. Here people would receive an introductory presentation about Braco and his work, and the many books and films made about him were available for sale in this one room. Countless people had reported spontaneous healings after reading Ivica's many volumes of books that he wrote during his lifetime. Ivica had written them as nectar for the people and wrote them from an altered state of higher consciousness. Now people reported similar experiences from watching DVD's about Braco. Also, Braco's own volumes, as well as other books written about him received similar testimonials. So these items were available to the public, offering another level of help and reinforcement of the energy into people's lives.

On the opposite side of the vestibule was a full kitchen in which the fulltime chef, Stevo, lovingly and skillfully prepared meals to suit everyone's likes and preferences. Also an office with a computer occupied a smaller space, along with a washroom and shower that gave everyone working at Srebrnjak 1 everything they needed through the long days and tireless schedule. These rooms were always active, especially the table in the kitchen that served endless espresso, Turkish coffee and ever something good to eat. It was also a choice smoking spot since everyone in Croatia seemed to still sport this habit, one that Ivica had enjoyed greatly, stating that it was good to focus the attention.

Finally, the third floor opened to a great room paneled entirely in magnificently carved wood, floor to ceiling, with skylight type windows in the sloping ceiling. Everything here was grand, including a dinning table of massive proportions of the same wood as the room, while a couch and chairs with a plasma screen on the wall and stereo made an inviting space to relax nearby. Here we would gather for the lunch meal each day, and enjoy lively conversations with playful joking and banter.

Off the great room, two bedrooms were housed, one that still held the clothes of Ivica. Braco was unable to discard these out of sentimentality. It had taken several years to complete the wood paneling and to install the onyx slabs below, but all was in perfect place. In its entirety, it represented a loving tribute to the place that meant so much to so many people, a place of healing and transformation that began with a simple Serbian prophet who only desired to help people improve their lives.

Inside the great room, several guests, including Braco's father, Viktor awaited us. He was a charming and quiet man with grey hair and a boyish grin, like his son. We shook hands and he said in Croatian that he recognized me from Braco's latest DVD about America. Braco translated for me and I was honored to be recognized in the Balkans. Many conversations, all in Croatian took place, so with only Braco to translate for me, I missed some of the lively banter but I felt completely enfolded in the group.

At this time I was struck by the music playing in the background. It was in the kitchen earlier but I thought nothing of it. Instead of ethnic, new age or Croatian easy listening, American 1980's pop-rock music filled these rooms. Everywhere I would go over my next three weeks, whether restaurants, hotels, shops, other towns or Braco's home, 80's music played on radios and stereos everywhere like a time machine had imported our old pop culture to Eastern Europe. I found the environment made it impossible not to enjoy anew this pastime. The spirit of openness permeated every corner of this place and each moment loomed full, bright and beyond the everyday rejections that create a false sense of comfort.

Lunch was served at 2 p.m. and was a bounty of vegetarian dishes, created just for me I was told, since Braco usually ate a simple lunch of boiled chicken and raw zucchini in olive oil. His breakfast was usually equally simple with a glass of milk with raw honey, a few spoonfuls of home harvested olive oil, a banana and piece of fresh fruit. My visit was a chance for the chef to show off his talents and I was very happy for the thoughtfulness. Braco told me he would eat exactly as I ate for now. When he traveled to other countries, he also ate what his host or hostess served without fuss. So I placed a few modest portions of each of the dishes on my plate, but my appetite was light as if the energy had already filled me so I could not do any justice to the tasty meal before us.

More gazing sessions followed after lunch and I drank them all in, feeding on them as others had feasted on our luncheon banquet. Then the day ended with the last group at six o'clock, and immediately afterwards Braco took me to his car. While pulling out of the parking lot, he told me that he had not driven in a couple of years. I was worried for a moment that he did not know how to drive, like some New York City people who only use public transportation. Yet he managed well and I discovered that he usually walked home between his house and Srebrnjak 1, as well as walking to work in the mornings at 6 a.m. When traveling on the road, one of the staff always drove and usually there were several others along. This ride was for my benefit after travel, and it would give us time to walk in Zagreb that evening.

Zagreb

We pulled up to Braco's home in a pleasant residential area. Here was a four-story house that appeared quite large, with a stone and steel fence around its front lawn. I had no bags to unload since my luggage, which had been located, was not scheduled to arrive until later the next morning. Thank heavens I had filled my mandatory zip-lock baggy for airport security to capacity with my essentials, and I at least had a toothbrush. I would stay in Braco's own home, something he usually did not do for guests, but he wanted me to see and experience all things in his life without exception. Later the reason why this was so important would emerge more fully, but for now my perspective was that I would gain good insight to help me write articles about him, since he was a mystery figure to most.

Inside the front door was a staircase that led in both directions. It turns out that Balkan homes are designed quite differently than American ones. The four floors boasted four completely self-contained apartments with two bedrooms each. Families in Croatia tended to stay together and as children grew into adulthood, they could decide to take over one of the apartments for themselves. There was a much richer closeness here in general, a deeper bond between children and parents. Rudi, one of the core staff members at Srebrnjak 1 lived for now in the top quarters. I was assigned the second unit and Braco and his family lived on the third floor. For the two summer holiday months, his wife, Dinka, and only son, Andelon, would stay at their vacation home on the Adriatic coast in a seaside village.

Braco ushered me into my new residence and showed me the rooms. The same heavy, carved wood furniture as at Srebrnjak 1 dominated the space. This furniture had an air of tradition and stability. Marble floors complimented all the rooms and a balcony was present on each floor off the living room. All was very clean and neat, with a silver tray of bottled water and glasses waiting on the dining table for me. Everything I needed was there to provide a more than comfortable rest for my stay. In the end, I would do little more than sleep here part-time because of our upcoming tour schedule, and trips to the seaside village.

Next, I joined Braco upstairs on his balcony and had something to drink. Fruit trees filled the long and narrow backyard and another plot below also boasted many edibles that were planted for their harvest. People here used the land to grow things to eat, and the food in general was organically grown as it had been for centuries. As we overlooked the back acreage, a stunning view of a valley surrounded by mountains greeted us. From the front of the house, there was no indication of the landscape behind and I was delighted.

On the lower plot, Braco spotted his father who took care of the fruit trees and land. He too seemed to love nature as Braco, and he enjoyed thoroughly putting his hands in the soil. We walked outside to greet him and he looked vibrantly happy. He presented us with fresh cherries from his trees and in the morning, we found a basket of greens he had placed there for our lunch. Viktor obviously took pride in the land and pointed out different trees and vegetables present. After a short conversation, he went back to work and we prepared to leave to take a walk in downtown Zagreb.

Soon strolling down shop-lined boulevards, I was surprised that the city did not have more old-world style structures. Modern dominated with old stone buildings rising up only intermittently. Stone streets were present in many places, however, that captured the spirit of the former Yugoslavian city. I began to ask Braco many questions as we walked, about his philosophy of life, about his gift and healing work. His answer then, and in the first week ahead to such queries was always the same; there was nothing to tell. I felt certain he knew many things in fact, but for whatever reason he was not going to tell me, at least not yet.

I tried again and again with this same line of questions, but after little gain, I decided to enjoy my new surroundings. He took me to an impressive stone walkway that led up to a massive ancient structure. As we climbed higher, a marvelous view overlooking the city appeared and we stopped near the top to appreciate the scenery. Folk music was playing in an outdoor café-style restaurant nearby and I asked if it was traditional Balkans music. Of course his answer was that he did not know, like a sheltered youth who was also experiencing these things for the first time. Laughing, I found him charming in this innocence, despite my earlier frustration with unanswered questions. Asking the same question different ways had done absolutely nothing, so I accepted the mystery for the time being.

That very first day, I felt a natural ease with Braco as if we had known each other for a very long time, and I trusted him. I could bring up any subject with him and he was adept at listening. He paid attention far beyond the norm and I think he read very well between the lines. At first it seemed like we were in dramatic contrast to each other, for I had traveled the world and had studied most things spiritual and related to alternative healing from a very early age. He had lived his entire youth in Croatia and had no interest in spirituality and healing until he met Ivica at the age 26. His knowledge was pure, his own and not acquired through the opinions of others, and he deeply understood that too much information drove the masses into living without real purpose and meaning.

That day in Braco's company had already begun to change me. He did not do anything specifically; his naturalness and his obvious self-trust gave me the tangible example I needed to do this myself to a new degree. It was simple, effortless and no words could have achieved the same depth of result. Our stroll continued down the other side of the hill back to the shops and we stopped at a café for something to drink. He asked if I was tired and I found to my surprise that I really was not at all due all the energy of the gazing sessions and his remarkably grounded nature.

Braco offered me a glass of wine and I wanted to accept, but I was too embarrassed. He did not drink alcohol at all. In fact, this unique man had never even had a sip of wine, and so I ordered juice instead. Soon, he would liberate me from such confining fears as if he subtly observed my self-contrived restrictions to reveal a more spontaneous side of myself. He would gently and naturally help me push self-conscious acts aside so I was no longer governed by this type of shadow, but instead by my own pure wishes in the moment which were harmless to others.

Although I could not get answers to certain philosophical questions, we had lively conversations at the café and walking about his 8-year-old son, the people who worked an Srebrnjak 1 and of course about Hawaii. Braco shared his feeling about what had happened with his father that he had not spoken of before to others. We discussed the city of Zagreb and his youth, his love of nature and his commitment to his work. After our stop, we went back to his home and called the evening complete at just after midnight.

I was invited to walk to work with him the next morning or to sleep in to rest. Without hesitation, I stated that I would be ready at 6 a.m. to walk, and so I went to bed that first night with a radiant contentment, filled with happiness of finding my spirit absolutely fed and nourished. My simple wish to see Braco again had come back to me magnified a thousand-fold with the generosity of the energy that had made all this possible.

Chapter Two

Day 2 – Tuesday, June 30, 2009

Making Wishes

My alarm went off at 5 a.m. and Braco was at my door at 6 o'clock to escort me on our fifty-minute walk to work. Incredibly, I felt fresh and ready to go, another testament to the energy that embraced me here in Zagreb. After walking down a few streets, we came to the vast city park with paths winding through forest. Few people were out; except for a handful we passed walking their dogs. The morning was crisp though mild, and sunlight beamed through the tree's canopy. Braco loved nature to his core and these times in a natural setting fed him well.

With his demanding schedule, I understood then more than ever his need of such contact with the natural world to balance the days. Such simple pleasures were too often overlooked in the lives of people caught in a whirlwind of high-pressure jobs with only television as a tool of relaxation. But this only drained away life's energies without real replenishment. Humankind needed nature to harmonize and reconnect to the spirit within, or it lost itself in an illusionary world of material gains that could not in the end sustain any true fulfillment. Braco knew and lived accordingly.

It felt wonderful to walk, especially since Braco indulged me with the brisk pace that I preferred. Later he would slow me down to appreciate the scenery more, but for now I viewed this as my exercise replacement to swimming in the warm Hawaiian waters with my dolphin friends. Surprisingly, I would come to enjoy these walks with him equally well. On the way we stopped at a street café and had a croissant and our first espresso. Expansiveness and a penetration of the moment was discernible while being at his side, and it allowed me to let go of my grip on my routine preferences to experience more new things with delight.

At Srebrnjak 1, Branko, always looking in command of things, greeted us along with other people I would learn to know as the stable, committed and devoted crew of the Center. Dinko, Rudi, Pero, Ljiljana, Miki, Davor, the chef Stevo and quiet Damir were some of the key people at the Center who had been around for years, and they did their jobs flawlessly and always without complaint. Branko, Damir, Pero and Dinko had all known Ivica and had helped him too, thus knowing Braco from his earlier days. They were more than co-workers; there was a camaraderie and friendship amongst all that created a sincere bond and ever-present harmony. Everyone was wholeheartedly committed to the energy that Braco's gaze brought and the work of helping the people.

That morning I met Ljiljana, the only female of the core staff; I had seen her in a few of the films about Braco, presenting in front of the groups at the Center. She was the only one who did not travel on tour and was always taking care of the visitors at Srebrnjak 1. A striking woman, she had lovely long flowing hair and a very warm demeanor with the air of being capable and sure. Yet all those who worked here had a balance and peacefulness about them, as well as a visibly evident inner strength. Especially the tour schedule and hours would require no less.

Gazing sessions took place for the flowing stream of people who came all day long. I would attend all sessions and each one brought me new insights and I could feel the light force growing within me. One of my dearest wishes, which I had not shared with Braco or anyone for a long time, was to be a novelist. All my English teachers had told me I would be an author one day, that I had that special talent. Yet an invisible noose bound me unreasonably and though I began many projects over my adult life, I could never get past a self-doubt that held me in check from such a large undertaking.

During the morning gazing sessions, my heart cried out this wish anew and asked for the strength to finally make this dream a reality. How could I possibly know that soon I would have my wish delivered directly through Braco and a wonderful, spontaneous idea he pulled out of the air? A second thing my spirit craved was to talk in front of large groups of people without fear or self-consciousness. I had an absolutely shattering case of stage fright, yet I loved public speaking and it was a huge contradiction in me. For years I had lectured at conferences, but it was pure agony and I knew this could be different if my mind could only trust something deeper.

Somehow, inner demons blocked my path on both of these sincere wishes and I did not know how to overcome them. So now I stood in a morning gazing session and my heart hoped again until I finally felt a stirring inside that told me these things were possible. Then I left the session without giving it anymore thought, not aware that the energy of Braco's gaze was immediately opening doors of opportunity. Late morning brought me a present of my luggage and I was finally able to change out of the clothes I had worn for almost four days in a row and across the globe. Finally freshly attired, I was now completely content in the generosity of my environment and the cadre of Srebrnjak 1.

Branko and others commented on my little need for sleep and also my strength to continue to attend the sessions, but I could not explain to them in Croatian that it was only because the energy was making me feel like I could fly. That morning, Coco, Braco's family pet cockatoo was brought in. This was a proud white bird with a demanding love of attention. Braco and I played with Coco in the gazebo during our breaks. He teased the happy bird, which looked so content as his feathers were tickled. Then we began to talk about Ivica and Braco's love of his friend, and the pain of losing him so suddenly. Everyone at the Srebrnjak 1 spoke with the highest regard for the Serbian prophet. I had heard Braco's story of coming to Ivica, and now it was time to hear about the man who began everything.

Ivica the Prophet

"The power was divine, not mine." - Ivica Prokic

Ivica's published his first book in 1992. Often, he had told friends that he would write thirteen books and no more. After his thirteenth book, he was killed in an accident that he predicted as well, and Braco was at his side when it happened. It was the young Braco who brought his body home from South Africa, where a rogue wave claimed Ivica's life while both men were enjoying the surf of a beach they had visited before and the prophet favored.

Born in the Serbian mountains on August 4, 1950, Ivica Prokic had an experience at age seven. While lying on the bank of a river with many other children, he suddenly cried out and became motionless. Later he told of feeling a piece of the sun entering his ankle and traveling up his leg. Mysteriously, this event triggered something profound in the boy that activated his unique abilities. In 1971, he would move from Serbia to the city of Zagreb and begin selling fish at the local market. Many visions came to him, especially through astral travel. By 1989, his powers and inner strength had grown and he realized that he could see past, present and future with great certainty.

It was a visit to a bio-energetic clinic that validated his abilities. He made an appointment for himself, and the healers told him he had great power and should be helping the people. On November 5, 1989, while lying in a bath tub Ivica saw a man falling from a cross. The cross hit Ivica on the forehead and left a permanent physical scar and blood flowing from his hands. Since that time, he had a special ability to heal and could touch someone and make him or her feel better. He realized he had been given a special gift, and knew he could never charge people for helping them and he never did.

His first prophecy then came on November 16, 1989 when he foresaw a local mining accident. It took him awhile to gain more and more strength, and to understand the images in his visions. Next he began using a little mirror, like Nostradamus, to see people's past, present and future. Ivica also started to see visitors one-by-one, offering advice for them and their families, and those they brought photos of for help. At this time Ivica had published his first book and began giving them to those who came for help. People to this day report that there is a strong healing power in his books, and Ivica wrote many, each delivering a different healing energy to the people.

Word of mouth would spread the news of Ivica's talents and abilities, and the number of people who came grew. Over the years ahead he would tour to other cities and make DVDs about his work to further help people to receive the energy gift. The many portraits of Ivica at Srebrnjak 1 show a vibrant man with a ready smile. Bold and direct, he always stated information for people without frills or restraint. All the pictures of Ivica show him adorned with heavy gold necklaces and gold rings on his fingers. This was because he had a message in a vision that he had to wear 2.2 pounds (1 kilo) of gold due to his work and the number of people he saw regularly.

Gold would help him to get stronger and protect him from all the negative energies from the people he healed and helped. It also brought in direct guidance from the sun. This was a harsh burden for the prophet, especially in the heat of the summer, but he understood that strength was essential and this was its price. Once Braco joined him, he too would wear a heavy amount of gold around his neck and on his fingers until his own natural strength increased to the point that he no longer needed this assistance. Now Braco, and so many who came to see him, wore a single gold sun necklace and ring to express the vibrant energy that permeates to help uplift and heal.

Spontaneity

We were then called for a gazing session and once we returned to the bamboo garden, I asked Braco if he was hiding any secrets. Since he ate as his hosts served him on tour, meat was sometimes a natural part of a meal, so he was not the typical vegetarian. Also, in Croatia everyone smoked without any social stigma, and so he occasionally sported this act too. Braco accepted the customs and traditions of an area or people without rejecting them. Often, in America, spiritual healers and teachers were pristine in their displays to the public, a seeming contradiction to Braco's mode of living. Yet in famous books about true adepts, such as Cyril Scott's book, *The Initiate*, such teachers would often adopt habits such as cigar smoking or swearing to break the projection of followers of a perfection that was illusionary. Perhaps Braco too acted as he did for this reason, but clearly he was also not wishing to set himself apart, his influence would work in other ways. I was searching to understand Braco more deeply with my question about secrets.

He smiled at my query and boyishly told me that he did have a secret, and so I followed him into the bamboo where he showed me an unseen hiding place. Quietly, he could disappear and no one would think to look for him here, and his freedom loving spirit had more than once led him to break away from the attentive eyes of his loving staff, especially ever watchful Branko, to have some time of privacy. It was a lovely spot to peacefully sit to appreciate the beauty of nature through the dark green bamboo leaves and the song of the birds. For Braco, this was a real secret, and the other things merely a facet of everyday life for people. It was another reminder to me that he did not set himself apart, but was truly one with the people despite his awesome gift.

It was time for lunch and we made our way to the third floor dining and recreation room where Stevo was once again laying out a banquet feast of vegetarian dishes, along with meat for those who preferred their animal protein like Branko. A seat was always reserved beside Braco for me, and this allowed me the opportunity witness all closely. Many of the staff joined us again while others continued to work. A few had a glass of wine with their meal, but I still abstained. Today Braco served my plate for me, knowing well my desire for small portions; he thoughtfully placed only a spoonful of each dish on my plate that filled it still.

Braco ate the same as I ate, only larger helpings, and said he would continue to eat vegetarian with me and I found this incredibly thoughtful and inclusive. It was not something most hosts would even think to do for a guest. Branko's healthy sense of humor made for many laughs, although I missed a few that Braco would not translate. They told me only later would I be ready for the full force of Branko's bawdy jests. Stevo announced that he had made a special crepe with ice cream dessert for us and our eyes grew big at the thought of more food. We shared a smile and I of course we knew we would taste what was offered without reserve.

Then the crepes came, and Braco playfully ate them with his fingers, despite the quickly melting ice cream. Earlier in the meal I had used my fingers to eat, saying it was more natural and that the metal of silverware changed the taste of food. To my surprise, Branko agreed. Perhaps it was another joke but he looked at both of us with conviction, and Braco too admitted that he liked to eat with his fingers, but no one had ever joined him. To me it was what indigenous cultures had done for eons and was very wholesome.

Fun and lively American '80 pop rock was playing in the background as David Bowie, Men at Work and Cindy Lauper filled the room. Spontaneity happened so easily here, and so we kicked off our shoes and Braco asked for my hand for a dance. We laughed and displayed a couples swing dance to everyone's amusement. Branko shook his head at us and told us we were crazy, but he enjoyed our antics, this was made clear by his wide grin.

More people had been arriving for the gazing sessions and it was time to go back to work. So far that day, the crowds of people arriving were predominately from Croatia with a few buses from neighboring countries. People continued to look at me curiously as I was always there at the front of the onyx room as they entered. Yet I was beginning to feel more warmth in their looks, and I directly attributed that to the energy that was already changing me to be more relaxed and less self-conscious. I would see greater changes over time as a special type of self-confidence also grew within that allowed me to feel connected to everyone despite mere surface appearances. Plus, word was spreading locally that a woman from Hawaii was visiting, no small news.

That afternoon, I walked with a group into the waiting area upstairs to witness the entire process that the people visiting Srebrnjak 1 experienced. I sat here watching as more people filed in off the street in a steady flow, most carrying flower bouquets that they laid on the outer table before entering to find a seat. A few individuals softly greeted others already present before finding a chair themselves. There was a quietly expectant atmosphere here and paintings of Braco and Ivica on each wall lent an air of potency. The floor was marble and everything clean and shining. This really was a special sanctuary devoted to the healing work at hand; it exuded from all the loving craftsmanship, the character and quality of the rooms.

Next the group was called to step forward into an adjoining room that was paneled floor to ceiling in richly carved wood with an ornate back wooden partition. On one side of this divide, the many books by Ivica and Braco were available, as well as the numerous DVD movies made about Braco, which were filled with people's testimonials that proved the power of his gaze. Finally, there was a shining gold sun pendant that so many who came wore - an asymmetrical sunburst design that Ivica had received in a vision long ago, and that Braco had fashioned into the current three dimensional form with thirteen raised rays emanating from its center. This too was available for those who wanted one, and I would hear over the days many stories of people whose loved ones were ill and were given this pendant as a gift, and it helped them recover.

Ivica had been shown in a higher consciousness state that the specific design would convey the Source energy to the people. Braco had placed the sunburst with raised rays on the stage of the onyx room, large and magnificent. Soon, Ljiljana, warm and caring, moved in front of the assembled group and gave a modest speech in Croatian, mainly speaking about Braco and Ivica. People would periodically nod their heads and smile, but the staff member translating for me only shared the general idea of what was said by her.

Then a break occurred in which those who desired books, DVD's or the sun pendant could acquire these things, and I noticed several people already carried books, obviously purchased long ago because of their well-read appearance. Ivica had stated that his slim volumes had meaning between the lines, and were meant to be read many times. Dozens of people would tell me over the days that they experienced deep help with health problems and much more just by reading the books or watching the films. The energy of Braco's gaze was clearly present and penetrating through these mediums of delivery too.

Shortly, we were all guided out and people received new bouquets before they made their way down the staircase to the outside, where we would walk toward the front of the Center to the great carved doors that opened to the onyx room. Those overseeing the group waited until all were gathered back together before opening those doors, and as people entered, the shortest in height or those with walking aids were directed to the front rows. Again, Ljiljana stepped before the group and mentioned not to take snapshots, then directed them how best to receive the energy, asking people to hold to their hearts any photographs of loved ones they had brought and a few other words. When she finished, the music began and everyone's attention was fully directed toward the stage. Braco came from the side and took his place in front of the group, and his eyes slowly moved across the room.

I found that all groups had an overall personality and unique quality, and those with younger people in their twenties and thirties were often noticeably affected. This group had a particularly soft and gentle feel, and I saw many tears streaming down faces afterwards, and even more with tissues in hand. People were clearly and distinctly touched by this energy, and open to the simple process of receiving it. Ljiljana came forward and gently asked if anyone would share what they had experienced, and several people volunteered, including a weathered old man who looked impenetrable - yet he spoke in an unexpectedly sweet and heartfelt way.

Finally I was introduced to the group as the woman from Hawaii who would bring Braco to the United States for a conference in the islands. Because of this, a couple of people asked different assistants to share their own stories with me. Rudi, another key person at the Srebrnjak 1, spoke English well enough to help act as a messenger or translator with these people to tell their accounts of their lives and serious illnesses miraculously healed by Braco's gaze. It was very moving to see faces, some old and chiseled, others so young, affected to the depth that I was witnessing each session. Over the days ahead, I would hear stories either directly from individuals or with the help of Rudi, Miki or Ljiljana, and I was so grateful for their bilingual talents.

Trip to the Zagreb Zoo

We finished early that day at 5 o'clock because of the holiday season, and so had extra time to go to the Zagreb zoo, which Braco was enthusiastic to show me. Walking there through the streets and the expansive park, we shortly came to the zoo looming ahead. Honestly, I would never have another zoo experience like that with Braco. He loved animals like nature, and wanted to pet and play with all the creatures. Unlike American zoos, there were no signs posted forbidding feeding or touching the animals. And the enclosures were not set back to prohibit public contact, just the opposite, they were designed so that people could get very close. Thus, Braco was able to stick his fingers through many wire cages and fences to at least try to pet some of the birds and furry animals, and he tried many places we stopped.

Needless to say, a few of the exotic animals were surprised and attempted to nibble or snap at the offered fingers, but that did not detour his innocent nature now on full exhibit. My own schooling on strict zoo protocol was overridden while watching his fun. I too wanted to pet the animals and offer a loving caress, but I was neither as brave as he, nor as free yet. People would walk by without giving a second glance as Braco gently stroked some smaller mammals that did not flinch or the many birds he enticed like his cockatoo, Coco. Having grown up in this city, visits to the zoo regularly had been a part of his childhood experience and I dare say he enjoyed it no less now.

Finally, the meerkat enclosure proved the great finale. The pen for a group of perhaps twenty meerkats was a waist high fence only, and all could lean against it. Braco quickly discovered that the fence was electrified at the bottom and he winced at the jolt. Then he reached over the fence, first as far as his arm and torso would stretch, which was not enough to reach a rather curious adult who came close.

This precocious meerkat was obviously thinking of food, which was not offered. So Braco had to find a way to extend farther. This he did by balancing his hips on the fence and swinging forward like a gymnast on a parallel bar. His feet came off the ground and I could hardly believe his determination to pet that confident meerkat who positioned itself each time just a few inches out of range. Finally I had to grab Braco's legs for fear of him falling over and I laughed so hard as I thought, 'come look, here is the famous Braco with the miracle gaze about to fall into an animal pen'.

One of Braco's favorite animals at this zoo, the tiger, turned out to be missing that day and so our viewing was complete. After stopping for refreshment, we strolled out of the zoo to walk by one of the park lakes as he told me of his fondness as a child of coming here to the many special spots offered. He had also fished in the lakes of the park, although only to catch the fish before setting them free. Heat filled the air and it was pleasant to find shade in the trees lining the water where we stopped. Silently, we admired the beauty and the sanctuary of peacefulness within the city bustle.

In those quiet minutes, I looked over at him and was suddenly startled and transfixed. As if two realities were merging instantaneously, I saw transposed in his countenance momentarily an Atlantean with a powerful, far away look. This image from the past was so tangible that I was shocked. Without understanding, I was certain I was witnessing an historical remnant of Atlantis, the ancient civilization Plato wrote about, coming to life. It was the most direct feeling of remembrance I had with him from another time and place without explanation. My whole body reacted from head to toe with an energy surging thorough me and it was almost overwhelming. All I could think was that I *knew him*, not in the conventional or ordinary sense, but outside of the boundaries of the five senses. Excitement and exhilaration filled me but I kept an outward calm, not displaying the impact of this non-temporal experience.

Instead I calmly asked him what he knew of Atlantis. Of all my questions, I would persistently bring this one up again and again over the three weeks, and my effort would reap a small harvest - but later, and I would discover through him that the time had not arrived to know and write about these things yet. So of course he did not give me much of an answer, but instead asked me what I thought. I simply told him that I felt that everything had begun in Atlantis, it was the fulcrum point, and now some were coming back again to finish what had been started back then; to bring something to completion so the world would be free again. Thoughtfully, he nodded his head in agreement and told me he felt something similar. Now I was happier than ever, it was a beginning.

Three hours passed between our stroll, the zoo, the lake and our many conversations. Heading back to Srebrnjak 1 to retrieve Braco's car, next on the agenda was a meeting with Drago Plecko, M.Sc., a scientist and paranormal researcher. This was my opportunity to interview someone of considerable knowledgeable who had studied Braco for the last three years and could offer his scientific explanation of the powerful gaze and the healings it created. Braco had made the arrangements for us to meet with him that night in a café in a nearby village.

Once back at the Center and in his car, Braco paused at the gatehouse and asked Branko to do something in Croatian. We waited a few minutes, and Branko came back with a box. Braco smiled and handed it to me as a gift from him. Completely taken by surprise, I opened the box to find a large jewelry case, and inside was an incredibly beautiful gold necklace with the sun symbol at its center. I had no words at first and could not fathom such a generous gift, but I expressed my deepest gratitude and remarked on its radiant quality. Braco looked pleased and offered to help fasten it around my neck.

I was told that he had never before given such a necklace to anyone in only two days; usually he gave such a gift to people who helped with the work over years. Mine was the eleventh of this design to be given over the past 14 years. It was a design that people could not purchase, because he had this one and others specifically designed as special gifts. His own was completely unique, as was one his son wore. Ljiljana had the same design he had just presented to me and I remained speechless, yet so happy to receive such a remarkable expression of Braco's glorious energy. I knew he perceived a role I would play for the work, but I would not ask and wait instead for time to reveal all itself.

Interview at Samobor

Next we drove to a village named Samobor to meet up with Drago Plecko. This was a small town 15 miles from Zagreb and it would reveal itself to be the lovely old-world style village of storybooks. The cobblestone streets and white houses were in the charming style dating back hundreds of years. We made our way to an outdoor café that had been prearranged, but Drago had not yet arrived and Braco wished to play a joke on him to see his reaction. So we went to the ice cream counter and Braco revealed his plan to order a dish with 50 kuggles (scoops) of different flavors of ice cream, a veritable mountain. Even more, he ordered several plates of a famous cake from the region. Sweets here were offered as a sign of loving care to guests and family, and so this was an over-the-top display meant to bring a smile.

Returning to our table, the waiter took our drink order. Now I was ready to have that glass of wine, figuring it would help digest all the bounty of sweetness on its way. Braco was certainly surprised when I told him the wine would go well with the ice cream dinner, but my experience of years in the California wine country made me the expert. This was innocent fun and Braco had me fully involved in the game, waiting only to see the scientist's face when our order arrived. Soon Drago came over, sat down and we reminisced over our last meeting in the United States at the Laughlin, Nevada conference.

Fifty kuggles of ice cream arrived in a huge bowl with two spoons as well as all the pieces of cake. We both innocently smiled and stated that we were very hungry, and hoped he was too. Perhaps Drago was used to this type of lark, but he looked surprised enough to satisfy us and we began to eat, although the vast majority ended up melting its way down the bowl to a thankfully large platter beneath. After a general conversation, I asked Drago if I could record our interview and we then talked for one and a half hours about the phenomenon of Braco's gaze, the sun symbol and much more. [*Interview follows in next section*]

After our poor ice cream eating display, but a very illuminating and thoughtful interview, we drove back to Zagreb. Stopping at Srebrnjak 1, Braco decided to show me the bamboo garden at night. It had been one year since he had last visited during the evening hours and that night was the perfect temperature to sit outside. As we approached the walkway, he found a switch and small lights illuminated our path to the gazebo. Here we enjoyed the breeze and a short chat before leaving. This was a final enjoyment of nature before thunder began to roll in the sky and urged us on our way.

Once at his home, I told Braco that I had brought him a gift from Hawaii and we only took time to freshen up before meeting again in his living room. My present in hand had a traditional Hawaiian village depicted on it, and it was filled with DVDs about the Hawaiian Islands. Instantly, he chose one to play and he went absolutely mad with delight over the wild beauty he saw in brilliant colors from tropical foliage, fish and ocean. For days to come, he would have these DVDs playing constantly. Soon, the late hour made me realize that my 5 am wake up time would come rather quickly, and we parted company after another full day.

Interview with Drago Plecko, MSc., Croatian Parapsychologist and Scientist

Legend: *A- Angelika;* D – Drago

A. Let's begin by talking about the beginning of Braco's gazing ability?

D. There was a woman who came to him at Srebrnjak 1, after Ivica's death, and handed a picture to him of her child. The child had a problem. She said I know if you touch the picture you can help the child. And Braco said no, I'm not some kind of healer. I'm not Ivica. She insisted. When they realized the child had recovered, they asked him to continue the mission. So he started. Initially he was talking to the people. It was quite a burden to talk to people because the questions are never ending. If you answer one question, two new questions are coming. Hundreds of people were coming asking all kinds of questions. Rumors later started that it was some kind of placebo effect, some kind of suggestion. It's common in situations like this one. So what happened was basically that he turned to a new practice of gazing, only without communicating to people. And then through the years, all kinds of stuff happened and people told of their experiences, they described a lot of things happening to them, having dreams with him, having some physical ailments cured, having all kinds of problems solved and everything. And so he started visiting other countries, he was invited all over the place. People started reporting various improvements in health ... marital problem were resolved. Stuff like that.

A. So it went completely beyond healing the body to healing the whole life?

D. Yes, that is the most amazing thing. If you observe, people are healed perfectly. If you move a person's psyche towards a certain direction it can help the body in healing. But how can you resolve someone's financial problems? This is highly unusual, people coming and telling their stories like - I have a horrible problem with my brother - we had a tremendous quarrel about money and inheritance. Suddenly, he came at my door, he was so friendly, everything was resolved easily. Nobody could actually understand this aspect.

A. It would instantly happen?

D. Within short periods of time would be normal. It couldn't be ascribed to the actions of the person. You know it was too unusual and it happened too many times. Everything is statistics so we can claim that some of these things happened accidentally. But you cannot claim that everything happened like that. I still remember the guy who used to come, he was coming from Germany and his boy had epilepsy, epileptic Grand Mal seizures. It used to happen once or twice a week, it started killing him intellectually at all levels. So he used to come and after a while he reported that his boy did not have any seizures within the last 12 months. This is considered to be absolutely impossible medically speaking. Then other reports came.

A. So this phenomenon is harder to validate, because it's not just validating medically that the body was healed, but that people's relationships were healed, or their job situations or financial situations had changed - that's harder to verify or to gather statistics on?

D. It's easy to verify that it happened because these case histories are very convincing. It's not that easy to explain it on the scientific level. I even think ultimately that there is not much point in proving it scientifically because it introduces the methodology of science. In some way, you destroy the essence of this transformation. If you want to enjoy the flower, you shouldn't grab it, cut it in pieces, look at it under the microscope, stuff like that; you destroy the essence of it. It's the same story in these spiritual matters; it's always the same problem. Scientists want to dissect it, they want to see what's inside, when they get some answers then they get new ideas to what they want to test next. Ultimately you are a guinea pig. There is no point in it.

A. But for people in general, to help them understand what is possible, has anyone gathered some of the medical healing cases together, just for the stories?

D. I did, I saw a lot of them. All of these cases, like this [raising his hand high above the table top], one-meter high. The problem is not in medical documentation, the problem is in something else. The problem is in follow up on studies.

A. To see if the effect is long lasting?

D. You would need a professional crew to accomplish that task. It's almost impossible. For example, a woman comes from Munich, I see the testimony and she brings the documentation, she had cancer, she improved enormously, she's back to her job. Then she disappears. She doesn't come back after another six months, so you can't follow these people around. If you could do that you would need a whole big crew. A follow up study would be possible in some form of Institute. There is no Institute officially in this country or any European country that would be willing to perform the task.

A. Right, but I've seen cases where someone has been able to walk who couldn't walk before. A transformation like that is something that is pretty concrete, right up front.

D. The problem is always like this - I presented a case to a neurologist and I said look, she had two strokes that hit her thalamus, she couldn't walk the last seven years, she was in a wheel chair. They always have this wonderful word called spontaneous remission that explains everything. It's not statistically significant or they would tell you that the placebo has some really powerful effects. So you always find some kind of a word in the scientific language that would suit the situation. So it's endless. If you bring ten cases, all of these guys get up and say that anything is possible statistically - they would never face it. It's strange that when this woman got up in Switzerland, two doctors gave a statement. They said yes, she's our patient. She's been in a wheelchair for seven years and it's unusual, we can't explain it. They did say this. But you know if you gather all this information, it would take you forever to objectify. If I tell you we have a case like this, it's strange, unbelievable. They would always find new questions that would question your results. It's endless; it's a mind game. It's intellectual mumbo jumbo. You know, it's like in medicine, if you want to prove something about a medicine, you can do that. Absolutely. You take one hundred patients, you are paid by the pharmaceutical industry, you distribute it to 100 people, twenty of them react properly and you take only that group. You add another twenty of them, you have a perfect scientific study that proves it works. It happens with many medicines. They would accuse you of doing the same stuff if you try to objectify it.

A. Let's talk about Braco's style as different to what Ivica did. Braco did not pick up the legacy of Ivica's particular type of healing. Braco manifested something unique.

D. Yes. It was the need of the time. Ivica definitely did not have so many people around him. He could afford to talk to someone for an hour for example. Or sit at a table with a dozen people and discuss for three hours. He could afford it. Braco can't afford it anymore because so many people are coming. It's a totally different situation; it's not the same story. Besides that there's always the temperament of a person. You have different teachers, different gurus, everyone has his own temperament. It depends on the personality. They are not the same personality, you know, education also. Braco is much more educated. So things develop, they are growing. Everything is like that. You can't stay in the one place with the same story and the same style forever. It has to grow and develop. If it doesn't develop it dies out

A. Do you think that Braco's philosophy is similar to Ivica's philosophy on life, healing and well being?

D. I don't think they had philosophies. If you put that philosophy in one word that would be spontaneity. Take it as it comes. Take life as it comes. So you have to accept the facts of your life. And if you do that, let it go through you, that bad vibration at that point, you can survive it easier. It's riding a wave more or less; it's not easy, it's very difficult.

A. This could explain why Braco has a very normal life. That he is married and has a son.

D. Yes, his life is normal. He is not a gambler; he is not a degenerate guy in any sense of the word. Yes he is projecting his own lifestyle to the people in front of him at a certain unconscious level. So you can say we are all connected unconsciously in this collective consciousness, all of us. More or less we are affecting each other all the time through communication, even if it is silent. So you can imagine him projecting his own qualities to the people in front of him, standing in front of him. So when they adjust to that way of thinking they spontaneously improve.

A. And yet Braco, unlike other healers and spiritual teachers and leaders, does not have a meditation practice, he has not been searching his whole life to find the secrets of life. He has had a very normal life in fact, and yet he affects people on this profound level. Why is he able to do this?

D. You see, I think of it as a manifestation of evolutionary needs. When people are in need, then somebody is there to serve that need. It's hard to explain it. It's like asking a guy why Wayne Gretzky was such a tremendous, unbelievably good player. It's impossible to understand. He went through the same training as all the other guys. His physical appearance is not a big deal; there is nothing special about him. Yet there's just one in the whole history. It's the same thing, you know. When the pupil is ready the teacher appears. When someone who is in need is ready, someone who will solve the problem appears.

A. You're saying in this case it's the collective consciousness of humanity that helps create someone like Braco?

D. Absolutely, of course. Otherwise it wouldn't work. Braco never gave any interest to the media - no radio, no TV, no interviews. Still many thousands gather at his place. Having 10,000 people on his birthday, for example. He had it in the days when people did not know anything about him publicly in the sense of media. You have to have that inborn charisma to attract people. I can understand why Michael Jackson attracted people. He has this tremendous machinery around him. Propaganda, marketing, everything was there. But here it is totally different - it is the opposite. You cannot actually answer exactly why and what is the reason. Everybody's a manifestation of the collective unconscious; everybody has a mission in certain ways. Somebody understands it and he's fulfilling his mission. The other guy is highly unaware of his own mission, his life is a failure because he can't recognize why he is here, but maybe he does before he dies. And ultimately you have people who are aware of the higher mission or larger picture, and they are born like that. I've seen so many gurus and yogis; a lot of them haven't actually accomplished anything after 40 years of meditation. They couldn't tell anything. They couldn't heal anybody, couldn't tell anything about your future in terms of your life, why you are here and all that. So it's also a possibility. On the other hand, you have people like Edgar Cayce, for example, who didn't do anything, but he was a sleeping prophet. He dictated 45 books. All prophecy - he didn't know anything about it. He did not meditate, he didn't go to church, pray to God or a power or stuff like that. It's the same situation here.

A. What is the synergist effect between Braco and everyone present for a healing?

D. It's called the radiance effect [or Maharishi Effect]. It was discovered by Maharishi Mahesh Yogi. They asked him about it, so he said he had ten particles. Each one has the emission of a certain amount of energy. If they work on the same frequency it will not be 1+1+1, it will be exponential. It's the same with meditation in his case. He said, if there are 10 of us, it will not affect 10 people, it will be like a thousand people, because this group effect is in everything, in nature. So there is this famous one percent thing. If you have a saline solution and you add one percent of a crystal to it, the whole solution will turn into crystal. So there is that effect of one percent that is significant. If there are 200 of us in one place, in synchrony with someone who is charismatic, then it will not be 200 people. It will be much more. If this 200 is one percent of a group, the potential effect will be a 100 times more people - 20,000. So it's proven, even scientifically, that organized groups - they are praying, meditating, whatever - there is always some change of consciousness in the surrounding area. I mean crime rates have dropped, you know, stuff like that. Accident rates dropped. It's rudimentary research, but it's there and it's obvious. So I think if you gather at the same time more people together in the name of something, it affects the collective consciousness much more. There's no doubt about it. It's scientifically proven. Even in nature you have these examples of one percent with crystals, with everything. I could tell you a lot of examples like that in nature - biological, chemical.

A. The way Braco lives, how do you think he influences people who want to better their lives? How do you think his example teaches other people?

D. No one knows much about his private life. Most of the people who come into his space are not aware too much about his private life. I don't think he is giving some kind of moral example. I think it's more or less at a subtle level. It's like Shaktipat. [Sanskrit word in the Hindu spiritual tradition that refers to the act of the spiritual energy of kundalini being conferred on a disciple or student, by a guru or spiritual teacher in whom it is already active.] If you have ever seen anybody who has the power of delivering Shaktipat, then you know that type of transference of energy. I would call it Shaktipat; it's the closest possible comparison. If you look at the person who has that ability and you don't blink and you concentrate on his figure, and there's a bunch of people around you and he is concentrating on you, these are the perfect conditions for something to happen that is called a transference of energy, whatever you call that energy. And I would call it Shaktipat. This is the closest, basically the only example. I have seen it with Poonjaji, for example, an Indian master. Then Ramana Maharshi was famous for that. Then even Muktananda was famous for that. He was selling, for $300, Shaktipat and he took the peacock's feather and he used to hit a person in the head and the person went into that tremendous bliss. There are many examples, and many forms of it. It's like bringing that inner feeling of security, of certainty inside to people. It supports you tremendously if you know there is nothing bad that can happen to you, no matter how bad things look from outside. So they develop that inner resistance towards this pressure from outside. I think it's activating your inner shield. Again, you can't change your reality instantly. It's impossible. You understand it's too complex. But what you can do is change your self towards that reality, your attitude, even on the level of energy, your power of dealing with the situation on that most subtle level. That's why people solve their marital problems, financial problems, stuff like that.

A. You start to attract things into your life. You've made that decision.

D. Yes. When the doors are open, you know the path. You can follow it. You already know that yes, that's a high experience. It's like a peak experience. For one second you know. More like that.

A. Eckhart Tolle talks about being in the now, and how important it is for all of us to be present right now. Do you think this is a major factor why Braco is able to manifest the abilities that he does, because of his ability to be present?

D. Not for him to be present, but the people. It's very simple actually - if you look at the people and how concentrated they are. When you are fully concentrated on any object, particularly on a person, which has energy and everything included. It's all you need actually for the best perception you can experience in that moment you are present. I think it's the same story. He wouldn't say that. He wouldn't explain that, but the bottom line is that if you are present fully then anything can happen because you enter the stage of all possibility, of all potential. When you are present, at that point all the possibilities are opened.

A. When Braco is doing his healing, he is not projecting his will to heal.

D. No, on the contrary. It never works. If you project your will to the people, it will only work for a small percentage of the people. Because, if your personality, your ego, who you are psychologically is projected to people, you would find one out of ten that would like it. If you project that inner certainty, that inner potential of solving all the problems in a life, then you would attract nine out of ten.

A. And this is why the numbers keep building for Braco?

D. That's right.

A. And why people can just look at his picture and be attracted without knowing fully what he does?

D. I have seen it so many times in temples in various places. If you go to the Hare Krishna Temple you will see the real plastic statue of the late Prabhupada. He was such a tremendously powerful charismatic figure, even if you look at him standing around you will see that face, you'll feel that energy still. Yes, that's it, that's the story. So you can. But you can't make it up. You can't do it willingly, organize yourself to be better. You know what I mean - on that conscious level, the intellectual level. You can't make a plan - now I'll do this because it will work better. That's one of the major illusions. You can't be what you're not. If you are trying to be what you are not, you are gone. You're done, finished. So spontaneity is the only route through which he can work. If you start making arrangements about things - it's like we would do this because it would affect people better - it's not good, this is on the intellectual level. You can't do that intellectual level; spiritually speaking you are lost. You lost the track. It has to work spontaneously.

A. I've noted with Braco that he does not read a lot of books and fill himself with information from other people. He's very busy just being present, living his life, and allowing spontaneity to come through him. But most people don't live this way.

D. That's why they come to him. They wouldn't need him if they would live like that.

A. So if you were to sum up for people how Braco's way of living and being could help other people to have a better life, how would you sum up Braco? How would you sum up the way he lives his day-to-day life while serving other people?

D. I call it resonance, the principle of resonance. If you resonate with some source eventually you are becoming that source - but not on that superficial level.

A. Not because you are trying, but because you are open?

D. If you are trying this is the way not to become. This is the worst you can do, to try. So what happens is if you are open minded you are open to it. That resonance creates similarity with the source, not on this intellectual, superficial level. You shouldn't dress like him, or smoke like him or have hair like him. You understand, like people usually do. Women come to India and they are all wearing Saris. It is bullshit. They can't become Indians like that because you are Indian in your heart or mind. It is the same story here. You have, on a certain level that resonance with the source. People are coming to be back with the source. To be reset, you understand? If you come to places where people like Braco are, why are you coming here? Not to build something new on an already bad foundation. You know what I mean?

A. Yes.

D. What you should do is reset your system and start anew. And try to resonate with the source and it will give you a solution. If you can't do that, it doesn't work for you. This is why there are a lot of people coming to his place who do not experience anything.

A. Many people want to categorize what a spiritual life looks like, and Braco breaks the mold in many ways for he smokes and does some harmless things?

D. Oh, there are many of them, in the past there are many highly evolved masters, Bugia was drinking and smoking. All Tibetan Lamas are eating meat … it's just a myth.

A. But many people on the spiritual path today think that they have to give up these many things?

D. Usually, Americans.

A. It's almost like you stop being human, that you have to discipline yourself so rigorously to fit into a certain mold. And Braco is teaching that you don't have to do it that hard way anymore. There is naturalness with the spontaneity, humanness.

D. You are paying the price for doing something you don't feel like doing. It's obvious, it's a tremendous stress and it's frustration. If you come to India, you will see at Sai Baba's place only the Americans are trying to be good Indians. There is no Indian trying to be a good Indian. Only Americans are trying. Nobody there is vegetarian, half of them are smoking. If you find devotees from California, they will do it because this is the way their minds work. Yes, it's clear. Everything which is not natural for you at one point you shouldn't do it. It's better to do something bad than be frustrated because you didn't do it. It doesn't sound nice, but this is the fact of life. And when Rajneesh told that to Americans they busted him, nobody wants to hear this there.

A. This is like people who want to pretend they don't have anger or negative emotions because they want to be spiritual, and then they become so frustrated inside?

D. It happens all the time.

A. Yes, that they go backward on their path.

D. Yes, that's right. Suppressed anger turns into animosity, hostility, aggression, everything. Look, it's the energy, it's never lost. So this negative stuff that enters your system, you have to release it somehow or transform it. You can't live with it otherwise.

A. But if you reject it or pretend it's not there...?

D. You will never ever make it. You have just created another frustration, and another one. What you do when you are frustrated, you are adding a new type of hostility, a new type... I am now vegetarian, I'll stop smoking. It's not enough, I'm missing something. Now I'll be vegan, I don't want to eat cheese anymore. And what should I add else, I should get up at 2 am and meditate for 2-6 hours. Well, enlightenment is not coming, Jesus, I have to do more, I have to add something to it - it's not true, you should subtract something from it. That's the worst thing you can do, you are chasing a dragon, and you know this is the worst possibility. Chasing a dragon, all the time you have that wonderful feeling, there's one more thing I have to do and I'll be there. And you'll never arrive at it. This is called the illusion. So spontaneity is the key. So someone is not terrorizing you with his books, with his ideas that you have to quit smoking, quit drinking, quit this, and live like this and live that. You are not yourself anymore ultimately, you are becoming someone else.

A. So when someone comes for a healing session with Braco, what is the best thing they can do to help themselves to optimize the potential of that healing?

D. I have a specific theory about it. I think that in Yoga there's that point, two fingers below the heart, there is a small sub-chakra that is called Kalpa Vriksha. I think if you concentrate on that, it's called the wish-fulfilling tree. And it was used in classic Indian yoga if someone wanted to accomplish something to solve a problem. I think you can help yourself if you at that point just feel, at the same time you are gazing at him.

A. So would you just be concentrating on the minor chakra at that point?

D. Just feel it.

A. So what about thinking about your problems?

D. No, there's no need for that because subconsciously you have already delivered your problems to the man in front of you. You don't have to spell your problems. We believe you have to spell it. It's there, no matter if you spell it or not. So every problem, it's like a thought. If you go deeper in your thought, ultimately it becomes so faint that you cannot recognize it. But still it's the same thought. The problem works in the same way.

A. So somebody comes with a very open attitude, once they actually step into a healing session with Braco, and you suggest they concentrate on that minor chakra right below the heart. This would be the most powerful way that you think they could receive the energy?

D. For some people more sessions are necessary. They are building up that energy in themselves. It's not for everyone that they can solve the problems instantly. Impossible. For some people it is possible, for some it's not. You have to build up high enough so that you may cross that barrier. Sometimes it takes time to transform. They need more sessions. Coming and coming, gradually they are basically transforming themselves to it. It's not always instantaneously. It can't work like that.

A. This is why people will come again and again, because they are building up an effect within themselves?

D. That's right, they feel they need it. They feel they need it.

A. And so the books and DVDs that people can get about Braco, these too will help build that energy within them?

D. It's a booster. It's a reminder. Different philosophies, religions have different reminders. You understand. It's like a reminder. You just remember. Just by remembering the feeling you had during the session, you are having it again. It's on the level of feeling. The problem of this civilization is the feminine side; people do not live their feminine side that is called feeling. They do not feel, they think. So already, when they switch on the feeling level they are starting to solve the problem already on that level. It's some kind of a mixture between what we call feeling and emotion, but feeling is more than emotion. Emotion is the expression of your inner state of mind; feeling is the way of how to resolve it. So if you accomplish that during this session that you have the feeling, then it works by itself.

A. Spontaneously, it just happens?

D. And there's another extreme. You enter the area of the emotion, and then you are becoming very emotional and everything, which is just the expression of what you experience, but it is not a solution for your problem. It's just the expression of your inner state, your current inner state.

A. What about Braco's sun symbol that people wear?

D. It has 13 rays and is of an ancient tradition. Only the 13-ray golden sun actually fits in Ying and Yang simultaneously, is the presence of both principles inside one symbol. This is the only symbol that contains both of the principles, both of the extremes in one. It's very rare in history. You have just one God in the Shinto tradition that is the male god of the moon. In the whole history of humanity, you have just one female god of the sun. It is extremely rare. One is Sumerian and the other is coming from the Japanese Shinto tradition. So here you have that unusual intuitive level on which Ivica realized this. It is that this symbol contains at the same time that grain of Ying and Yang, and that grain of Yang and Ying. It's the perfect combination. I traced it to other civilizations and traditions. I see it clearly, it's very clear.

A. So when somebody sees this symbol, or when they wear the gold sun, it continues to give an individual the power, it continues to build that power within them to transform?

D. Everything is devoted to that, everything is for that purpose.

A. Yes, I mean specifically with Braco, the symbol is a potent ally to his work. It embodies it in a way?

D. It became part of the human perception of him because people always see him connected to this symbol for 14 years, it's normal. Somehow they became one, it's very big; it's the matter of the authority on the level of the reflex. It's always interconnected, but the meaning itself goes far deeper than the individual personality. It's a unique symbol, a historically significant symbol that unites this principal in such a way that is extremely rare. I told you they are found in only two religions in all of history, and you can count at least 20,000 different religions on the face of the Earth. So if you trace it properly you can find the roots for an explanation of what it actually does mean. It's a highly complex issue, why it contains both types. There are reasons for everything. You can reference some historical facts, it's highly complex. In Japan, you have the number four, which is the symbol of everything bad. Numbers are symbols and 13 is a specific number, but it was never been incorporated into the symbol like the sun itself. It's highly unusual.

A. And the symbol, the way it is presented today on all of Braco's material, is something that Braco himself had the vision of?

D. No, it was Ivica actually. He was the one who picked this from the collective consciousness.

A. So Ivica picked the symbol, but didn't Braco bring it into its current form?

D. You can say that. You know, there are no real borders between these two. When Ivica was alive, Braco already was in a way on that path. It's actually hard to say all these details, you can't put it as in historical books. On that date, I saw this. On that date, this happened or that happened. It doesn't work like that. It's all intertwined. The birth of the symbol itself – it's gradually manifesting itself physically as your subconscious is manifesting itself on the other level. So there are parallel paths. You can't say this is the date. It's not like when America was born. It's more intertwined.

A. Do you understand how the mirror works, how Ivica was able to use the mirror?

D. There are many theories about it. You have a lot of practices throughout the world, throughout history. Like Dr Dee in Great Britain was the first one describing the obsidian mirrors in which he could contact different entities from parallel worlds. He could see the future. After that, I think it was the sixteenth century, you have new broader techniques, methods, theories connected to mirrors, the way mirrors work. In every Eastern tradition, in Shinto temples you have a mirror in front of you. Then you have that famous exercise in which you look into your own eyeballs in the mirror - so you can see your faces from past lives. There are innumerable techniques and methods of using mirrors in the history of humanity, on all continents, so there is probably some connection. And I don't think Ivica was reading about it. He came to that spontaneously. So he could see stuff in it. Now you have plenty of things. You can see your own aura if you switch on a red light in your room, and look at yourself in the mirror but from the profile, you can see your aura clearly. There are many techniques involving mirrors. It's very hard to tell precisely. He didn't like to talk about it too much. He did not give any explanations.

A. But the sun symbol that Braco uses is that more to stimulate the subconscious to give more an archetypal symbol from the collective consciousness, than the mirror which is meant to reflect back information?

D. Exactly, it's not solely a one-dimensional issue. The symbol itself has more aspects to it. It's not only the sun principle, which is basically the Yang principle, the active principle, the light principle. The number 13 has the moisture, the dark principle, the moon principle in it so it's a mixture as we all are. So it's a multidimensional effect that it has on the consciousness of people. You have to study what it actually means from the point of view of the other civilizations and traditions. Even more than psychology. This symbology is very tricky stuff. Because it's very well known that the symbol has tremendous power itself.

A. I'd like to end this interview discussing something that Ivica said. Ivica made a prediction that Braco would come to America once a transformation in the psyche of the American people had taken place?

D. He said more like to the new lands or something similar. In Europe you don't say America, it's the new land, New World. He said something like that. He would go to the New World. Which means he knew Braco's mission, there's no doubt about it. He said to him, you know, when I will not be around, there will be thousands around you here. So he knew that goal in these things.

A. This particular statement about Braco going to the New World when a change in consciousness took place? In February Braco went to the United States for the first time. Now he's going to be going back. Braco has had a huge effect in many countries in Europe with his healing work. What do you think is in store for the American people and other countries of the World that Braco is now going to be visiting in the future? How do you think his healing talent and what he offers is going to affect these new countries?

D. There are coincidences, it's very strange. He was invited to America exactly at the point Obama was elected. And now he is going to Hawaii, and Obama was coming from Hawaii, yes. There are many coincidences like that. I don't like to discuss that stuff. It sounds like a marketing story. There are many coincidences. These are just two. You know you can find support for a lot of them, coincidences like that. Well the time will tell. I don't think projections into the future, what will happen, and what will be the effect on people in America, in which year, and how. I just don't feel like making any projections. I don't know. He can create something unbelievable. I don't know.

A. I'm thinking more in terms of the incredible opportunity. There's a catalyzing effect going on here. So Braco is soon going to be coming more to the United States and then other English speaking countries and beyond. So it's more about letting people know that there's this incredible opportunity coming.

D. Well it depends. I see it as whatever has to happen will happen. So all the information needed will be there. It's like when you are reading the newspaper - I don't know if you have observed this, I did with myself, I read an article and when I had finished with the article, my wife was reading the same article. Suddenly she makes a comment, and I realize I haven't remembered that part of the argument because that wasn't meant for me. You know it happens all the time. It's like with books, with conversation. If you, for example, have a discussion with some friends for an hour while you are having a coffee, you will not necessarily remember everything. You'll memorize what is needed for you at that point. So usually, we take in the information that is needed at that point for our evolution.

A. It's right back to the Now, being present.

D. It's easiest. It's here now and that's what you should deal with. What comes, comes. It will come by itself. Anyways, it's beyond our power to decide. So there is something much more powerful that is making decisions. You can have dreams - sometimes they are fulfilled, sometimes they are not, it depends. It's the greatest mystery ever. It's the mystery of life itself.

A. Thank you Drago for all the great information.

Chapter Three

Day 3 – Wednesday, July 1, 2009

Slovenia – Rogaska Slatina

Already I had come to understand a very important element of Braco's work. Braco was not a healer, and he would never call himself one. An aspect, however, of his work was that people were healed, sometimes of severe illnesses or injuries, and at other times of overwhelming or problematic areas in their lives, which improved greatly. People would feel better and stronger due to the energy of the gazing sessions. Yet Braco was not trying to heal individuals, instead he wholeheartedly had devoted his life to serve a Source energy so vast, delivered to us via the sun, that a name for it was not in our language, and perhaps it was too sacred to have one. This was a divine wellspring that we could only meagerly associate as the All That Is.

He served this energy that was the force that decided when consciousness would wake up and evolve on our world; humanity could not decide such things. Therefore, instead of a healer, he could more accurately be thought of as an awakener for those open to receive the gifts the divine power bestowed. Our fates and destinies were as they were, already written, but this unlimited power of divine consciousness had the ability to do all things and make the impossible possible at its will. Our wishes from our hearts, not our wills, were our best connection to this energy. Our wills were propelled by our chaotic minds and our myopic views of reality. Often our desires had no alignment with that of divine will, and so our lives could be filled with so much suffering and pain.

The power behind our heartfelt wishes was that they were honest and filled with our true integrity. They could be effortlessly granted if they came from this source within us. Now I was in the midst of someone capable of being a vessel for this profound light, and he could only be this because of his absolute commitment of service to this highest power. And so the healings took place through his work, but in fact they were actually transformations within the individual activated by this energy and the divine will that triggered one's light and a deeper connection within to Source power.

Never before, in all the healers and spiritual guides I had encountered, had I felt or seen a gift that effected so many people to the degrees that I was witnessing. Yet I was just beginning my real journey of understanding, and only later in Macedonia at a gazing event would I experience myself a taste of this ineffable Source. For now, I only yet glimpsed to a small degree the scope of what I still had to learn to better penetrate of this great mystery of Braco.

I awoke that morning, once again with only a few hours of sleep, which I came to realize, was a test of sorts. To do this job, it was required to go beyond the normal boundaries of the body and mind's limitations. One had to dig deep to find resources within that could be tapped so that when work was required, no hesitation or denials would arise to stop what had to be done or accomplished. Spontaneity had to be embraced too, for this was how the energy flowed and it would use all opportunities at a moment's notice that required immediate action. To deny spontaneity was to block the flow of life energies that was hallmarked by an effortless grace.

On the first Wednesday of each month for the last year and a half, Braco and his staff had traveled to a village in Slovenia to do his gazing work. At 6 o'clock, a car picked us up to drive the hour and half drive to Rogaska Slatina. Once a thriving vacation spot prized for its natural mineral springs and frequented by those of affluence, it was now a town filled with resorts that attracted only a modest crowd since the breakup of former Yugoslavia. Economies had changed and now once prosperous areas were challenged.

Wide-awake, I appreciated the beauty of the drive to our destination. We passed lush green valleys and sweetly quaint villages. Forest lined the hill and mountaintops, where no clear cutting at all had taken place. There was so much untouched natural land that I was quite surprised. In the car, a CD played of music by one of Croatia's most popular singers who had devoted an entire album to songs of gratitude for Braco, who had helped his own life. The music was cheerful and had heart, and I would grow to thoroughly enjoy listening to that same album on many drives.

When we came to our village, a variety of lovely resort buildings greeted us with a charm of an era past, yet they were all well kept and the grounds were spotless. It was not evident in the outside facades that a dramatic drop in tourism had occurred. Between the many buildings, a wide walkway with trees and benches acted as a spacious courtyard. We all strolled down this long walkway to view all the surroundings, and stopped at an outdoor café for espresso and a morning snack.

A very pretty woman named Marjana, youthful and well dressed, who I had met at the Laughlin conference, greeted us. She had traveled all the way from Slovenia to the United States conference to have the opportunity to see Braco at an event for seven consecutive days. Since Braco began coming to this location in her home country, she had attended regularly once a month and had also helped with the arrangements of the event itself. We hugged and exchanged words of happiness at seeing each other again. She, like Ljiljana and now I, wore the same special sun design necklace that was Braco's gift of generosity and thanks.

It was time to set up and we all headed to the place for our event, a theatre-style room with stage, in one of the nearby resorts. The space was fresh and clean, but I had expected an empty room with only a raised platform for Braco. Yet this layout worked quite well as people could sit during the presentation and all rise for the gazing session itself. People were always asked to stand for the gazing unless they were in a wheel chair, or disabled, and I thought that the straight spine would probably conduct and receive the energy best, as was standard practice in all eastern forms of meditation for this reason.

Dinko, Rudi, Miki, Branko and others stepped into action getting all set up while Braco, Marjana and I went backstage behind the large stage curtain. There were two long tables set up, one with and array of fruit baskets, cookies and sweets and bottled water, and the other with chairs all around for eating and conversation. Each event I came to on tour always had fruits, sweets, snacks and water set up for Braco. The organizers would not only provide a private space for him to await groups, but they also took great care in making the space pretty with flowers, tablecloths and food served on trays. Unquestionably, Braco was shown great respect in all places in this way.

Branko was ever vigilant in security and ensuring all went smoothly, checking everything so all was as it should be. He had an ever-watchful eye that seemed to constantly read and penetrate people, and this I was sure from all his years in law enforcement. One could always feel safe and secure around him; he had that mature and capable air of a man of authority. While Miki, Dinko and others set up the book and DVD tables, Sead, the filmmaker who had also accompanied the group, came in backstage for a snack and we chatted.

Suddenly Braco came up with a spontaneous idea. He loved to change things around and try new possibilities. He looked at me with his ever-confident demeanor and told me I would present him here in Rogaska. "What do you mean," I blurted out, my heart missing a beat. Enthusiastically, he explained that I would help to open people up to the energy. Of course I had no idea what to say and adamantly expressed my lack of confidence in his suggestion. But he continued to vaguely outline a few points for me to touch upon and I was asked to simply state what I felt. I was terrified, thinking of all the times I had stood before audiences in utter torment inside. Normally, I would take months to prepare myself mentally for what I would face, but this offered no such opportunity.

I did my best to refuse, but his mind was set and I did not know how to say *no* more firmly, especially when he had been the most gracious and considerate of hosts. And heaven knows, I had asked for this wish only yesterday and here it was blatantly manifesting before me. So I numbly agreed and my mind raced with what was before me. It was obviously my time of initiation in a way I had not expected, but he seemed convinced that I could do a good job. Not yet finished, he next looked at Marjana and told her she had to translate for me in front of the group, since she spoke excellent English and Slovenian.

Marjana was more reluctant than I and she very firmly refused at first. She was coaxed and encouraged by Braco, who now loved and was fully committed to his idea, but she denied that she could do it, besides not wishing to do so. Not to be thwarted, Braco then declared he would not do the gazing for the people if she would not translate. We were all breathless with this threat because it looked like he was serious indeed. Some would look at this as high handed, but he knew this was an important step for Marjana in the work, and she finally agreed despite her reluctance.

Braco called his normal staff presenters to let them know about the change in plans, and then Marjana and I were escorted to the front of the stage and walked through what would take place. We were given hand microphones and tried them out, told where to stand and when to begin. At first I was told to talk five or ten minutes and then it expanded to fifteen, whatever I felt. All headed back stage and the first group was called of over 150 people, and it would be the smallest of the day.

At this time I realized something I had noticed before, I was growing stronger, more natural and self-confident. Inside of me I actually believed I could pull this responsibility off with some grace, and then Marjana and I stepped before the group. My stage fright, though present in my racing heart, was so diminished that it felt almost exciting to step in front of this new challenge to help, and I was so grateful. Marjana began by introducing me and then I told a simple story of finding out about Braco in America, coming to his gazing sessions and the incredible energy and change I had experience in myself.

Mentioning the sun symbol and its energy, I also talked about Braco coming to my Hawaii conference and I closed by letting everyone know that they had already made their decision to receive the gift of the energy by walking through the door. My final words accentuated the importance to focusing on feeling the energy and allowing the heart to guide the way. There was a bond of hope and a desire for better in all of our lives that united us, and I understood that only the heart knew how to embrace without limitations, and this was the key. Truly I was honored to stand with them for Braco's gaze, and I thanked them before leaving.

People clapped, which I had been told they do not do in the Balkans unless they liked you, and I walked to the side of the audience for the gazing. Sead filmed us this first time and how I wished he had done so later, for Marjana and I each grew a little brighter each time. Branko, Dinko and others were all watching in a back row, and though this was daunting at first, afterwards they all spoke with Braco in Croatian, and both Marjana and I had their approval. Of course Braco smiled and had the look of satisfaction. We would be the ones to bring a new level to the opening presentation to assist people to be heart centered and to feel. Marjana and I turned out to make a good team together, ever supportive of each other.

By the third presentation, I felt invincible and Marjana was beaming. We had both met our challenge well and we knew it. After that time, each audience I stood before in the days ahead was easy, and I could be grounded and relaxed. This was thrilling and empowering, and Braco was entirely to thank. As the day went on and we presented to all of the groups, it became clear we were affecting the people as tears began to roll while we talked. Many people nodded in thanks and appreciation that day to me as I left the stage, and I was so overjoyed and content.

Backstage, Braco would change little things about my presentation to keep me on my toes, and I discovered the rule of thumb, flexibility, ever around him. Yet always, his obvious support and trust helped Marjana and I to be our best. A total of 916 people came that day to see Braco; I had spoken before most of them, honing each time my words until I knew I had a very good speech that people responded to openly. I was now a pro ready for more action. Inside, I wondered about Braco, if he somehow felt my wishes because he had the uncanny ability to push me exactly toward these specific things with such graceful spontaneity.

Braco never appeared tired, the gazing energy fed him in abundance, and he had worked as much as 36 hours straight in order to see all the people who had come to him at an event. He required his staff to work without fail for the people, no matter the lack of sleep, food or breaks. The needs of the people were always first and all present around him accepted this wholeheartedly. At 5 pm the last group was brought in, and I was surprised how quickly Braco and I were escorted to a waiting car, driving away only minutes after the group was finished. Others would stay behind to pack up, but we were done with our part.

The drive back seemed to fly by, and in an hour and a half we were dropped off at Braco's home. We would watch Hawaii DVDs for hours, which I greatly enjoyed since they were all new to me. Before departing for Croatia, I had visited local shops and bought every single one I could find, and now I was able to enjoy my islands playing tour guide, as his enthusiasm only seemed to grow.

Day 4 – Thursday, July 2, 2009

Germany - Kraichtal

Thursday was a day that Braco never worked upon, because Ivica had a vision to take this day off, to make this day like a Sunday, and so Braco honored this too. Usually, he would travel to other countries on this day instead, and I was able to sleep in and came to Braco's door at 9 am. I brought green tea, which I always traveled with, but amusingly, Braco did not even know if he had a kettle to boil water. It became immediately evident that he did not know what was in his kitchen at all. This was only one of the ways in which he had lived a sheltered life a bit unlike a normal man. I did not ask if he knew how to cook because the answer seemed obvious.

I quickly surveyed the kitchen myself and found a pot that would do the job. He joined me for tea and we lounged on his balcony, enjoying the warm morning, the beautiful view and chatted about the upcoming event the next day in Germany. Then came more Hawaii video fare, which he insisted on watching with undiminished delight. Later I would take some time to pack and rejoined him at 1 pm. Rudi, a key person at Srebrnjak 1, was there, and I had taken particular note of him because of a special warmth he displayed when working with groups. A dedication that was particularly apparent in him. Yet I felt his reserve too in my company and I wondered how he and others must feel since Braco spoke of me taking him out of Europe, which meant away from the Center and them.

Rudi offered to make coffee and a farce ensued as both men entered the kitchen, insisting they could take care of this job. I heard them discussing different containers, unsure of their contents, then much clanking as sugar ended up on the counter and floor. Yet a short time later Rudi happily emerged with three cups of Turkish coffee. Smiling, I drank while they watched with expectation, and I nodded politely but was really quite alarmed at the taste. Had they cleaned the pot, I wondered, because it tasted a bit off. Both men drank and Rudi remarked that it tasted good because it was what we had on hand. Later I would discover this really was the flavor of that style of coffee. Though I would drink it many times, I could not develop a palette for it and eventually stopped trying.

Now Braco and I declared that we were hungry, but he did not know if there was any food because his wife was at their seaside home vacationing with their son. But Braco bravely endeavored to find us something and finally came back with two carrots. Then Rudi went upstairs to the apartment that he was living in part-time during workdays, though he had a dearly loved wife and his own home in another town. The schedule of touring and the Center did not allow him the time to travel day by day back and forth, and so he spent his days off and vacation with her only, a sacrifice many at Srebrnjak 1 made for the work.

Soon returning, he had in hand a half loaf of bread and some cheese singles wrapped in plastic and we happily ate what we had. It was enough and we were contented, much like Rudi was with the Turkish coffee. By 3:30, we were all off to the airport to fly to Germany. Filmmaker Sead, Branko and others from the Center met us at the airport and together we checked in, had a café stop for a dearly appreciated espresso (by me) and then we were off.

Tedo, a Yugoslavian born man living in Germany for the past twenty years met us with a van at the airport. He was tall and lean, with shortly cropped blond hair and looked very Germanic. I would come to greatly appreciate his gentlemanly ways and his great devotion to the work with Braco. For the last 6 years he and his family had rented a lovely, country style hotel and restaurant in the town of Kraichtal, and held an event twice a month on Friday and Saturday for Braco to do his gazing. The village was richly old world, with lush green surrounding in the countryside. Once it had been prosperous, but now the biggest draw for the hotel were the engagements with Braco, which brought in thousands of people each time.

At 9 pm we arrived at the hotel, crisp, white, sprawling and clean, and were each shown to our rooms upstairs that were spacious and comfortable. I was pleased to have a table to write at and wireless Internet downstairs. After dropping off our luggage, we descended and I was introduced to Ida, a Russian born beauty who would show herself to be a petite powerhouse of energy and enthusiasm. We took to each other right away, and I was so impressed with the quality and kindness of the people who Braco attracted.

Ida had followed Braco for eleven months, and came every weekend to see him. Because she was born in Russia, she very much wanted to bring Braco there, but for now had arranged an event in Stuttgart, Germany, our next destination. This would be her second event and her first had brought 1300 people in a day, and now she hoped for 2000. A long time vegetarian like me, she spoke excellent English along with other languages. Her spiritual desire for something more had caused her to leave her job to now organize events because she had found, as so many, something so special in the energy Braco shared that she wished to also help bring it to more people.

We all sat down outside in the hotel courtyard for a late dinner. Braco would now have me play the role he had alluded to on the phone in his original invitation to me. I was to tell those loyal and loving people who supported the work here that Braco's time to leave Europe was approaching. My own conference event would be that doorway out to new countries and new audiences. He had also had an offer to come to a conference in Australia that next March, and we were planning on cultivating some dear friends and organizers I knew in Japan too. So the dynamic trio of new horizons was mine to deliver to everyone, and I did my best to enthusiastically and happily talk about the merits of these opportunities.

Of course I could see sadness in many faces, those of his staff and supporters, because they knew they would lose Braco to the world. And yet they were openly supportive and delighted for him too because they knew this day would come. When I was done fulfilling my job with the conviction and self-confidence that helped to sway everyone, wine glasses were raised by all to my Hawaii event, and I knew all was well. As we made the toast, Braco too took a small glass of the wine and drank the contents like a shot of whiskey. I watched Tedo's jaw drop and face go white, while Branko jumped up objecting, grabbing for the glass.

They informed me that Braco had never had alcohol before, not even a sip of wine. Braco confirmed this while several shook their heads in disbelief. Everyone revealed that they believed Braco would not cross certain lines, mainly because they looked up to him, but Braco could not be defined in this way and had just pushed the boundaries. People asked why and he smiled - he had just had the wish to do it. The simple reason he had not done so before was the same, he had never had the wish. I thought this was my influence somehow, but Braco had stated the first day that he would eat what I ate and perhaps this was just his way of fully fulfilling that promise.

So I teased him that he drank it so fast that he could not have tasted it, but he made it clear he had to do it that way because of Branko's lightening quick reflexes. Branko would protect Braco in all ways he saw fit. Next dinner was served, which was an excellent mushroom pasta that Tedo himself had prepared. It was a culinary delight, but again my hunger was meager and I only ate a small portion. Since I knew that Tedo had gone to all the care of making it and I did not want to hurt his feelings, I waited for the right moment after Braco had finished his serving. Then I scooped the untouched half portion of mine onto his plate.

With fingers he began to eat it as we had playfully done now on several occasions at Srebrnjak 1, and he asked me if I would do the same. So I did and he was happy to share this ritual with me. Eating an elegant pasta dinner with my hands made me feel pleasantly rebellious in a childlike way, and so I challenged him to a race. He suggested five minutes timed to see who could eat more, and I made it three minutes so I would not have to eat so much. Hands hovering over our plates, we waited for someone to be our timekeeper and start our match. Tedo assumed this role and set us in motion.

Braco used both hands and held back nothing in the intensity of challenge. I chose to use one hand, but was able to hold my ground. We shoveled our mouths to capacity and I could hardly chew it fast enough to keep pace, but I did my best. Sead was beside himself as he watched because he did not have his video camera, but Tedo pulled out his cell phone and videotaped us. At the close of three minutes, Braco won with his face bulging with noodles and sauce in his hair. His showing was spectacular and mine a good try.

I reached over and shook Braco's sauce covered hand with my clean one and gave Sead a description of our match on camera, which he had by now retrieved. I lamented with a straight face the poor showing I had done for my country by losing. After taking turns in the washroom, we were full but well amused by our spontaneous game. Thankfully, it was time for an activity which everyone always partook in during his visits, a long walk down country lanes after dinner.

In the warm night air, the movement felt wonderful and relaxing. Ida and I came together naturally for we had the fastest strides, and chatted away on our many common interests. Tedo, Branko and Braco walked together behind. I genuinely liked this woman who had a sureness and grace about her, and we spoke of her home in Russia and my own in the United States, and the things we valued in life. It was well over an hour before we came back to the village and climbed the stairs of the hotel to our rooms. Everyone now needed to rest to prepare for a big day to come in the morning.

Chapter Four

Day 5 – Friday, July 3, 2009

Germany - Kraichtal

I came down for our first group gazing session that day which began at 9 am. Our staging area and rest area would be the in bar, which was closed to the public, since it led into the large and elegant banquet-style room which we would use for the event of the day. It held a stage with a platform atop for Braco, along with fresh flowers in abundance. People would gather in a large white tent set up outside as they arrived, and here they would state the language they needed, and be organized into groups accordingly and await their turn. They would also pay a 4 Euro fee that was the maximum Braco allowed all event organizers to charge to cover their own expenses for room rentals, flowers, staging and more. Braco took nothing of this for himself.

Warmly, I was greeted by Braco, Tedo, Ida and the others and was ready to see what the day brought. Slovenia had an attendance of nearly 1000 people in a day, and now I would experience the same steady stream over two consecutive days as people poured in by car and buses. Everyone was cheerful and knew well the job at hand, but of course Braco was ever spontaneous with new inspirations and changes, and decided that I would present him that morning with two translators. The early audience was a mixture of German and Croatian, so I would have the challenge of keeping my thoughts clear for the duration of two side-by-side translations of my words.

I thought this would be difficult, but as I stepped before the first group my heart opened to the people and the energy had me. In that energy it was easy to stay focused and certain, and I found that I had no problem at all shortening my speech while maintaining its rhythm and keeping track of its many topics. My stage fright was indeed gone and I could thoroughly enjoy sharing my own experiences that appeared to resonate with the audience who warmly received me, especially when I told them that my own mother was a native of their country and that it was my first visit, a very happy occurrence for me.

Then I continued with the job from last night's dinner, announcing Braco's visits to upcoming new countries, and everyone truly accepted the news with goodwill for their beloved friend. In fact so many considered Braco as a part of their own family because of how deeply he had touched many lives, and so he was like a son prospering well for them, along with some notable sadness at him leaving for far away. Again, tears came to some faces as I talked and several people throughout the day touched their hearts and waved. I was so fulfilled in my job that I beamed and I wanted to continue to do this without end.

Then the music began and Braco walked on stage and the energy began, that marvelous, unexplainable energy - some people swayed as they stood, many cried. Now and again someone was overcome, and needed the quick assistance offered by the strong staff members always present for the audience. Perhaps one third of the people carried pictures of loved ones, which they pressed to their hearts to receive the energy too. As Braco's gaze touched the room, a softening took place over all and bodies relaxed as if dropping burdens and cares.

Once the music ended, Braco slowly left the stage and no one said a word. They, like I, only wanted a few moments to continue to feel that beautiful feeling inside that the energy called out for most. How many came, I wondered, who had no specific reason, but just wished to feel good in the energy and to take that boost home. As I spoke with people who came throughout the day, I found many traveled a good distance for this reason alone. After

Braco left, one of the staff finished with the group as a few people in the audience shared their experiences. Then I left for our rest area and rejoined Braco.

He wondered how it had worked with the two translations, and I told him all went well, as did my translators themselves afterwards. Ever pleased by the success of a new idea, he joined me for an espresso and some fresh fruit that adorned a table along with sweet rolls and more placed out by our host, Tedo. I told him how happy and strong I felt once again and this too pleased him. He truly loved to see those around him reaching for their best and more, and he did everything to encourage it. If something were wrong, he would be honest and blunt, but never with a punishing attitude. He just liked to see things done properly when it had any impact on the people who came to be helped. Everyone needed to be treated the same, which meant everyone deserved our best without fail.

In the next session I came beside Ida after my presentation to stand with the audience for Braco's gaze. She politely told me that I should turn away from Braco and watch the people instead since I had already done a gazing session before. She could not know my special arrangement and so when I told her I stood to watch all of the gazing sessions, she looked surprised but graciously accepted it and stepped aside. Then I felt my too sensitive empathic antenna hit a ripple and it disquieted me. But the energy that day would help me to grow beyond my ultra-sensitivity. I still felt most people without effort, but I had gathered the strength to maintain my own balance in the face of this empathic connection. That was another milestone for me, and now my empathy was no longer my rollercoaster curse, but my stalwart helpmate.

Braco and I joked at my growing espresso consumption, but even my system was fortified to handle my intake with a new balance. As always, we came together each break to chat. One conversation made very clear that Braco did not have the power - the power had him. This was a vital point for me to grasp in order to understand the nature of this energy and the gift of Braco. The power had all the control, not the other way around. Braco's first dedication to life was to the Source energy, and he had made the pledge that as long as people came, he would help them. Braco gave himself fully to the energy - to all the other people, including his family and best friends, he gave equally the same.

Currently Braco felt a certain way during the gazing, but he too was changing. In time, he would develop the ability to maintain the same feeling during the gazing and in life. That would come naturally. Now, silence was becoming more important to him and pursuits such as watching television, reading the newspaper and other common habits were losing attraction. Even talk, which he described as often *killing the feelings* since it was not possible to express feelings with mere words, was of less interest. Words could only describe material things and a feeling was too big to describe with words. A spiritual force, feelings were body and soul, and of prime importance.

Nature and its peacefulness was ever important and a dear part of Braco's life. He knew it was difficult to live as a regular man, and he could not do so. If he did, he would not be able to bring forth the energy in his gazing. Inherently, he recognized that the problem of civilization was that there was too much information and it extinguished people's feelings. Current information in fact made most people afraid; watching the endless parade of strife, chaos and catastrophes in the news greatly exacerbated this condition. The worse enemy of the people was fear, to be afraid and scared. To Braco it was worse than poverty or war and its weapons.

In the late morning the crowd was more easily separated by language and I was relieved of one translator. The people kept arriving, spreading themselves out through the day in a way that allowed a steady and fairly equal flow into the banquet room. At 9 pm the last group was taken and I had presented to all but the last two, from which I was given a break. My appreciation had grown immensely for people like Rudi and Dinko who sometime worked such days to the end, giving the opening and closing presentations without the luxury of taking some sessions off, and sometimes the workday was much longer than a mere twelve hours. I was having the pampered version of this experience.

Professor Alex Schneider, a Swiss engineer, physicist, parapsychologist and President of the Para-psychological Association of Switzerland joined us that evening. As the founder of the Basel PSI Days / World Congress of Healing, he had invited Braco to the congress in November 2006 after watching two of his DVDs and being personally affected. He was studying Braco's gift and had become a friend. As earlier suggested and immediately decided by Braco, I would conduct an interview on film with the professor. This delighted and intrigued me. Alex was very warm and vital at 82 years of age, and our subsequent interview led to a discussion on the topics of spirituality and how Braco's gift could change the world, which was absolutely electrifying. I was enormously honored to meet such an intelligent, broadminded and heartfelt man. The combination was rare and inspiring.

After Braco's idea of the interview, he had another that would startle me greatly. Not only did he want me to do another interview to publish on my news column, but something much bigger. He read possibilities hanging unseen in the air and became enthusiastically animated over this newest one. He suggested I write a book on my experiences with him and even named it, '*21 Days with Braco*'. Encouraging me wholeheartedly, he was certain I could write a great book for an American audience and others. Once again he was innocently delivering to me one of my dearest dreams and empowering it into a reality.

Through the years, good friends had often encouraged me unrestrainedly to write a book. Even my own partner had suggested that I should use this trip to Croatia with Braco for the foundation of my first manuscript, and had bought me a voice recorder for the project. Yet none of these sincere encouragements and shows of support had been enough to override my own doubts or empower me. Only Braco was able to do this, and it happened as if by magic. The strength of the energy he carried was able to instantly overcome all of my social programming, the imbedded beliefs from my family that artists only starved and any other obstacles acquired over the years.

Only that Source energy itself was able to reactivate my own dearest aspirations and wishes to make them stronger than the blockages I had subconsciously accepted despite my will and positive desires. It was as if my original template of spirit was washed clean of rubbish. And this was the very reason why so many could find healing and transformation through Braco's gaze. I was somewhat speechless as I quietly agreed to the project, but I was also luminous with my own joy. Now it was finally real and nothing could stop me. It was decided that we would work together over the next day to outline all the events that had transpired thus far, and all was set into motion.

Our day finally ended with the ritual of the long walk to refresh ourselves after a rigorous but rewarding schedule. We once again strolled out of the village to a country lane and as soon as I saw a stretch of grass on the side of the road, I took my shoes off and left the road for it. At home I walked barefoot often, and now the cool grass was a delight. Braco immediately noticed and took off his shoes and joined me. We walked carefree like children, and once the grass ended, we continued barefoot on the side of the road in the dirt, through puddles, brush and pavement. All felt good on our soles and spirits. Along the way, we came across a cherry tree orchard and entered to have our fill of the season's final fruit. Even Branko and the Professor, as well as Tedo and the Srebrnjak 1 crew partook in the sweet and crisp cherries, the perfect dessert to compliment the end of our day.

Interview with Professor Alex Schneider, MSc.,
Swiss Engineer, Physicist, Parapsychologist

Legend: *A- Angelika*; D – Dr Schneider

A. Welcome Professor Schneider, I'd like to begin by first having you talk a little bit about your credentials and your background with Braco?

D. Yes, I'm a scientist, natural science and I'm very skeptical of all the supernatural things, but I've studied them and now I accept them. And so in Basel [Switzerland] we had for years a very interesting congress of the border sciences called Basil PSI Days [Spiritual Healing Congress] and we had many healers there, excellent healers. But one day a man from Croatia came and told me to look at something, he had brought me DVDs about Braco, and said Braco was someone you couldn't compare with the other healers. Well, he was a nice boy, I liked him and once home I studied the DVDs he gave me and . . . oh, really, I felt something! Me, me, I felt something as a scientist, incredible! After having watched two DVDs, and I don't like to see films, but I watched two and then a backache I was having went away.

A. Just by watching at the DVDs?

D. Yes, I had been ill for five days in a Spa because of this backache, but that didn't help. But just by watching the films - that helped me, that's incredible! So a lady and I went to Zagreb. She was organizing a fair in Zurich, also a fair for three days, and we said yes, let's study this man, maybe we can invite him for our congresses. Indeed, when Braco came to Basel he was a very good success. Many, many scientists gave statements that his session was excellent.

A. At this conference other doctors and scientists came forward and they also validated that this was a very real phenomenon?

D. Yes. Yes. Yes.

A. Now have you conducted any studies of the people going to the sessions and experiencing changes?

D. No, that I didn't. It's a very big job to evaluate all these healings. I'm only convinced by the rate of healings, and the rate of improvements in physical things and especially social things. That's very interesting for me. So many people told me they had problems and then came home and all was good. It was just incredible.

A. Everything was harmonious after seeing Braco?

D. Yes, yes. Well, you could say things looked a little bit more harmonious but you can't explain this. Also, other people told me, "I came to my office the next day after I saw Braco, and it wasn't so morbid, everybody was so nice." So that's a real phenomenon. That it has this effect, that it affects even the social life.

A. Well this is something that I found fascinating that I experienced myself. I heard about the physical healings of illnesses in the body, but going there without an illness myself, I experienced a transformation that was incredible in all areas of my life. Emotionally related, spiritually related, my connections with everyone else. Can you explain?

D. That's my explanation. I am very interested in modern physics of course and modern theories of how the world is comprised, but we can't explain what has happened here – not by natural science, everyday science in the last century. You need modern science, and you need a more expanded science. The reality is not what we touch here. The reality is something we can't see. We have a long way to see reality, and that's touching these things. And we have other realities. With these other realities, we can see only aspects of the reality. It's a little bit difficult, especially if I have to translate it into English. Let me say, here is something happening that *can't*. That's the first statement. It can't be explained by the natural science of the last century. That's clear. And what has been the explanation for it is very interesting. And for this explanation it gets very complicated.

A. Could you try and give us a philosophical explanation in your own perspective?

D. Simple, there is the very ancient view of Plato, maybe you know this? Mankind is in a cave and mankind looks at the wall behind in the cave, and they see shadows going by, and they only see these shadows. They think this is reality, but they don't turn around and see people going by. And so we see only shadows if we look only with natural sciences. And so maybe we see different shadows from different sides. When we put all of these shadows together, maybe we can gather the reality and Braco is leading us to this reality. And we must discard all this nonsense. I say nonsense. I heard you do an introduction and you felt that you received the transformation itself.

A. Yes, instantaneous knowing.

D. Yes, that's it. And this is so important that this happens in our days, because otherwise, it's finished for mankind.

A. Well people have asked me why can't this be taught. But I think this is a special gift. It's almost as if it's pulled out of the collective consciousness. That this need has arisen, and the person arises to deliver the gift, to heal the need.

D. Yes, that's it. That's it.

A. And I think it's so important that people understand that the best thing to do is just step forward and receive the gift.

D. Yes, and I tried a little bit on the side to give an understanding with words, thoughts and so on. But the main part is what you stated.

A. So I know that we can't really put this in scientific terms, but I'm going to challenge you here. Is there some way you could define this phenomenon with science, physics, and quantum physics, with the study of consciousness that could help people to appreciate what is taking place?

D. The first step is that we agree that both my eyes see you, a nice lady. I see you, but that's not you. That's an outer shell. Unfortunately, we don't have the senses to see what you really are. And that's where Braco is leading us, to *feel* what you really are, and maybe with science we can get a little bit nearer to this concept that man is not only the body. Yes, he has thoughts and for the very hardcore scientist thoughts are just a thing of the body. No, no, thoughts are not a thing of the body. It's something separate, but above these thoughts is something else. We call it spiritual, but we don't know what spiritual is. So we have two ways, one is yours, to experience the spirituality, and the other is to get it from different sides of … we can call it science, to understand that man is not only the outer body

A. Well I know that science usually does not like to participate in the experience but only to observe. But I think quantum physics is now showing that by observing you become a part of the experience.

D. That is one of the steps towards the goal. But only one step.

A. So you said at the Congress at Basel other scientists and researchers stepped forward to say something was happening?

D. Not really. It was just in personal talks afterwards. There was not the space to do that, unfortunately. But many people contacted me and said, 'oh yes', and gave their opinion in their ways.

A. Now, I've heard one explanation from Drago Plecko that our bodies are water, mostly water and there's work done by Dr Emoto now showing that we can influence water with our thoughts. Do you think there's any connection here in how Braco affects the individual? Why is it possible?

D. That's what I said before, that's one of the shadows of the reality that maybe true. It's also true when we talk about energy flowing from Braco to us. But that's only one aspect. In another aspect we are one. When Braco is standing before us we are one. There is no space. There is nothing to flow. We just together alter in a way that Braco already has, and so we have different aspects. And it's one step to say Braco influences the water in our bodies to make a change . . . little steps, in the whole goal we have. You can get videos of the work of Braco. There's information coming through that you can't explain with words. You see the pictures, you see the healing, 'oh that's wonderful this healing', but there is something in these videos that can heal you. Everybody knows homeopathy, there's nothing in it of the ingredients in the beginning, and it has information in it. And so in these videos, his healing is harmonizing information.

A. I've read that many people have bought the videos and the books. They get these to support the healing process they have initiated by coming to the healing sessions.

D. Like homeopathy.

A. But now I'm hearing to that people are coming in groups just to hear the recorded voice of Braco. Braco's not even present. They're just hearing his voice, and people are experiencing the same levels of healing taking place?

D. Sometimes. I think if you touch several levels it's better. It's the same with normal long distance healing. There are many healers that put hands on you, on your shoulders or whatever. Then you can do long distance healing. The healer only looks at the photograph and he can give a healing. And I always find it's OK if you can't do it in another way. I prefer to sit before Braco and to hear Braco, and to be with him. Of course if you can't, just look at the video.

A. Now to me this is really a challenge to our minds to understand how Braco, in these long distance sessions, is doing what he does; he's not looking at the people's photos, he's not looking at the people, he's not even present. Yet the healer who looks at the photo and does the long distance healing is a different phenomenon than a healer who's not even looking at the photos or the people, and yet still gets results.

D. You see the theory that he is sending energy, let me say to New York for example - this is a way to explain, but not a very good way. If the people look at the video they get into contact with Braco in a way.

A. I think Braco is challenging civilization at this time, because the modern thinking is that things have to slowly progress. That it's difficult to change. But what Braco brings into our lives is a gift that instantaneously unfolds when you just open to receive the gift. It's so simple.

D. That's a wrong understanding of cause and effect, this is old thinking - for everything you need a cause and so on. No, no, no, that's only for natural science to make steam engines and electronics, but not for our personal lives. Something can change immediately on our human level.

A. Yes, it's as if time is taken out of the equation, linear thought is taken out of the equation, and now anything is possible in a spontaneous moment.

D. Yes, but of course I admit that usually something is happening in you when you have been in a session, but you don't even feel what is happening. When you get home, slowly, slowly that enters your body and heals your body. So maybe sometimes it takes time, but sometimes it doesn't need any time.

A. From my personal experience I have felt afterward for days and weeks and even months afterward, a series of answers were coming to me. Things that had been completely unclear and muddled, poor relationships with things all of a sudden cleared up. It became clear to me within myself. It's as if something were turned on within me that was giving me the answers that had eluded me before. And I find this absolutely fascinating that this phenomenon that Braco sets in motion within us – it's as if he initiates the healer or something larger within ourselves.

D. Yes, it's just as I understand it.

A. I'm wondering what are your thoughts on what this could mean for the world? In a larger sense this opportunity is set before us.

D. Yes, the little thing with the work that comes with the next stage and everything is harmonized. That can mean bigger groups. Braco always especially says take a photo with you of your grandmother and others, so he makes a point, it can grow in this way also.

A. Yes, as you live your life better you influence other people too in a positive way.

D. Yes, yes, so a whole nation can alter in a way, in the only way that is today possible. Otherwise, I said before mankind is finished

A. I find it very fascinating that so many people say that we need something to change our world. We need something quickly now to transform our world, and our worldview and our consciousness so that we enter into a more balanced relationship with all things, especially nature.

D. Yes, and also with nature.

A. Yes, here now all of sudden we are starting to hear about this healer in Croatia who is going across Europe and delivering this gift, this spontaneous healing gift that's transforming everything.

D. Yes, yes.

A. So where next? What is possible now with Braco?

D. A bad thing is especially the social alternations for the normal mind that ask, 'how can this happen?' 'I am here with Braco, the next morning all the people around me are just different - that's nonsense.' A healing, yes, one can understand, you hear these days so many things about healers and you can understand it better on a social level. Yet, for it you may need a more modern view of the world. You said it before, that time and space are real for when I work here, when I eat, when I walk and so on, but it's not the real world we're in. As a human being I'm not living with my inner self in a world of space and time and so on. We must understand this; then it's possible that also the whole world can change.

A. I think that we as a people, in all countries, are taught to question what we feel. We are taught to analyze it, to consider it with our mind how it will fit into our life. And yet really in these healing sessions it seems that just by opening up and accepting what you feel ...

D. Yes, that would be the right thing.

A. ... accepting what you take away. Do you think that this will influence science in the future?

D. Yes, maybe inspire science because you see that really these things, these social things that people are talking about are happening. So scientists can say, ah yes, we have here an experience for our new ideas. Modern science is very complicated. I'm an engineer, but on physics, but I can't read modern science because it's so complicated. And so most can't, only a few people can go this way, on the step of science, but maybe you can grasp some results of modern science and put them together.

A. What you have discovered working with Braco over the last three years?

D. Yes, I really didn't know a lot of things about him in my first meeting with him. He's such a nice man and one must love that in him. And that for me is always a sign that it's a special person. A loving person is a special person. I have met so many healers with good results. I admire them but sometimes they are very nasty. These healers who heal some real damage in the body; again to point it out, that's one way. I would not say a healer is not as good. The doctor, that's the first level. And then comes the healer. All are repairing certain things, but the right thing is to bring people to a stage where illness and other thing don't exist. They just don't exist. That's like room or space, time like you said doesn't exist at a higher level. So illness doesn't exist there. Similarly, a cup of coffee doesn't exist there. It just doesn't exist.

A. I've heard Braco say that he cannot explain his gift?

D. I know. You must not if you have it . . . if you have it!

A. He just accepts it's something larger at work and accepts the role in a way?

D. Yes, Yes. And if you really accept this high level found, you are just fine.

A. Yes, that's true, I found that there seems to be such constancy in his nature and energy.

D. Yes, that's the proof for being on this level ... you are not on the level of eating, you have to eat of course. But you are not on the level of thinking, yes of course you think. But you are not on the level of emotions; yes you have your emotions. But above, there is peace, harmony and so on, and here, I think he is. I never said things like this - only to you.

A. Thank you. Thank you. Well I think it's interesting another aspect of this constancy is that he has healed up to 36 hours in a row. He can take group, after group, after group doing sessions. How is this possible?

D. Because he is at his level.

A. Most healers are burned out after running a certain level of energy through their body, and seeing a certain number of people and they must rest. But I've never seen Braco needing to rest.

D. A normal healer works a little bit with his own thoughts, his own emotions. Of course maybe he still has the influence of the spiritual energy too, but at one moment his bodily energy is finished. But, if you are at the right place then . . .!

A. It's almost as if Braco has removed his own personality or ego from the equation in order to achieve this level where it's more than him. I know that doesn't do justice to explaining why he is able to stand up 36 hours in a row and still be perfectly filled with energy and ready to continue.

D. We must put together all these little things, and then maybe in time, get an understanding of what is really happening. If you just mention one element, such as a person is healed from cancer. Oh yes, that can happen yet another healer can do this too. So you must put all together and then you have it.

A. Well that's it. There are many healers who work at a level where people are cured instantaneously of diseases, cancers etc. but the shear scale of what is taking place here among people seems unprecedented?

D. Yes, and if you don't just count the cases where bodily healing occurred, it's even more. Last time, people contacted me, and everybody said, 'I feel better'. I'm paraphrasing, but everybody felt better.

A. And they attributed it to the session?

D. Yes, yes.

A. In my own healing experience, I feel now like I literally have more light inside of me, and I can't help but wonder if over 200,000 people came to see Braco last year alone, and other people are feeling this sense of more energy, more goodness, more brightness or whatever you want to call that inside, how that will exponentially build and affect different countries and then eventually the world?

D. Yes.

A. Are there researchers now who are looking into this to understand this phenomenon better or is it still something the scientific community is just appreciating for the moment?

D. Again, for the normal healing there are some scientific approaches to get the information together to prove that absent healing or healing by touching occurs - many cases where the doctors said, 'you are finished, in a fortnight you will die, there is no cure'. There are scientific approaches, yes, but not to really understand what happens because all of the scientific people work in the frame of the old natural science, and with this you can't understand it. You can't understand with medical science why a person was cured from cancer in this way, so they just admit now a day that there are interesting cases that they don't understand. 'Let them do the healing, these healers, if they can help us great doctors a little bit.'

A. There are so many DVDs or movies made about Braco and his work. And in these DVDs there are testimonials from many, many people who say they were seeing a doctor before hand and after the session they were having these miraculous healings that were verified by doctors. So perhaps just for people who are interested in learning more about Braco, watching one of these videos to see the real life testimonies of people's experiences probably tells the best story of all, to hear it directly.

D. That's a good idea to put these stories into the videos and they say more than the statistics about cases curing this and that. If a person speaks with emotion, 'that I was lost and now I'm fine', that's good. But of course I would say as a scientist, it would be a good thing for a scientist to go to Zagreb to collect all these testimonies, they have a lot of testimonies...to collect them to bring them into an order and maybe to check on back cases and write a thick book, but that would be a quite a job. And it wouldn't explain *why* the healings happen. It would only explained *that* these healings happened. And that's why I'm not so interested. I want to learn *how*, *why* does it happen. For this I don't need 10,000 cases, but it would be interesting.

A. It would be interesting but really the bottom line is that you need to be open to go and experience the phenomenon. That'll be the telling of it. And healings can happen for some no matter what. Even some people in doubt have gone in who thought, 'I can't get anything from this, why am I even here?' I've heard these testimonies from people who say they had the most incredible healings! Afterward they discovered something very tangible took place despite themselves.

D. Yes, I know this old story of a man who went into wrong hall, not with Braco, but with another healer from the United States. He wanted to go to an election debate and he went into the wrong hall because he couldn't hear. And then just down the hall, the healer said now everybody who doesn't hear will be healed. And he heard.

A. Amazing.

D. Yes, and he was in the wrong hall! Maybe in a higher place it was the right hall. And so it can happen here too. A man comes in, 'this is nonsense, my girl friend wanted me to come and I'm forced here', and then he gets healed.

A. Well it seems that we are being shown in all these different ways that we aren't really controlling things. We are brought to the right place at the right time when we are ready. And then the magic can truly take place.

D. Yes, that's it.

A. Whether we think it can or not, it still can.

D. But what we like to do is to help people to open themselves and that's the most difficult part of it, and maybe you are right, it is not necessary.

A. Maybe in the beginning, the first time, it's just enough to have a taste of that which is offered. And then, I know that people come back. Session after session, whenever Braco is in town, because they feel like it just keeps giving them more and more each time.

D. They can control more and more the thoughts and emotions and so on, and get really into this open state of mind. That's what one hears, yes.

A. So perhaps you are given as much as you are ready for at the time. As much you can handle because of the changes it will create.

D. Oh yes! I especially heard that from other good healers ... 'I have to be careful, if I give a person too much healing, they would go crazy. Some people can't handle too much opening with too much healing.' So maybe for some people coming it's even a lot if they feel a little bit, and next time more and so on. And then after two years ...

A. I know for myself I felt like I received certain dreams and aspirations that I had given up on in life, that I was given them back. But then I found I needed to find a degree of strength within myself to clear away all the debris that I had put because I believed I couldn't have those things. So as I'm given this gift I have to have the strength, which the energy gave me too, to accept what it takes to reorganize my life so this gift can be fully present. It brings change and I know it can happen very gracefully and very easily, but I find at least for myself there is a degree of strength with the acceptance that we can have so much more.

D. I must say you are an excellent witness of that which is happening around Braco. I have heard several witnesses on the DVDs, but never such a good witness as I heard now from you.

A. Thank you. I want to ask you about the symbol of the sun that Braco uses, and that Ivica, Braco's mentor, used previously. Do you know anything about his symbol of the sun and how it relates to this phenomenon?

D. It's a pity that I don't experience these things very easily, so I didn't experience the sun myself, but what I said before about homeopathy, there is information in it ... a very powerful information and it's clear that if someone is open to this information, they can have it.

A. I have heard testimony where people have brought one of the gold sun pendants to a sick loved one, and they stated that their loved ones were healed – just by having this symbol with them.

D. Yes, the information was in it and the information fit for that person. Maybe for another person, it wouldn't give any results. We have in former times amulets ... the wise woman gave people a certain amulet. Even the church, the Catholic Church, does it. Maria or Mary is on an amulet and you carry it somewhere on your body - so why not the sun?

A. So it's generally just another reinforcement of what's taking place in people?

D. Yes. I don't wonder *if* it takes place when someone gives the sun to someone, but I don't understand how this information can be given through the sun … from the sun to the sick man or woman?

A. So here we have another mystery on top of the mystery of it all.

D. That's it, we don't see the reality, we only see the shadows.

A. So here we have a point where we can't really understand right now?

D. But in a way you can understand … take a building, you make shadows of this building. If you make it from different sides, in the end, the building must look like this. One only gets maybe a square and asks what is that? You have shadows, different shadows, that's all. It's the scientific way.

A. Now you yourself have brought Braco to other countries?

D. Yes, a little bit I have, a little bit.

A. And when Braco now expands his work to go outside of Europe, can you make any comment on where you think this is all leading? And your own role with this?

D. Ah, I never have thoughts like this, I just try to do my best in where I am standing.

A. So we all just do our part.

D. Yes, I think that it's important that people with a good philosophy are with him. Like you, I'm sure that you in Hawaii will have many people, and bring Braco over in a good philosophy, not just in the end as a healer. Of course everybody seeks healers, 'I will go to Braco, he will heal me.' That's the first idea.

A. I find it absolutely incredible that the first visit Braco had to the United States was to the Las Vegas area in Nevada. The least spiritual place in the United States you could possibly think of, and where you find him coming. It seems like a joke of the universe in a way, and a test too. And yet it was very successful and people came to see Braco despite a casino being downstairs. And he did healing sessions above in a room where you could hear the chink of the slot machines, and yet still Braco did his healing work and people were walking away and telling friends and having this sense that something incredible was happening. It's quite a phenomenon.

D. One thing is that Braco is not afraid to work, or to work in a casino. Other healers would say, 'oh no, in such a bad vibration, Las Vegas, I never could work. Spirits and the Holy Spirit wouldn't come in'. But Braco did it. And read the bible, Jesus went just where the need was, the real need.

A. Lets end with this for today. I would really like to thank you Dr Schneider so much for your time today. It's been a real pleasure. Thank you.

Chapter Five

Day 6 – Saturday, July 4, 2009

Germany – Kraichtal

Braco greeted me warmly that morning and we had our morning espresso together as others busily prepared for the day. He would always impress me with his great care with detail around the organization of all things at events. The upcoming travel schedule was also always clear in his head and he could give it in detail at any time. There was a grounded clarity in his mind, and it allowed him to make quick decisions that were always well chosen. All the staff members looked to him as a leader, and he played this role too with much grace. Yet he also greatly appreciated individuals who thought for themselves and took the initiative, and this was something necessary in those who would organize gazing events in new locations.

While we waited for our group to be gathered, I chatted with my German translators, Detlev and Jelena. Detlev was a German man who had toured with Braco for a time, presenting him for over a year on the road. His wife had brought him to a gazing session, and he ended up as part of the team. Now he worked in an executive position for an international German company, but he still assisted with the website and joined Braco when his schedule allowed. Detlev was gentle and well spoken, with excellent English to assist me around others.

Jelena was a court interpreter who had also come to Braco for some time and had become friends through her own assistance to the work. She had a German reserve that melted throughout the previous day, especially when Braco asked her to translate for me, something she had never done before in this situation. She had taken it gracefully and put up little hesitation before squaring her shoulders, and walking before the audience with my promise to keep my sentences clear and short. Jelena embodied that wonderful trait of German determination, and also she possessed a warm and caring heart that balanced her as someone suited to perhaps play a larger role in the future with Braco.

I could feel a little nervousness from her that first time, though she did not outwardly show it, which I admired and I knew it was a good experience for us both. Yesterday, she had been asked to come back to interpret once again, and today she looked particularly pretty in a crisp white blouse with striking blue earrings. Already we were talking as old friends as her natural warmth came forward in the energy of the experience, and she literally became brighter and more radiant after coming from a group.

Professor Alex Schneider also presented about the scientific aspect of Braco and its spiritual implications, so audiences were opened to the possibilities of the gaze by both of us at different times before Braco came out. Our team worked beautifully, and we all did our part to touch and open people's hearts, the best preparation for the gazing. Once again I felt a strong connection to the predominantly German groups and was surprised at the warmth of the people in the face of a reserved German stereotype. I especially enjoyed watching the younger adults in their twenties who were often strikingly affected by the energy.

I had brought down my computer to start recording events for that climb up the mountain of collecting material for our book project, which Braco was equally excited about today. I was certainly jubilant inside too, but felt somewhat small, as the scope of the process loomed tall. Braco sat across from me as I typed away, wanting me to write and also pulling me into conversation. He was impressed that I could talk and type at the same time, and I glanced up at him regularly to engage new points. Yet, the computer would prove inappropriate for both of us to catalogue the days, so a red notebook was assigned the duty of holding all notes, and I would use it the rest of my stay instead of my computer. It became my constant companion; it would come out at all times to document events, people's stories and bits of conversation.

In my heart, I was beginning to see Braco in a new way, as a hope so great that it could affect the entire world, and I was left awed by such a vision. The dialogue with Alex Schneider had brought this into perspective for me. Now I looked at the man who was so natural, peaceful, fun loving and spontaneous; and I had a new appreciation for the commitment that drove him to be a beacon of light to so many. This was an incredible responsibility most would flee from or be burdened by, but somehow he had achieved a perfect balance between being in the world and being something vastly more. Braco set an example; to become more like the children of the world, who were the purest because they could just feel honestly. He, like they, did not turn away from life with a mind full of excuses and reasons to limit, and put boundaries on the natural flow of life.

As we sat, reviewing the events of the last days, I jotted down detailed notes. Braco was a great help with place names and people. In the midst of this meeting, I was brought a fragrant, white rose elegantly wrapped as a gift from a Croatian woman from the last group I had spoken before. Pleased, Braco explained that white was clean and that Croatia was showing me respect. The next day, I would wear that rose on my dress in appreciation. This was an added sign of a connection to these people and I was grateful.

After another session, Rudi came to me because a woman had approached him from the group who said she too lived in Hawaii. Surprised, I asked if she was still about and together we found her in the outdoor restaurant area. Her name was Margrit and she was a medical doctor who lived in Switzerland half the year, and the other half on the Big Island in a town called Pahoa. Happy to meet me, she shared her dream of bringing Braco to Hawaii to share his good energy. She worked in Hawaii with veterans and impoverished indigenous people, and we immediately made plans for her to host an event after my conference, specifically for these two groups that could greatly us such help in their lives. On tour I would make many such connections through the divine symmetry of an action through synchronicities.

Conventional and traditional, the majority of the people who came to Braco here and in the Balkans were not those on a spiritual quest of transformation. They had not experienced life in an ashram, Vipassana retreats or tai chi. Meditation and yoga would be practiced by only a few; yet there were medical doctors, psychologists, dentists, famous pop singers, lawyers and scientists of many fields who assembled with the masses to feel and receive the gifts of the gaze. Several times a day individuals from the crowd would come forward to share their stories of healing. Braco never encouraged people to stop medical treatment with their doctors. Because of this there were countless cases that were well documented, before and after, that people such as Professor Schneider or Drago Plecko could study.

I spoke with individuals who had been relieved of a myriad of different kinds of back problems. Several mothers told me of their daughters, medically diagnosed as unable to have children, who came to one or more gazing sessions and soon bore healthy children. Depression was another common malady that was often healed in the face of this energy; it not only mysteriously rebalanced the body chemistry, but also infused qualities of resilience and strength so that emotional wellbeing was more stable. There were even cases of people getting up out of wheelchairs and walking, regaining eyesight or having their financial problems solved. Truly, the stories were endless from curing alcoholism to saving marriages.

The Lake

Ending the workday at 5 pm with the last group, we were all immediately off to our rooms to change into swimsuits. I had earlier expressed a wish to be able to swim and was informed that there was a local lake nearby. Immediately, an excursion was planned and now we were on our way. Often, I teased Braco and the others of our entourage about taking Braco for long swims once he came to Hawaii to be with dolphins, whales, sharks and mantas. They all knew I was a seasoned ocean swimmer from my many stories about the waters of my home. Now Branko and Miki looked genuinely concerned about Braco going in the water and they asked me wholeheartedly to take care of him, so I pledged to watch carefully their treasured leader.

Some rustic lake was what I expected, only accessible via fields, but this was not what met us as we pulled into a car park. Here was a huge, manicured, beach park lake that was bursting with people, espresso stands and local snacks. A person in our group took care of all the entrance fees and we strolled in the gate to a sandy shore with dive platforms offshore. Hundreds of people were on beach towels around the perimeter, and we walked to find our perfect spot, near a café so Branko could enjoy some espresso, since he had no intention of joining us in the water. Only he and Sead would decline the opportunity to swim, while Braco, Professor Alex, Detlev, Rudi and I were all delighted to partake in the cool pleasure of the water.

We found our spot, and Braco and I were first in the lake. Because of Branko and Miki's concerns, I was not sure if I needed to really keep a close watch on Braco or not. Yet I told him I would take care of him in the lake, but this soon proved unnecessary because he was an excellent swimmer and strong. Later I would realize that he grew up with summers on the sea and had spent much time in the water himself, so I was glad to find a kindred spirit in my favorite joy, the water. He kept a good pace swimming free-style and occasionally we flipped on our backs while continuing along to engage in short conversations. For a whole hour, we swam side-by-side across the lake, and I felt bathed and cleansed while Braco looked contented.

Once back at the shore, we miscalculated our group site and ended up walking half the distance of the beach back to them. Sead began to film us walking toward him and in a moment of mischief, I grabbed a handful of sand and threw it at Braco. Instantly, he joined in the spirit and our intensity escalated. It became all out war, playfully between us, as we moved in on each other scooping sand until even our mouths ended up with the gritty granules. Spitting and scooping, I laughed almost breathless and we finally called a truce. Our trusted filmmaker was happy at the footage and we charged off to the lake to rinse off, since we looked like walking sand sculptures. That was when Braco dove in too briskly into shallow water and ended up with a stomach full of scratches.

Almost proudly, he later showed them off to Branko, who immediately came to me and asked if this is how I was going to take care of their beloved Braco in Hawaii. Protesting my innocence in the matter, I scolded Braco for getting me into trouble with Branko and we all came to laugh. Later, I began looking in the clover patches for that lucky 4-leaf talisman as everyone rested peacefully, enjoying the very warm evening that kept light until 10 pm. Soon, I noticed Braco as well as Branko joining the search, but after intense scrutiny with no treasure to show, I wandered to the sand to draw spiraling designs instead.

I became so intent on my artwork that it startled me when I looked up and Braco was at my side. He looked at my design as some ancient hieroglyphic type language, and it inspired his creative side to also draw until it was soon time to leave. At some point we began talking and I asked to know much more from him about life and his insights. But he only smiled and asked for my patience because it was not yet time for more. I would have to learn to understand certain things yet.

Patiently and gently, he offered that I was like a baby bird in the egg, pecking through the shell and sticking my head out for the first time. My first job was to breathe, for this was necessary to all life, and then I would next watch and then touch. There was a wisdom to this that would unfold, but at the time I thought it quite ridiculous. More than two weeks ahead would prove his perspective valid and I agreed to be patient again for now. Next, we all rose, found our cars and departed for the hotel. Our morning start would be particularly early at 3 am, but this was necessary for the journey ahead to our next destination of Stuttgart.

Day 7 – Sunday, July 5, 2009

Germany – Stuttgart

In the early morning hours I packed my suitcase and prepared for a big day. Ida, the Russian woman I had so enjoyed, was opening her second event for Braco and she had gone to great lengths to make it a success. In Stuttgart, the town's conference center had been rented for the event, specifically chosen because of Braco's love of water and nature. Here we would find a lovely tree lined lake next to the conference center, and once we arrived, Braco and I strolled around its perimeter on its walkway. The morning air was cool and felt refreshing after our last days of intense heat, and Braco told me of Ida's passion and ingenuity in organizing this event.

We came across attractive posters advertising the event on a building near the lake, and she had taken out full-page advertisements in the local newspapers. Determined, Ida had committed herself fully to reaching new people with the work of transforming lives. Her enthusiasm and inspiration was shining that morning as she supervised her volunteer staff to arrange all areas; from setting up the rooms, flowers and product displays to registering people as they arrived, organizing them into groups, and much more.

After our walk, Braco and I found an outside balcony with chairs and sat down, and spoke of his leaving Europe and differences between how countries would receive his gazing work. To me, Japan and its people would become one of his dearest followings. I had been on a speaking tour in several cities there and had found their love of the alternative healing arts to be exceptionally open and warm. I felt what Braco offered and represented would appeal to their hearts in a great way. Interestingly, Braco too felt a great affinity for the Japanese culture and spoke of dreams he had as of child that made him feel a connection to this particular country.

Touring in Europe had presented many challenges; because the numerous small countries did not have many venues where larger groups of people could be gathered. Many cities had threatened to close down an event if the numbers attending grew too large. Unlike the American stadiums and event centers, Europe was not as prepared to handle huge flows of people, even in many cities. In September 2008, Braco was in Macedonia and nearly ten thousand people showed up in one day. If that happened in Germany, Austria or his other tour stops, this would cause civil authorities to end the event. Braco knew he needed to go to places that could handle the growing crowds to come.

Viewing next the conference center itself, I was greeted by a bustle of activity and Ida's warm welcome. This building had two levels and the gazing would take place on the second floor in the main hall. Everything was clean and attractive, the building well maintained and manicured. A stage was ready with a platform for Braco with fresh flowers to both sides. Our rest area was a comfortable room off to the side of the stage, and here Ida had filled tables with fresh fruit, bottled water, cookies, cheeses and more. She even had an illuminated picture of a water scene on one table, and yellow onyx bowls on another table for him.

All of the organizers respected and appreciated Braco beyond words, and they all wanted to honor him and his work by pleasing him with nicely set rooms, flowers and an abundance of food. Braco left to work with the lighting crew to ensure that his face and eyes were well lit for all in the room to see, and I wandered downstairs to take note of the set-up. It was something I would duplicate in Hawaii after my conference, when I took him on tour of neighboring islands. A great foyer downstairs was perfect for holding groups as they waited their turns, with an inset desk for registration. Impressively organized, everything was almost ready to go for the people already beginning to gather outside.

Today we would in the end see over 1600 people for the gazing sessions, and because of the room size, groups would be larger, between 200-400 people each. Again I was reminded that it was the holiday time when people traveled, so numbers would be smaller than at other times of the year. Despite this obstacle, Ida would have a success and have three hundred more people than her first event. Yet it would become a day of trials for her as well, as her expectation of two thousand people had a shortfall, and some staff problems would cause Braco to question her control of her assistants that led to a confrontation between them. But the morning progressed smoothly and everyone worked to prepare for the crowds.

Now it was time to gather back stage and await the instructions and spontaneous influences of the day. Braco initiated change first in the form of having Professor Alex and myself both consecutively present before each group instead of taking turns. This meant I would work extra hard that day speaking before all the people who came. Happily, I was up for the challenge and looked forward to the bigger groups, because by this time, I realized that my energy grew each time I presented, and I knew I needed all I could gain to tackle my book project and conference once I returned home. Fortunately, a new short film would be shown to each group before our presentations, so this would give us a few extra minutes in between in the break room.

Detlev joined us again to interpret for me into German and I greatly liked working with him because of his professionalism and calm. Well educated and thoughtful, he spoke of a repressive societal conditioning in his fellow countrymen that he rigorously questioned. He would regale me of stories of past tours when he was presenting, a time he said he dearly loved and valued. Yet he had left the work for a more conventional career that left him a bit dry, and I wondered how this choice now affected him. At least he was able to assist now and again, and this was a prime opportunity to be well nourished by the energy.

Our dear professor stayed out in the hall at a café style area and chatted with people he recognized. He had been late in coming to a presentation the day before, and he was spotted outside talking to two very attractive women who had his full attention. So today we teased him to not let the women steer him away, and he good heartedly took our jokes. Alex was easily found when someone was finally sent to escort him to us before it was time to begin. Our first few groups began smaller with about 200-250 people each, but they were all back-to-back without pause throughout the day.

I was always struck by how hopeful most people looked when they stood in that room, whether rich or poor, educated or not, men and women alike wishing for better in their lives, good health and for their difficulties to be made better. They were regular people who believed or were at least open to miracles and the idea that there was a greater power, no matter the name or definition, which could grant a new possibility through Braco. Each time as he took the stage, I saw people waiting for things impossible to be granted or others who only wanted the pure, sweet energy to take away. Every instance I stood for the gaze, I felt something turn on, and though I felt it in different ways many times, it was tangible and alive all around me and through me. And I could see clearly that many felt this too.

In the fourth session of that day, as I stood for the gazing, the energy struck me in an awesome way and I had a complete sense of my life changing. Dynamically clear in those moments was the fact that I had to serve this work too. Not just as a part-time commitment as I had originally envisioned over the days, but I felt that I could not do anything but the work. My head was alive with the feeling of energy pouring down on it, and I left with a sense of the profound and absolute. Nothing would be the same for me from that time onward because my heart had answered a call that rendered everything else subservient. This was more real than anything I knew in my life.

Walking into the break room afterwards, what could I do but smile at Braco with the gratitude of greeting someone who had made such an experience possible without saying a word? His effect on people was utterly astonishing, and he did not try to make anything happen, it always flowed naturally of its own accord, and he merely encouraged and allowed it to happen. Espresso's arrived on a tray with Ida checking on us, and the next moment Detlev entered the room too. We drank and snacked on fruit, enjoying the brief time before we had to leave once again for the stage.

Braco was ever warm and waiting for us to return, often asking how all was going, how we felt and our impressions of different groups. He would enquire about my energy level and stamina, and offer a break to me if I needed one, treating me like a conscientious friend, ever caring and thoughtful. I could see it pleased him when I swept aside the idea of being tired or needing a rest. Spiritedness he admired and appreciated. There was always a special camaraderie in the break room that few others were allowed to enter. It was all of our sanctuary, and coming back to this room always felt special because of the company.

No matter how long the day went or how many groups came, Braco himself never became tired or ever looked worn. The energy fed him in so many ways, and it made it possible to have a stamina and constancy beyond regular people. I had the amusing opportunity to watch a few rare instances when he was caught off guard in the timing to go on stage. Sometimes a conversation would become animated and the music cue would go momentarily unheard. But he could change his focus in a split second to be taken by the energy to do his work, and the people always received the same from him, never less.

During the sixth session break, I stated to Braco how much the people loved him. Yet he discussed the idea with me that in fact people came because they loved themselves and wanted the good feeling of the energy. People put first what made them feel good; it was natural. He illustrated his point that when a loved one was lost, people cried for themselves, not for the person. This idea of how others make us feel and its significance was one we discussed several times over the days.

By 3 o'clock, we were still waiting for a promised special vegetarian lunch and when Ida finally came in, Braco used this opportunity to talk with her about her staff. Branko had visited several times earlier irritated, and had a conversation in Croatian with Braco that I did not understand. But now it was made clear as Braco challenged Ida about her staff abandoning posts with crowds left unattended. Unfortunately, Ida had obviously understaffed, so there was no one to offer any replacement to her assistants for breaks. He questioned her authority over her staff, and very firmly stated that the people attending came first. Staff had to work without breaks if there was no one to substitute for them, and that was beyond discussion or people arriving or leaving would not know where to go. Such a lack of supervision would create a chaos that broke the flow of this healing sanctuary space that had been so carefully created. A further tension was added because one of her family members had been involved in the desertion of a post to have a beer.

Ida felt that in Germany, however, she had to put a smile on for everyone and not use what she called the 'Balkans authoritative way'. But Braco would not have any of this excuse, and asked for firmness in her leadership. Several conversations over this matter would ensue, and I left the room a few times because things became heated and Ida became emotional. Yet Braco's unflinching point was to protect the needs of the people, so that they were met with the same consistency in all ways. It did not matter if her staff did not get the breaks, this was the work of service, and it was her job to oversee the enforcement of responsibilities. A challenge was laid before her, questioning her own ability to oversee such work with strength.

Organizing for months to set up this event, Ida had worked very hard to make it a success, yet this area of failure was a real issue. I think Ida felt hurt by Braco's bluntness, but a truce would be reached by the end of the day. After the event, she would have to contemplate her real commitment in the time ahead, and if she could adapt to its challenges. The question was only if these setbacks would prove too much, or if she would rise up with renewed enthusiasm. Braco would have been very sad to lose Ida, but he would not change his requirements. I really liked Ida and wanted to see her prosper and thrive in a work that I knew her heart called her too with a real passion, so I was rooting for her breakthrough.

Scheduled for 5:30 pm, the last group came delayed, and Professor Schneider was particularly concerned that we would end up leaving too late to catch our plane flight home. I offered to shorten my presentation, but Braco declared that the last group would get as much as the first group, no cutting would take place. Thus, I gave my presentation, as with all other groups and once the gazing was over, the time was late but not dangerously so. Once again, like lightening, Branko came and ushered us both past the crowd still gathered outside to our car, and away we drove as people waved and smiled at Braco. It felt a bit like being with a celebrity, walking quickly out with escort to a waiting car, and I enjoyed the experience thoroughly.

On the drive to the airport, a conversation led me to volunteer that even though I did not smoke cigarettes, I would be open to smoke a small cigar during the right occasion. That was all I needed to say, and the next thing I knew Braco was walking into the duty free store at the airport and I was requesting Dominican Cigars, which they had in many sizes. I selected a slim cigar pack of five and Braco gave these to me as a gift. In fact it had been over seven years since I had my last puff on a cigar, but the idea seemed to hold the potential of making special circumstance more memorable. Then we were off to board our plane home without further delay. That night we would sleep again at Braco's home, and spend half the day at Srebrnjak 1 before heading for our next destination on the Adriatic coast.

Now my first week was complete and in this short time I felt like I had lived many months and had known Braco equally long. As for the changes in me from the energy of the gazing, I now recognized that it unlocked within me what was actually already present and always there. Yet it intensified, strengthened and illuminated my real self to flow more freely within my life. Once done, there was a certainty and focus, which I had never mastered before to this degree, that burst forth with a splendid intensity. Now it was mine and it could not be taken from me, it could only grow with a fresh life of its own. His grace filled gift gave me nothing less, and now it was for me to use it and allow it to make anew my life. Joyously, I would watch it lead the way into my life and initiate many positive changes.

Part Two

Family & Friends

Braco

Core Staff of Srebrnjak 1: (Front) Stevo, Branko, Braco, Damir; (Middle Row) Davor, Rudi, Ljiljana; (Back row) Dinko, Pero, Miki

Onyx Room with Braco's Sun & Gazing Platform

Braco in bamboo garden,   *Croatian Scientist Drago Plecko*
Srebrnjak 1   *with Angelika*

Braco, Professor Alex Schneider & Angelika
after a swim at a German lake park

Braco takes a break in between Gazing Sessions at Kraichtal Event

Angelika & Branko at Stuttgart Event

Gazing in Kraichtal, Germany

Stuttgart, Germany

Outside Srebrnjak 1 on Braco's Birthday

Chapter Six

Day 8 – Monday, July 6, 2009

_____

Srebrnjak 1

After rising, I had to repack once more for the journey to the Adriatic coast, our next destination on the seaside. When done, I met Braco for our 6 am walk through the park to Srebrnjak 1. Another warm morning greeted us and as we strolled, Braco shared his birth story of coming into this world. He was born premature at seven months, and his mother almost died in labor. For two months, he was in an incubator and his mother's milk was placed in a bottle for him. Coming into the world he only weighed 2.6 pounds (1.3 kilo) and was 18.5 inches (47 cm) long.

Next he told me something I had never heard of before. Braco was born with skin so dark that he looked like an African parent's newborn, with hair black, coarse and wavy. The doctors asked his mother afterward if his father was black, and everyone was very surprised. Soon after, Braco's skin color became Caucasian like his mother's and father's; and his hair turned fine, straight and brown. I could not be help but review in my mind all of the ancient tales and prophecies, especially from India, to see if I could remember one in which a special child was born in such a state and later transformed.

As hard as I tried, I could not come up with any firm memory at that moment, yet I felt there was something to this very strange beginning for Braco. Certainly mythologies of the ancient gods and goddess, heroes, sages and wise leaders often begin with odd events like this, and perhaps we had intellectualized our lives too much to understand the deeper meaning underlying the spontaneity of the natural world. In the end, I had to let this mystery go to come back to it at another time. Another unusual phenomenon of his early years was that until age seven, Braco did not like to eat and he would always throw up his food. Despite this, he was healthy and strong during that time.

His childhood would otherwise be normal, and he would spend much occasion in nature alone. Although he had many friends, he preferred this to playing with the other children all the time. Braco had such a peaceful constancy to him that I asked him, the first time we met, if he was always this way from childhood, or if something had changed him? He answered that he was the same as a child. In the end, I believed his connection with nature, and his love of feeling this connection kept him from filling himself with as many distractions as most other people. I would learn that Braco always had a concrete purity to him and an innocence that was never tainted. His balance was connected with his spontaneity and respect of feelings. These simply conveyed so much more than communication through language, television, books or computers.

At Srebrnjak 1, I end up speaking to the first group of the day and something had noticeably changed for me. I could feel light from the sun in me reaching out to the people, and I could see them subtly appreciate it. This light was my new found connection to Braco's work of service, a commitment to an incredible energy that superseded all else, and I felt a happiness fill me in all ways imaginable. An earlier doubt I had that made me consider standing at the back of the room, to be more inconspicuous, vanished.

In the morning sessions I came to fully appreciate my own feeling that I *had* to attend all the gazings, and I needed to be seen and I knew people would understand later. To be in the presence of this power day in and out was liberating me in so many ways. After presenting to a second group, people's warm smiles and hand movements to their own hearts displayed clearly that they had accepted me now. And I recognized a few faces that had come before or to a tour city, and I saw how they came back with a true love of Braco, indeed like he was their own precious family member.

During a break, Braco talked about his Center. Ten years ago, Braco was working in one of several flats in the building at

Srebrnjak 1, and it was only 50 sq. meters. Eleven people originally owned flats in the building, but Braco would buy each one over the ten-year period and design the bamboo garden. It was also a decade ago that he told his staff that once everything was done in creating the Center, including the garden, someone would come from outside Europe to take him to new countries in the world.

He also reminisced about childhood visions of a brown skinned people with palm trees, exotic fruits, fishes and coral. Braco described happy smiles on the people's faces and they danced on the beach. They did not have what people had in Europe, but in fact they had everything, and were happy. Even handmade canoes were a part of this picture. Once only a beautiful story, I was certain Braco now saw this as a possible reality, and it was in fact the reality of my own home in Hawaii.

Braco had also always admired the Japanese; how they wore kimonos, drank tea, built bamboo houses and especially their martial arts, which tapped into a great, unseen strength unlike the physical strength of the Europeans. Having never met a Japanese person, he still felt that inner connection. It was at age six or seven that he discovered this interest, and it had stayed with him. Now I was discussing with Braco my dear Japanese friends, especially a remarkable conference organizer named Sakae Ozaki. She had brought myself, my partner and several other speakers to Japan for events in three cities, and I was hoping to bring them all together in Hawaii.

At some point in our conversation, we grew silent, and a clear feeling overtook me. I then solemnly told him that I had not believed that there was a force in the world stronger than my attraction to the islands, but now I felt one and I would even leave my Big Island for it. Fascinated and so surprised by this feeling, it strongly conveyed that there was something more. Then I mentioned a shaman I had worked with in Zacatecas, Mexico who had told me that I would one day be before more people than the Pope himself, and have the love of the crowds who would look to me. At the time I thought this prediction outlandish and gave it no attention at all, but in those moments I shared this for the first time.

Finally, I also told him of my former stage fright, a double-edged sword that had made it so difficult for me to say all that I wished to share. It was his spontaneity in asking me to speak before groups had broken that barrier. To all I had to say, he showed a warmth and kindness that encouraged me, and I felt in him a true friend that I could tell anything without self-consciousness or fear. He had that gift of honest openness that allowed everyone to be natural around him.

I was dreaming a lot during my stay, and though I did not share this with him, I had dreamt that night before that my mouth was filled with a foul substance. As I tried to spit it out, huge masses came out that were lodged in my throat. Upon awakening, I instantly knew that this evil waste represented all the things that had been crammed down my throat through life that were rubbish. It was clear then that my dream was communicating to me that this refuse was finally leaving my system, and Braco and his energy was the reason I could spit it out. It was all that was contrived and unnatural.

In the onyx room during the fourth gazing session, I had a vision of Braco as the sun itself and then I felt myself illuminate too, and we came together in absolute excitement and a love of what was possible to create together for the work of service. I did not think of this as my fantasy, it was something that came from beyond me and offered a glimpse. To me, it was another gift of a real opportunity, which spoke of an underlying purpose for my presence at Srebrnjak 1, and at Braco's side that was deeper than the surface reasons.

At some point, Braco began talking about his beloved friend Ivica. Ivica used to see the future when he was driving. He would put the seat back and begin talking. Once he told Braco that he saw great masses of people coming, a sea of people that had no end. There would be no limit to them, and he stated that only when the sun stopped shining, the people would stop coming, only then. At another time he told Braco that he would answer any questions he had, anything at all. Braco could have asked about the future, past lives, Atlantis, individuals, any subject, but the young man had not asked anything. Perhaps this was one of Braco's regrets with Ivica, but at the time he did not know what to ask, he was not driven to know the things that the prophet could have shared through his gift. Yet I was coming to understand his lack of questions, for mine were dropping away to be replaced with an overall peace that did not require probes into the future or endless information gathering.

Before lunch, we went to the great room on the third floor and I pulled out a DVD from my handbag. It was of a boat trip excursion I had guided for a group of people to swim with spinner dolphins in Hawaii. A videographer had taped in and out of the water for it. Braco wished to see it, but admitted he did not know how to use the DVD player, and so he called for someone to help. Ever low-tech, Braco did not have a cell phone, computer or any of the usual fare. He was not interested in all of the latest technology, yet he was open to it if it could serve a purpose in some way directly for the work. In practice, if he needed something, someone else was always there to assist, or he would do without and not have a care.

The video showed my group playing in the water, the dolphins swimming around us, and some of the other sea life we encountered. It was short and fun. Braco displayed the same enthusiasm he had earlier with the Hawaii DVDs, and the same persistence in wanting to watch it over and over again. As new people would come into the room, it would be started anew, each time like it was the first. Then a game began between Braco and Branko of trying to guess which blond I was underwater, since there were several of us on my boat that day. Turtles, manta rays, dolphins and pilot whales were our swim companions in the video and everyone who watched enjoyed the idyllic show.

After lunch, I moved into the bamboo garden to lie on the grass and write in my red notebook about the morning events. It was delightful to lie in the hot sun with bamboo leaves shading my face. However, I soon discovered that the slightly damp grass had made the back on my white skirt not only moist, but also covered with grass stains. When I was through writing, I showed Braco the stains in dismay, since more groups were coming. Surprisingly, he only smiled and said how natural it was, and therefore good. He further explained that we could not be perfect, and even placed a smudge on his own shirt to demonstrate his ease with such natural things. He was incorrigible and insightful, just like a child demonstrating innate wisdom.

Once the last group was finished for the day, it was time for Braco to begin his annual vacation. Each year he took off one month, as was standard in European culture and business, to go to his summer home on the Adriatic coast. Because of a special event arranged in Macedonia, we would depart for a few days and return afterwards. So we stopped again at his house to pick up our luggage and were off on a three-hour drive to the sea with Damir as our driver. Soon I would meet Braco's family.

My first impression, when I finally glimpsed the Adriatic Sea, was like seeing the city of Zagreb. To me it looked like a giant lake, and I was expecting water to the horizon. Most would not understand my hesitation, because the Croatian coast was just like travel agency pictures of the Greek Isles - beautiful, clean, deep blue waters and charming villages that rose from its shores. But I held my wild and vibrantly exotic Hawaii ever close to my heart, sighing at this well dressed, fashionable, worldly and sophisticated sea. It was at first barely real, barely breathing to me.

Fortunately, my view would change and evolve in Braco's company, as he showed me the place that was his childhood vacation spot with loving eyes. What I would soon come to respect and appreciate was a gentle quality the sea and area possessed. Even the sun here was mild, and in the summer season no waves crashed at the shores, no swells rollicked, just a constant placidness. Now was Braco's time to rest, and this was a perfect place to do so in a lovely and pampering environment.

Adriatic Coast

We arrived in the seaside town, which was upscale and elegant. It boasted its main activity at the shore where all of its commerce took place on the edge of the sea. It was alive with people strolling and we drove through some narrow streets up a few blocks from the water's edge to Braco's vacation home. Terraced up the slope from the water, its garage lay at street level, with the house above rising in two stories. White with wood doors and shutters, marble patios and a green lawn, it was a typically beautiful Mediterranean-style home.

Braco went upstairs and retrieved some keys and led me to the first floor, which offered a completely self-contained apartment with two bedrooms. I had a large marble balcony and a table and chairs outside to sit at to enjoy any spare time. Damir brought up my bag and I was asked to come up to the top floor as soon as I was settled. Taking only a brief time to open my suitcase and hang a few items, I shortly went up the marble stairs to the upper part of the house and I stopped at the open door, hearing conversation and laughing within.

Then I entered and met Braco's wife, Dinka, and his eight-year-old son, Andelon. Dinka was a beautiful woman with a warm smile and happy eyes. She had long brown hair and a very nice tan from her time at the water. Andelon was a handsome boy, a heart breaker for all the little girls at school, with hair down to his waist and an endearing, sweet wildness about him. I was immediately offered refreshments and Dinka genuinely welcomed me into their home, as we chatted away with Damir joining us. Conveniently, she spoke English very well, although Andelon had not yet learned more than a few words. For this first visit, Andelon was shy towards me, but this would change completely after Macedonia.

A gracious hostess, Dinka took care of all of us on that warm evening as we gathered. There was an easy, relaxed mood amongst all as we enjoyed the late dinner she prepared, and partook in animated conversations, especially between Andelon and his father. After a satisfying day, I was happy to rest in this pleasant and comfortable environment. I went back to my lower apartment after thanking everyone for the kind hospitality, yet that night Braco and I would have a bit of a miscommunication. After we parted company, for what I thought was the end of the evening, Braco came back and invited me up again to spend some more time with him and his family.

Now I assumed that Braco would like to have some privacy at this point, and was only being polite, so I stated, 'that's okay', emphasizing the declined invitation with my American euphemism. Unfortunately, Braco did not understand my nuance and instead thought that I would come back shortly. I had planned to retire early, but the apartment was very hot and I knew I could not sleep, so I had the inspiration to go exploring on my own and to take a long walk. The warm night was perfect for this activity. Quietly, I left and set out down a maze of streets to the shore and the main walkway through the village. I took special note of some house numbers and landmarks so that I could find my way back up the dark streets.

For the next hour and a half I walked and felt the peaceful energies of this pleasant place, passing a variety of restaurants and outdoor cafes filled with people. Later, thunder rolled in the sky and lightening flashed in the distance. Dearly, I hoped for a nightlong thunderstorm, which was one of my favorite shows of nature. So I perched myself on a large boulder at the water and watched the horizon light up, until a light rain began and I decided it was time to go back. I arrived at my lodging without getting lost and took a shower before going to bed. By now it was raining hard and I climbed into bed and fell asleep.

Suddenly, a knocking on my window woke me and I saw Braco standing there. I got up and came to the door and invited him out of the rain. He was absolutely livid and asked me where I had been. Still half asleep, I did not understand his mood and I simply said I had gone for a walk. Then I found out that he had been expecting me upstairs. My assumption about him wanting privacy had been wrong. I think Braco, like I, was still charged with all the energy of our past schedule and an immediate quiet time was not yet necessary. My assumption was based on past references, not an attention to present ones - my mistake.

He, Damir and his family had been waiting for me and when I did not come, he had come down to see why I was taking so long and discovered me gone. He had sent Damir to walk in one direction downtown and he had taken the other, but they were not able to find me. In the Balkans, people took their jobs as hosts with a deep seriousness and accountability. As his guest, I was taken care of in all ways and never had to look out for myself in any way. Obviously, he felt responsible for my safety and even though I found the town perfectly harmless, he was worried I would get lost or some mishap would befall me.

Because of his genuine concern, I was now awake and sorry for causing everyone worry, but I was not contrite because I still felt my act had been harmless and completely understandable. Though I tried to explain that I was used to traveling alone in other countries, and a sleepy, posh village was no problem, he did not see it that way. Firmly, he made me promise not to leave his house again without first telling him where I was going and for how long. I was so speechless at his heartfelt insistence that I meekly agreed, though I was still baffled at the protectiveness of this act. Then I acknowledged that some cultures had different standards of etiquette and I had just found one.

From that day forward, I was on a bit of a tether that I had to slowly dissolve away with my effortless, independent ways. We were no longer on tour now with duties and responsibilities to guide our choices and actions, we were on holiday. The freedoms of a holiday were calling me and so this point between us became a type of game, and I would have fun playing the coddled guest or as I had been earlier called, the 'baby bird'. Little by little, I would push through. Two days later, Braco would remark about wishing to show me a walk on one side of the town that we would have no time to do, and I told him it was I good thing I had already walked it that first night and not missed out. This made him laugh at my stubbornness and our game was in full swing.

Chapter Seven

Day 9 – Tuesday, July 7, 2009

Adriatic Coast

Waking up early, I dressed and had tea on my front balcony overlooking other rooftops to the sea. The morning was warm and bright, the rain having passed, and I knew we would go later to a new property a short distance from the village, which Braco had acquired over the last few years. It was a 40-minute walk away, or a short car ride. This was a piece of land directly on the water with a small home on it. It had become the gathering place for all his friends and family when they needed rest and relaxation, and I would soon see why. For now, I waited for Braco to come down from his flat above to see how we stood that morning.

At 8 am, he came to my open door looking as if he had just risen, and hugged me to let me know all was well between us, and his sternness the night before had just been because of his concern for my wellbeing in a new environment. Then we went for a walk, an activity we would repeat first thing every morning together on the coast. He showed me the easiest way to the main street and water, a path I had not discovered in the dark the night before. Happily, he pointed out those favorite childhood spots; the bridge he fished on, where he swam and walked in youth. The town was awakening to the activities of the day and we went over a drawbridge to the other side of the village, and began to head away toward a wooded path by the shore.

After showing me a spot off this rocky side of the shore, where his parents had brought him everyday in the summer as a child, we strolled leisurely back to the area where the shops began.

Soon we stopped for a croissant at a bakery. Then we found a table at an outdoor café and ordered our morning espressos. Beginning the tether game from the night before, I was told exactly how far I could swim from the shore and instructed to go no further. It seemed a joke at first, but everyone had boats here at the shore and the traffic in the water was constant, so his desire to have me stay out of the boat lanes later revealed itself to be very good common sense for my safety.

Mischievously I pushed, pointing to islands in the distance and commenting that surely he would have no problem for me to take the one hour swim to them and back, and he patiently responded by repeating the distance in meters that I could stray from the shore. But of course I could swim, hypothetically, close to shore for hours in either direction at my leisure so as not to overly restrict my fun. We laughed as I prodded, but in the end he was truly concerned for my welfare and meant what he had said, and I had agreed and would honor my bargain.

Some interesting topics came up over coffee. Yet Braco wanted to talk about what he could prove, not what he thought. Otherwise he knew only more questions would be raised. This was why so many films have been made about him; people's own accounts of their healings and life changes were the proof of what his gaze could do. And so he did not speak in public or offer his personal thoughts in general to the people. He did not want to play the role of a guru, he only wished for the work of the energy to reach as many people as possible and stand on its own merits.

That night, Braco himself had a dream and this was odd for him, because he usually slept deeply without dreaming. Yet he shared that he had dreamt clearly about Japan, about seeing two very elegantly dressed Japanese businessmen. I was there, very happy, and the two men were much shorter than I. They were in high spirits and pleased too, but did not show it openly. Braco would sign a contract they had and this was making me smile. All took place in some hotel in Japan, and when Braco woke up, he also felt happy. My desire to introduce him to my own Japanese friends certainly made me look at this as a possible glimpse of the future. I hoped so.

I wished to bring him not only to Hawaii, but Japan, Australia, Canada and other new places.

By a certain time, we had to be finished at our café; to walk over a drawbridge to the other side of the sea, before it rose for thirty minutes, allowing ships through a narrow passage. So we continued over this sole route of crossing, and then stopped at a second café. It would become our destination for meeting others at in the future, and today Damir awaited us here. Braco would partake in milk with honey, a staple of his morning. After some Center logistics were discussed, we left and climbed a steep set of stone stairs, up a long passageway leading directly to Braco's home. There we put on our swimsuits, packed our day swimming supplies, and drove less than ten minutes out of town. Winding down a gravel road in a completely undeveloped area, we arrived at his seaside property.

Dinka, Andelon, Damir, Braco and I arrived at a large gate, which he unlocked and we strolled onto a property that had beautiful stonewalls stretching in many directions. Braco had employed a man over the last year, and he had worked full-time, grooming the property and creating stone work to accentuate areas; especially around a 1000 year old olive tree and an upper terraced level with a great outdoor stone oven. Olive trees grew in abundance, and the house was small and rustic. But it was suitable for the family to use, and for Dinka to prepare the meals for all the guests who came through, which she did with loving care and sometimes with help from a visiting friend.

We came to an area down from the house, and near the water where trees shaded two long, stone tables with benches. Here we would eat and talk over the course of the day. Then I was shown the short stairs leading to the beach front, with a sunning area and stone landing with a boat mooring. That morning Braco had bought me a set of fins, and I borrowed Andelon's extra mask and snorkel, and soon I dove into the water. It was warm and clear, with a seabed filled with unusual shells in multitude. Each day I would take a swim along the shore in either direction and lose myself alone for an hour in my favorite medium. Only on this day would Braco stay with me in the water to make sure I became familiar with my surrounding, and was aware of the boating routes.

Beverages, fresh figs and snacks had been laid out on the table when I returned happy and refreshed from my exercise. Soon Braco's mother and father would arrive and when I met Ivanka for the first time, I felt an instant affection for her. She was an elegant woman, while being wholesomely natural at the same time. Soft spoken, she had a shy smile and sparkling eyes. Her chestnut hair was always groomed nicely in the days ahead, even though she would sun and swim everyday. Because of her own love of the water, she would swim for hours on end regularly.

Ivanka's smile held genuine warmth, her tan was the best I had ever seen, and she had a voluptuous and trip figure with that air of eternal youthfulness. Like Viktor, she was charmingly sweet spirited and had retained an innocent quality through life's many challenges. Because of the language barrier, we would share many more rich looks of hearty communication than words. We would often sit next to each other, while Viktor quietly watched the coming and going activities. He said very little, but he always had a ready smile when someone met his eyes and Andelon chatted with him regularly.

I wanted to interview Braco's parents, to get their unique perspectives, and I was told Viktor had never spoken to anyone about the past. So I asked anyway, with Braco's assistance, and while his father was quiet and thoughtful, his mother instantly agreed to help in this way. So later that afternoon, I had my red notebook in hand and wrote down her words exactly as she expressed them about Ivica, about Braco's time then and how this impacted their family's life.

Ivanka - Story of Meeting Ivica

Neighbors told me about Ivica. I had always had headaches for years and was taking pills. A neighbor said she would bring me to a man who could help my headaches, see the past and future, and who never took money. Friday afternoon we went, there were about 30-50 people. People were waiting and one man was giving an explanation of Ivica; he said photos could help also. So I went ten minutes and got a picture of Braco. Ivica would come out and tap shoulders of people he would then take. No first come, first serve – Ivica decided.

Those Ivica touched went into a room and I was one of them. The room had six or seven chairs, and some people sat, and the rest had to stay standing. I was the last one in the room with Ivica. He was looking in a mirror and he said to me my problem was very difficult and he may not be able to help me. He gave me special water and said if it helped, I could come back in one month. I bought a book before leaving. My headache did go away. It took one year for my friend to convince me to come and I only went because my headache was so severe. Now maybe two times a year I get a less intense headache. I used to get them regularly all the time.

Ivica intimidated me. He was wild and in people's faces, but I had a pleasant feeling with my first meeting. After that meeting, I cried all the way home and I felt Ivica could really help me. I began to read the book. Then the headache began to go from my head, down my body into my legs and lessen. This was the beginning of the healing. I did not mention this to my husband. The next Monday, Braco went with me. There were many people waiting at 7:30 am. I asked Ivica how long we would have to wait and he said it could be ten minutes or all day. Braco stayed until the end to about 1 pm.

At this point, Braco himself told me further events that happened after he stayed that fateful day. [This story is told in Chapter 1, *Braco's Beginning*.] Ivanka then continued her story in the time after Braco's relationship with Ivica was accepted and he was released from the army. After this episode, Ivanka and Viktor would become friends with Ivica, and meet often.

Ivanka Grbavac - Conversations with Ivica

Viktor, Ivica and I were in the house together. Ivica told us our Josip was no longer Josip. I said, "First you took my son and now his name!" Viktor said, "He was born Josip and he will stay Josip." Ivica said that two hours ago he had received a message from source that their son's name was Braco and he was witness to this. Viktor began to pace. Ivica said only for you both is he Josip, and to all others he is Braco.

Another time when Braco was not around, Ivica told me that my son was his connection between heaven and earth. He said that my son was a child of Atlantis. I said that I did not understand, and he told me I did not understand anything. [Mother laughs] Ivica wrote in one of his books, a child of Atlantis is here, but he did not write then who it was.

Ivica said there would come a time when the people of Atlantis would start to return and one of them was here. They would come when it was time for the golden period. Now is the bad time and the golden time is coming. When they come, they will be everywhere, but normal people will not recognize them.

(Pause)

Before going to Africa [Ivica died there], I told Ivica the night before not to go because I felt something would happen. He said that now everything was finished and he must go. One day before this, Ivica said to me that he felt something was going to happen to him and he wanted to put the flat at Srebrnjak 1 in my son's name. Braco refused this and said he did not want it. Ivica said it would be good to put it in Braco's name because he was leaving, spirit was leaving.

On the birthday of Ivica's wife, two or three weeks earlier, I was showing Viktor all the things he had built in his family home.

On the last night, Ivica asked me what I would like from Africa as a gift. I said something beautiful and he said he would bring me back a diamond.

When Ivica was helping the people and selling books, he signed all the books. He would tell the people to please buy the books now because they were originals, and in the future they would only be copies.

While Ivica was helping the people, the last few months before he died, there was a terrible story in the media about him. He told me that after he died, his bones would not rest but be taken up. After one or two years after Ivica died, so many people came to his grave with candles that they took up his remains, and moved them to a bigger grave.

Viktor never wanted to tell anyone, not even me, what Ivica told him.

Ivica once said the time would come when he would not want to be in Braco's place. A difficult time would come for Braco and it made him angry.

For Ivica, Braco was like his eyes, the most valuable diamond. Ivica then said Braco would become a leader of the people. He said Braco would write books and be on T.V. and I would watch him. Many times Ivica told me that my son would travel everywhere, to all the continents and I must prepare myself.

Ivica wrote in a book that he and Braco were one spirit in two bodies.

Often, Ivica's voice and look changed as if he was a different person, and he said it depended on which spirit came into him. I noticed this, as did my son, although Braco never spoke of it.

Ivica would have nightmares and be attacked and he said someone was after him, fighting. He said he could be attacked as long as Braco was not touched.

Evening at the Sea

Braco's mother then said that this was all she could remember and smiled. I thanked her for sharing her memories and we all went off to swim, partake in the gentle Adriatic sun, or in Braco's case - play with his fun loving son. Andelon was constantly at his father's side, and the strong bond between them was obvious. Despite Braco's demanding work schedule and travel, it was clear that the boy was well nourished by his father's love. Braco gave his son his full attention throughout the days, whenever we were not engaged in adult conversations, and Andelon thrived with this companionship. Together they walked up to a specially built bocce ball playing field for a game. Completely unexposed to this sport, I wander away mystified by the rules.

Later Dinka would make us special bread cooked in the outdoor stone oven and a tasty pasta dinner with fresh tomato and cucumber salad. Ivanka, Dinka and I all had a glass of red wine together and toasted while the men had other refreshments. Viktor was ever contemplative and Braco talked with him, and then told me that his father had agreed to give me his story from those early days with Ivica. Honored at his trust and delighted, I thanked him and he said he would begin writing it on paper. Tomorrow I would have it.

Braco felt this would be a good choice by his father to finally share his feelings, since he had never done so before. This was an opportunity for all of us to finally chronicle pieces of a greater story that people would one day appreciate and value. It was especially important now that the lives of Braco and Ivica were revealed. Fortunately, we also had gentle, quiet Damir with us too, and he had worked with Ivica in the healing work. The next day I would hear a short story from him about the prophet, and I knew all of these stories together would tell an interesting and unique tale.

At the end of the day with the sun going down, it was time to walk off the late dinner and so we packed up all our supplies, and Braco and I headed down the gravel road while the others loaded up the cars to drive back. By the time we had walked halfway, rain began to fall, which grew heavier. We still had about 20 minutes to walk, when Damir drove up behind us with Coco, the cockatoo taking up the front seat in his cage, and Braco's mother and father in the back seat. They let us in, but the only way for all four of us to fit in the back seat was for Ivanka and I to each sit on a lap. Without hesitation, she moved onto Viktor's lap who did not blink and eye and helped her. It was touching to see them this way during that ride home; this act said so much about both of them and their own special relationship.

Day 10 – Wednesday, July 8, 2009

Adriatic Coast

At 6:30 am I woke up, and shortly afterwards Braco arrived for our morning walk. At home, I would wake up everyday and make my morning cup of green tea and meditate. Each day I would spend an hour in the morning and before going to bed in this activity, but since I had arrived I had not meditated once and I did not feel less balanced for it. In fact, I felt the opposite. This energy of Braco's gaze had filled me with a heightened appreciation and zeal for life. Living fully in the moment, each moment, was becoming natural. With this came a dynamic spontaneity that flowed from me with youthful ease. I no longer needed to find my center and balance in a reclusive environment; I was finding that balance living life fully aware and zestfully.

Braco's way of living and behaving was teaching me this new facet of being present in life, which I had once known well but had forgotten. For years, I had strengthened my intuitive skills through meditation, and I was grateful for this training and discipline, but now I could apply all that discipline to life itself. A new strength was emerging in which I did not need to leave behind the world for previous reasons, even for an hour. Now I would use mediation again, but as a compliment to this work, to augment a way of life that would become gradually more and more present as an evolving spiritual expression.

Here I had discovered a great gift of energy that turned something on within and granted great strides in a life spontaneously, without integration periods, and more searching and balancing. As Professor Schneider and I had discussed in our interview together, here was something that represented the step forward for humankind. And it helped people from all races, all circumstances and all walks of life to embrace their given lots; and achieve through them, not run from these circumstances. One no longer had to abandon the difficult for a lack of certainty and strength to triumph over it. So now that stride forward had come, and I believed that this was true in the greatest social sense.

Opportunity was present on the planet, and the Source itself had delivered its first measure of the antidote in the form of Braco's gaze. Perhaps this was indeed the first stage of the return of the children of Atlantis that was Ivica's prophecy. Maybe Braco was that first child to step forward in full remembrance of what is our birthright as children of a divine and magnificent origin. I had my own ideas, but now I would turn my attention to Braco fully, and head out for the morning walk I so loved.

Once again crossing the drawbridge to the other side of the village, we strolled along the shore of the peaceful Adriatic, in this season at least, and afterwards came back for our two espresso stops. At the first, a waiter recognized us and brought our drinks without taking an order. We did not spend as much time at our second café, perched with open sliding glass doors on the water, for Braco wished to visit his parent's house. It was only a short walk up one street from the sea's edge, and only a few blocks from Braco's own home.

Once here, Braco's mother came out with a smile to the front marble balcony, greeting us, and immediately went back inside for refreshments to serve. Then Viktor came out and we all sat pleasantly in the shade and chatted over cookies. Damir was staying with them, and he next strolled out, taking a seat. He was ever at Braco's side as a trusted member of Srebrnjak 1 and a friend. We came up instantly with the idea of him sharing a story with us since he worked with Ivica too. Of course Damir smiled in his boyish way as his light colored eyes sparkled, and he agreed. It was clear by their relationship that he would have moved a mountain if Braco asked.

Damir Dumic-Kambicek - Ivica meets Braco

I was living at Ivica's home and that morning we had coffee and Ivica said that someone very special, who he had been waiting for, would come that day. And later Braco arrived with his mother. Ivica told me how beautiful he was, he did not mean physically, but beautiful as in spiritually pure. He told me that if, and when Braco came back after that day, I must let him know immediately, even if he was with people doing healings. The next day Braco came back, and I immediately knocked to tell Ivica, and then I brought in Braco.

Ivica had a woman who cooked for him and made lunch each day and Ivica said from then on, Braco would eat with him – eat what he ate, drink what he drank. Then when Braco would go home in the evenings Ivica was sad.

The day Braco arrived; Ivica changed and became more calm and peaceful. Prior to this he was always running around, up and down, in front of people, frenetic. But Braco's arrival instantly had this effect of bringing him peace.

Damir was the longest with Ivica. He was the first, and Ivica said Damir would be the last to leave Croatia as things expanded over the world. Damir also arrived at Srebrnjak 1 the earliest in the mornings at 6 am, and he was the last to leave.

Next Braco's mother, who was sitting and listening, volunteered another story about Braco and herself.

Ivanka Grbavac – Braco's Birth

Braco was born at 5 am, November 23rd in Zagreb. I was in labor four days and finally delivered him naturally, but I almost died during the process. At this time I was taken ill with gallstones and suffered greatly.

After the birth I recovered quickly, but I had another attack one month later and was told by the doctor that it was probably something I ate that poisoned my stomach. But I then became worse and I was hospitalized. They performed surgery, opening me up from my lower chest down to my belly and discovered many gallstones and much illness. The doctors told my husband that night that I probably would not survive the night. Yet I knew I must absolutely live for my son.

As I sat and drink Turkish coffee with everyone, I felt the love that Braco's mother and father had for their son, and I was deeply touched. In turn, my own affection for them grew. Viktor was quiet and thoughtful, but I could see his desire to finally share his story and the emotions that this was bringing to the surface. Today would be an important moment in his life when he no longer held alone this information. Ivica had said that Braco would continue to grow, but the real power would not come to him until after the death of his biological father. The power could not come while Braco had two fathers, the biological and the universal. What Braco was manifesting now was only a shadow of what it would become.

Soon our visit was over, we said our good-byes and planned to meet everyone again at the property on the water in a short while. Today one of Braco's dearest friends, Nikica Stimac, would visit with us there, and he had heard about my love of cheese and promised to bring some fresh from the sheep and goats of his home on the island of Pag. We walked back up the now familiar steep corridor of stone stairs, and met Dinka and Andelon at Braco's home. Again loading up our supplies for the day, we drove off to our sanctuary on the water's edge.

After getting all set up for the day with fresh fruit and water on the tables under the olive trees that shaded the picnic-style tables of stone, we all went to the water and I had my long swim. Exploring the shore a longer distance each time, I found deep happiness in the water's warmth. This too was a meditation practice for me. Boating activity that day was busy, however, and a few times boats came in so close to the shore near me that I did feel a bit nervous. Again it was made perfectly clear that swimming across the channel to another island would be hazardous. Thus, I found my tethered lot fully acceptable and enjoyed the shoreline views underwater to its fullest.

Around noontime, Nikica arrived along with the promised cheeses. He was a big bear of a man with a mischievous and boyish smile, black hair and dark eyes. Like an old friend, he gave me a warmly energetic hug, smiling and laughing as he spoke in Croatian to Braco. He was the type of person who exuded such a positive nature that one could not help but like him, and wish to stay around for the fun that would follow in his wake. I knew Braco admired this man for leaving a more material lifestyle to now live quietly and simply on a beautiful island, which made his heart happy.

After an introductory conversation in which Braco acted as my translator, we headed off to different activities; including bocce ball for the men and Andelon, and rest for me in a lounger. At our leisure, we eventually regrouped at our sturdy meeting tables. Since Braco had already asked his friend to talk about his own connection to the healing work, Nikica was ready to share a story. Diligently, I pulled out my red notebook to write, and found out that he had known Ivica first. Then he told me about a severe illness he once had that had led him to Ivica for help.

Nikica Stimac – Healing with Ivica

Fifteen years ago I came to Srebrnjak 1. I was ill with skin cancer and systemic lupus that was affecting every part of my body. When I fist saw Ivica he asked me what problem I had and I said health. Ivica asked if I was happy. He then said I had a wound on my right leg, and that it was open and this had saved my life. [This is where Nikica had skin cancer.] Ivica then said he would try to help me and he touched my body three times. I felt so happy, like a bird and as if I lost

150 kilos, when he did this. Then I bought one of his books and went home, and tried to read it but I was tired and had to sleep.

For the next three days I always wanted to sleep, and then after this time I finally read the book on the fourth day. Then I went back for a second time, half believing. I asked for help for some problems in the family, some relationships that were not good. Ivica said this was normal. He then told me to open up my down pillow; I would find dirt and things that did not belong there. I went home, got my pillow and opened it up with a knife, and found these things; so I threw it in the river as Ivica had instructed.

Next time I saw Ivica, he said I only half believed. He asked me why I had not thrown all the pillows in the river since I had the money to replace them. Then I bought a second book of his, and went home and threw the rest of the pillows in the river. I began to feel better in a general sense, and then began to read the second book. By this time severe cramps and spasms began to happen in my body. So I placed the book on the areas of pain and this helped.

Three months later I went back to Ivica and the cancer on my leg was 50% better without any medical treatment. I had had that cancer for ten years. After ten months, and again going to Ivica, I went back to my doctors and they said I was the healthiest man in the world. Now I no longer go to doctors. They said then that I could never go in the sun again. Now I am in the sun all the time.

Nikica continued coming to Braco after Ivica's passing. At one of Ivica's birthday celebrations, to honor his memory and work, Braco and his organization needed help to handle all the jobs to prepare for the thousands of people who would come to that event. They asked Nikica if he could assist and he did. Slowly, a natural friendship would evolve between the two men, and Braco told me that he simply liked Nikica. Now, whenever Braco was able to make a spontaneous visit to the coastal town, he called his friend. This burly and cheerful man always responded, and came to visit despite the long distance of a several hour drive from his home in Pag.

After we finished, Viktor came over and handed Braco and I a notepad. It contained his story. He had been writing since the day before, and I thanked him wholeheartedly. He smiled shyly, slowly walking away after exchanging a few words with his son. Then Braco guided me to another set of olive trees with chaise lounge chairs underneath. Reclining in the chairs, I had my red notebook in hand as Braco began to translate Viktor's manuscript for me.

Viktor Grbavac – Braco and Ivica

> A few days ago I came to Srebrnjak 1 where my son Josip introduced me to a beautiful blonde woman named Angelika who came from Hawaii. After a few days I am again in the company of Josip, Angelika and some other people on the sea. We are enjoying the sun and swimming and we were talking the most about how Josip came for his first time to Srebrnjak 1, about his work and his first meeting with his teacher Ivica. About the work when Ivica was with Braco.

> In one moment Josip, my son, asked me what I thought of Angelika. It seems like he was reading my thoughts because I was thinking about Angelika. And I told my son I think that Angelika is a very spiritual person and this is a part of her life, she is thinking of this way and now is probably thinking about you - how you are, what you are doing and how you are doing this, about the energy you have and about your incredible wish to help the people. I said to my son that this woman believes incredibly in you, something similar to how you believed in your teacher Ivica. After a few minutes Angelika asked me if I would like to tell some stories about

Ivica and Braco, because she is writing a book about Braco. My son told me this a few days ago.

I said I would like to do this and that I am happy that it would be just her, the first one that I will tell something of what I thought about Ivica and Braco. So first, my name is Viktor, and I was born in a village. There were five of us brothers and I finished elementary school. Afterwards, I was living in this village doing agriculture and after that I finished the army. In the year 1963, I came to Zagreb where I started to work for the police and while working as a policeman I went back for another four years of school. Then I finished university for law and received a master's degree in economics. In 1976, when I was 36 years old, I became a manager of a company. In 1966, I met my wife, Ivanka, and got married and in 1967 Josip was born.

This time after Josip was born, I worked as a policeman, was going to school, and everything was great in our marriage. Josip was a happy child. We tried to give him everything. After Josip finished elementary school and all the other schools, he was 24 years old. He also earned a master's degree in economics and opened a private company named Viktoria, whose owner and manager was Josip. The company was going very well and everyone was surprised how well everything was. Then the biggest changes came into our lives after my wife, Ivanka, went to meet Ivica and after bringing Josip to Srebrnjak 1. I found this out a few days later.

After a few days, I went and found Ivica and Josip together. He was smoking cigarettes and drinking coffee with some man that I had never met before. Before this moment Josip never touched coffee or cigarettes. I cannot believe this and I felt like I would fall down to the floor, and my son and Ivica were smiling at me. Suddenly, I got myself to the doorway and I succeeded to sit myself on the floor. I felt completely without power, without energy. I felt completely destroyed. This evil man, Ivica, is telling me something but I don't understand anything. Black thoughts are coming to me - he took my son, he took everything, everything I was living for.

So now my ship was going too easily and suddenly the big storm came. I felt like I was a captain without any sailors around me. I did not know what to do but I said to myself, I must go on, I must go on, because of my son, Josip. I gave myself room to figure out the situation and began to speak with Ivica. It was very difficult because Ivica was a very unpredictable person, but at the same time so was I. Many people were around us when Ivica and I were talking, and they told me I was stronger from Ivica. Ivica also said that I was strong, but I did not think this way.

Soon I became like an empty football, hit from all sides, and I was born without power. My only choice was to cooperate with Ivica because it was the only way for me to be close to my son. Ivica and my son came to visit my home from time to time, but at the same time my wife and I began to visit Ivica's house. A few times I was traveling with Ivica and Josip to the places Ivica goes to help the people. And Ivica liked me to be with him so I could see what he was doing.

In my deepest memory will always remain Ivica's last visit before he went to Africa. In his home were Ivica and his wife, Josip, my wife and I and another 10 people. It was about 9 pm in the evening and Ivica invited me to go out in his garden. It was very cold, almost frozen outside, and Ivica started to tell me how he and Josip and a few people would go to Africa, and he did not know how everything would finish. He wrote 13 books and he saw in his destiny that he would write 13 books – he had finished the job he had received from the divine. He told me he started something and that he was preparing Josip for all he too would have to do. It will be a very difficult period for him but in the end he will succeed.

At the end he told me that I must be proud that I have a son like him, to whom the whole world will admire soon; that people will love him wherever he will come. He told me that no one could stop him because he was prepared for this way from the divine for a long time, it will be difficult but then he will succeed. I told Ivica, but you are young, healthy, you have big energy and you will continue to help the people and that I have nothing against Josip being with you, and like always as your right part. Ivica was always talking that Josip was his right side. Why not think positively, I said. Ivica said he must follow the divine will and he was getting an order. We spoke for almost two and a half hours and then came back inside his house. After that I went home with my wife.

One day before leaving for Africa, he came with my son Josip to say good-bye. We were talking for two hours and then he said good-bye, but the kind that means forever. These words were in me for a long time and even now I can hear these words. Always he said good-bye, we will see each other soon. In my opinion, Ivica had powerful energy, he could see the past and future - what all of us can see in his DVDs and in reading his books; he really helped the people. He wanted a big challenge and challenge wanted him. He was unpredictable. One did not know if he would be nice or rude sometimes.

He was the happiest that he finished his part of the job and that Josip would be able to continue it. After the tragedy of Ivica's death, Josip had to continue his life mission. Ivica had told him it was very difficult, and Josip was doing without stopping with his people, from day to day, from year to year. I can say as his father that the power is stronger. Many people in the beginning did not believe that Josip would succeed and continue, but the time has revealed all. I, as Josip's father, don't like to speak about him, about his power. Like my son always says, let the people see and talk.

What I can say is that people are coming in bigger numbers, he is trying to help the people in more places, not only Zagreb, but Slovenia and European countries and now I can see he is soon to leave Europe. There are many books written about this and DVDs. Many people ask me where my son is getting such powerful energy, and I just say I do not know. I just ask God that he has the energy to be protected. I am thankful for the people around him, who are following him around everywhere, and also thankful to his wife, Dinka, and his son, Andelon, who have such a big understanding for his way because he is not often at home.

As we came in the translation to the part in which Viktor told of the final meeting before Ivica left for that fateful day in Africa that cost him his life, tears filled Braco's eyes. He was deeply moved as he read his father's account about the man who had meant the world to him. I reached out a hand in comfort and gently said we could continue later, but Braco shook his head to go on because it would be easier for him than to wait. Braco had never shed tears for his dear Ivica before. So much had happened so quickly and responsibilities immediately had come. This was the first time in all those years that his tears could finally flow for his friend, and I was so touched and somehow grateful that I could be with him at this time. It bonded me even more deeply, spiritually, to share in this moment of grief. I came to regret deeply that I had never been able to meet this exceptional man during his lifetime.

Once we were done, we paused and Braco reached for a cigarette. He occasionally liked to smoke a special brand imported from England. In the Balkans, the majority of the people smoked unlike in Europe, which was changing. As he was smoking, I reached for his cigarette in a spontaneous moment and inhaled. It nearly made me fall over and I gasped, I was not ready for the potency of the tobacco. He could not believe I had done this and we both laughed, and I was so happy to see him smile again. Later we had a feast for dinner and I could only admire how hard Dinka worked to take care of everyone with such love and grace. Once again, the women all toasted with red wine while some of the men had white instead, and Braco abstained. After we all ended our meal on that special day, we packed up and went back to the village. There we would meet all again for a final round of joking and banter before going off to sleep finally well after midnight.

———

Chapter Eight

Day 11 – Thursday, July 9, 2009

Adriatic Coast

Shortening our morning walk to meet with Nikica and Damir earlier than usual, Braco and I stopped at our first café for a brief chat while still alone. I raised the topic that we seemed to come into this life with certain themes and experiences that governed our individual lives. My empathic/telepathic dolphin friends had helped me to realize mine. It was that the universe was kind, and this theme had governed my life journey like a beacon, although for many years I thought the opposite true. My focus switched in my life, once I began swimming with the dolphins, to one of a deeper appreciation and connection with all things. They were wise teachers on many levels. Braco smiled warmly at me, happy too that I felt such a positive force present.

We soon left and found our comrades standing before the drawbridge. Nikica wanted to watch it rise, and I had not fully witnessed this event. We stayed the whole thirty-minute duration, observing the many boats and ships line up, and pass through the narrow channel. All the men conversed in Croatian, and I simply listened. I could not understand any words, but it was enough to feel the bonds of caring between them. They all were so open, and filled with goodness and light; and they constantly demonstrated that even the small things in life were worth note, and could be simply enjoyed.

As I turned to look at the people, the shops and the cafes, I felt as if I was in a protected bubble. Noticeably immersed and vitally present in the world of Braco, his family and friends, I distinctly felt separate from the rest of the experience of the seaside village, and its sweet summer atmosphere of an idyllic Adriatic community. All its many activities, diversions and entertainments felt a world apart. Tangibly, I watched the town from an invisible protected shield, as if being in some alternate dimension in which I could observe and participate without fully entering anymore.

This was a highly unusual and very intriguing experience. It offered a clear view of a distinction, in consciousness perhaps, that prevailed because of the everyday people's materially oriented relationships to shops, appearances and money. I felt I had truly entered a field of energy of a more natural existence, into Braco's world. It felt more than alive, it was denser with life somehow, and I was in awe of its feeling. I would have it now continuously in the days ahead, that experience of a reality of wholeness tangibly side-by-side one of an aimless coarseness, with its chaos and distractions that interfered with a *real* life. Imagining the entire world this way, I sighed. It was a possibility.

After the drawbridge lowered, we walked next door to our chosen café, joked good-humouredly with Nikica, and then stopped at a bakery to buy fresh breads and pastries for our communal breakfast with Dinka and Andelon at their home. Dinka provided fresh fruits and honey and we feasted together with Turkish coffee, as I made my final try to acquire its taste without success. Soon, Braco's father and mother joined us. An excursion for the day was planned to visit Ivan, a swarthy fisherman, and Braco's other best friend, at his home an hour and a half drive away. I would see open sea finally to the horizon this day.

The Home of Ivan and Lida

Everyone came in a caravan of cars, and as we drove along the coast, I saw the water to the open blue sky and finally the temperate Adriatic looked like a real sea. We passed village after village, all white, charming and postcard perfect in appearance, until we finally arrived at our destination. Ivan's home was located directly on the water next to a pier, with much construction going on as he added upward to his large, old-world style house. Immediately, Ivan and his wife, Lida, greeted us and I recognized him from one of the latest films about Braco. He was a jovial, smiling man with a burly build and the look of a true Adriatic fisherman. At his side was his wife, equally genial and gracious, with expressive blue eyes as she welcomed us all.

Unloading our cars, swim supplies went to the front shore of the house, and all else to a great kitchen set with tables pushed together to accommodate everyone form our large group. It was clear that this kitchen was the gathering place for many events, and it was filled with love and good cheer. After the introductions were made, and some friendly conversation, I headed to the shore for a long and leisurely swim down the coast. Ivanka prepared to enjoy the sun on the beach; and the men gathered themselves together and laughed with words that remained the mystery of a foreign tongue.

After over an hour of sightseeing the shore from the water, I came back and lay in the sun while much activity and pleasant aromas wafted from the kitchen. Dinka was helping our hostess prepare the 2 pm feast, the second of three that day. My tan was improving on its already good base, and I collected polished stones from the beach as I relaxed and hunted for unusual shapes. Spontaneously, I had the thought of asking Braco to pick out one rock for me as a souvenir, instead of bringing home the piles I was accumulating. I got up to join the men near a porch swing to make my request.

Immediately, Braco came forward and told me he had a special rock for me. I was taken aback by the coincidence with my last thought, and simply said, "Really!" The day before, Braco and Nikica had told me about a nearby island on which a UFO had been witnessed to land. They knew my interest on this subject, and told me next visit they would take me there. Not only had they visited this island in curiosity together, they had also gathered some rocks, and now Braco had chosen the best one for me to take home as a gift. It was a very strange stone and I did not recognize the type; like a whitish marble with a perfect circular hole near its top peak. Of course I loved it and would cart it home to Hawaii despite its sizeable weight. It was better than I had wished for a few moments before.

Our lunch was a spread of absolutely sizable proportions, including fresh squid from the sea for those who enjoyed it. I tried some different cooked greens that I had never heard of or tasted before; and large lima beans in olive oil were a staple. After eating more than my fill, to my surprise a special cake was brought out made for me to try, a local favorite with raisins and nuts, and I did justice to my plate for once. Good healthy food, always home prepared, sometimes self caught or home grown, was a joy of life here.

When not another morsel could be eaten, most drifted outdoors. Then there was an opportunity to talk with Viktor a bit more about his memories and gather more information. Braco was at my side as interpreter once more, and I began to ask some questions about earlier times.

Viktor Grbavac – Getting to know Ivica

> V. Ten days after seeing Ivica, I was consulting with some people who understood about him such as psychologists and doctors. They told me it was best to leave Josip alone and to let him make his own decisions. Time would then tell. I had to think about this and I fought with myself. I only changed my opinion about Ivica after the army experience.

> A. *What happened after you accepted Ivica?*

> V. I had a problem with stress, my brother died and a few times I asked for help ... and things got better each time. Yet frankly, I only really did this to spend more time with Josip at Ivica's. I had no experience with this area and I did not really understand.

> A. *Do you understand this work now?*

V. After I saw everything, heard people's stories and the DVDs, I eventually came to believe this was all real before Ivica died. Ivica said that because of what Josip is, he had to be with him all the time. He said Josip would continue his work, but in numbers far greater than he.

Ivica told me that he cannot change this, even he cannot stop him, he tried to send him away several times - but the divine controls Josip and no one else has control of him. At this time we are both thinking of what to do with Josip, but Ivica knew he had no control. He saw when the time came no one could stop this power; only the divine could stop it if it chose. After this time, I came to understand and accept that I could not change this.

Before Africa, a moment came when Ivica was in a big crisis. The church, health profession and media attacked him, and he started to loose some power. Ivica said only Josip could continue this work because he was completely unafraid. That if the church, media, doctors or blackmail, anything came, Josip would not ever be afraid or stop. Nothing could stop him. Ivica said Josip is this child of Atlantis, he said to let Josip do as he feels.

A. What do you think of Braco's work now?

I believe very much and I admire how Josip can do this with little sleep, long hours etc. And I miss him because sometimes we do not see each other for a long time. I believe all the people and reports.

Ivica knew that if Josip did not continue, then no one could continue the work and all that was built would end. A few days before Africa, he was talking only about this subject.

Now I come a minimum of once a week to Josip's gaze, not only for myself but also for my family. I have received a lot of help, as have others. I have read all the books and I wear the sun symbol.

Viktor then stated that he was satisfied with this and there was nothing else to tell, and we ended our talk. I looked deeply at this man and found him to be a rare person. One who had completely changed his perspective, delving into things beyond his comprehension at the time, for the sake of not separating himself from the son he loved so dearly. Life had placed a tremendous challenge before him, and he had come to peace with it and the destiny of his own life, and that of his son.

After more sunning and swimming, we all went inside to change and dress for another venture out. Braco has been invited to visit and dine with a couple that owned a hotel and restaurant on the very popular Island of Trogir. It was a very special circumstance that Braco would accept such an offer, but he had known this couple for years and along with Nikica, they were the only ones he would visit when occasion allowed. Braco had little time to himself, and he valued those opportunities fully that offered him the company of his family and friends.

Ivan's son, a strapping blond man, had joined us for the lunch, and now he and his father readied a small boat for us to travel across a straight to get to our destination across the water. All the women came aboard in high heals accept for myself, in Hawaiian-style sandals. Perching ourselves on the front deck, I sat next to Braco's mother and as my shoes came off, we smiled at each other in the knowing way. She too loved the water intensely, and took pleasure in our transportation.

On the way over, we would stop in the middle of the sea straight while Ivan's son dove into the water with a large bucket. He came back up from the bottom with it filled with small fish, shells and more, and set it on the deck. Once he was aboard, he picked it up and suddenly emptied it on the rear deck. My love of all creatures made me sit up straight, concerned with the possible intent behind this act. The little fishes were floundering on the deck, and he refilled the pale with seawater before he and his father began scooping up the fish, and throwing them in the pale.

Immediately, I came to the back deck and helped to quickly rescue a few back into the bucket, but quickly thought better of this and threw the rest I could catch back into the sea. They assured me that they were only for a large aquarium at the hotel we were visiting, and they would be okay. Even this did not sooth me and Braco, who had joined us in our work to get them back into water quickly, looked at me apologetically; he understood. His empathy was always active, although he was strong and grounded, and this gift did not make him unduly sensitive to taking on the pain of others. Instead I watched him value other people's feeling while maintaining his own equilibrium. Braco told me in a kindly way that I was very sensitive, especially to the plight of animals and creatures, but that the energy would give me more strength to handle such things.

Island of Trogir

Our destination was a small island that proudly displayed a great fortress of centuries past at one end, and it's ancient, cobblestone streets were filled with posh shops and innumerable restaurants. Clearly this was a famous spot, told by the line of millionaire and billionaire mega-yachts lined up at the shore. I had never seen so many of these in one location before, and was told Bill Gates came here and many celebrities. There was a vibrant bustle in the air of both leisure and commerce intertwining.

Ivan parked our boat aptly in a tiny spot that he made bigger amongst an array of other small vessels at the shore, near our hotel destination. We all gathered together, Braco at my side, and he told me that our hosts were special people with big hearts. They spoiled him each visit with a table full of their best fair, and showed their love in this convivial welcome of hospitality. Shortly we arrived at a lovely European-style hotel with rooms each uniquely decorated by our hostess in elegant charm.

Franka and Mate, proprietors of the *Hotel Pasike Restaurant*, had created an atmosphere that was distinguished with quality antique furniture, while the rooms were fresh and bright with great attention to aesthetic details. Their daughter met us first, dressed in a traditional Croatian long dress, and walked us inside. The restaurant was set with elegant tablecloths and sparkling glasses, ready for the evening clientele. Ivan's son carried in the bucket of fish, and went to a huge fish tank in the restaurant, and poured them in. A few of the men made a point of telling me that none had died in transport.

A young son of our hosts, a bit older than Andelon, emerged and the two boys instantly bonded together at the aquarium. Lobsters were in the tank too, and the children were fascinated with watching the sea life. Then something unexpected happened as I watched. I saw a lobster corner one of the little fishes, and though its claws were tied shut, it managed to begin eating the fish. Soon many of the fish were gone and though I said nothing, I was distressed. Young Andelon watched me intently and looked back to the fish. Braco came to my side and let me know that they had not known that this would happen, or they would not have brought the fish. Later Andelon stated that when he saw me look like I would shed a tear, he too felt sad for the fish. But that boyish curiosity had both boys watching the tank for a long time like a movie screen, laughing the whole time together.

Franka came out and hugged Braco dearly, then everyone else and showed her warm delight at our arrival. She had a full main of white-grey hair, a rollicking smile and a vivid love of life in her eyes. This woman truly glowed with an inner joy. Finally Mate entered, and as his wife, gave Braco a hearty hug with a genuine smile before meeting us all. His bearded face held peacefulness as bright as his wife's joy, and I was taken with both of them because of this radiant quality they possessed.

Plainly I could see in them a happiness that was a constant, not the typical up and down relationship that most people had in life. Demonstrated in them was a real foundation that did not teeter with the passing moments. These two people had fully received the gift of the energy, and it radiated from them tangibly. I felt serene just watching them. Franka and Mate had been coming to Braco for 8 years now, once every month, and the energy danced in them exceptionally.

Next, a cheery faced woman entered the restaurant with an elderly woman behind, and was greeted as family. She was a cousin to one of our hosts, and she spoke English to my gladness. Hers was also a genial nature that made no one a stranger, and we all began talking in lively tones. Before dinner was served, we would all have a tour of Trogir. Our latest arrival, Marina, would be our guide to share some history and nostalgia about the island. Working in Southern California, she still maintained a Balkan's charisma, and her knowledge of the town was a wonderful introduction.

Marina would stay at my side and conduct our excursion in English for my benefit, and I was touched by this courtesy. We began at the fortress and saw other special places that were seeped in a history dating back to other eras. As we strolled, I noticed a strange effect in me. As our group was divided in the narrow streets and masses of people going in all directions, I was acutely aware of Braco's absence. I realized that in a very short period, he had become important to me, as one of those rare friends whose company one always treasured and wished near. Several times, I found myself casually attempting to note his whereabouts, and I appreciated with amusement that my tether had taken on a life of its own.

After our walk around and through all of Trogir, small as it was, we came back to the hotel and our hosts showed me their establishment. In the reception area, one of the many films about Braco was playing on a plasma screen television, and I was told that his DVDs played all day and night. They had unconditionally welcomed the energy into their lives, and told me that they felt that the films kept that energy ever flowing into their home and work. With a deep respect for Braco too, they paid tribute to him in this way. Later I would chronicle their story, and find out why their loyalty and love was so great.

For dinner, two great round tables had been pushed together and it was enough to accommodate all of us. I was seated on Braco's right side, with Marina on my right, and Dinka to Braco's left. Our meal began with appetizers big enough to be the main course, and food only kept coming from that moment onward. Animated conversations took place around the table and as soon as the meal had a lull, I asked Mate to share his story of coming to Braco. He looked pleased to be asked and pulled a chair next to Braco, who would play the role of translator with Marina, as I pulled out my red notebook in readiness.

Mate and Franka Buble – Life Transformation with Braco

> My wife and I worked at a shipyard. We were fine economically and had a good life. I was prominent with computers, bringing advanced technology programs in for the ships. My wife supported me all ways.
>
> At the time the war started, my wife lost her job and we both lost all our income. We had a little house for coming together, and we decided to work from scratch to begin a restaurant here. The first two years were okay. Then many problems came, and we thought that jealousy from the neighbors was responsible. My wife began to have pain in her hand and it became so bad she could no longer work in the kitchen. I took care of provisions and supplies, but I had asthmatic attacks and they stopped me from doing simple things.
>
> We put in so much effort with little effect. One morning my wife came to work and saw plants and trees all thrown at our entrance door. Before this, we told Marina about our problems, and she advised us to seek answers as to the cause. So one of our cousins saw our condition, and recommended to my wife that we see Braco.
>
> We were not open and we were raised in a different system, not spiritual, and we were not open to this. Finally the last

blow was the mess at our front door step. Even though we had so many unusual problems, we could not comprehend it being something beyond, so when it continued, our daughter told my wife to go to see Braco. She said what are you waiting for?

At that time I was so severely impacted that I would end up at the emergency room every three months and they tried to save my life. So my wife went to Braco. It was May 2001. At the same time that she was at Braco's, I was with my doctor at the emergency room. However, while waiting, I felt different and could breath easier, I was lighter. My wife returned from Zagreb, and I asked what happened up there, why do I feel better? She said nothing happened, I just spoke with Braco for about ten seconds.

After her visit, I started to experience a gradual shift in myself – I started to think differently and even though I still had problems, I dealt with them differently. Suddenly, I had a need to go to Braco, and Franka and I spontaneously decided to go. I have to emphasize that each time we wanted to go to see Braco, obstacles would appear. For instance, while driving, our steering went out, and the car went to the side of the road. But we were not dismayed or detoured, and since, the beginning of every month I am going to see Braco.

Since I am seeing Braco, my life changed so much that I can barely recognize it in every aspect – not just how I approach work or my children – it is indescribably different. Even though there are still problems, like my daughter's divorce, the way I react has changed, and everything resolves itself in a positive way. Before it would be hard, even though I did not want it to be so, and I tried to resolve it with psychology etc. But now I understand it can be well without effort.

As far as the results go, this hotel and whatever we have achieved, we are deeply convinced that it is thanks to Braco, because we were with nothing and our background is as shipyard workers. Nothing would have been possible without him. When we were looking for the way out of crisis, we sought out Braco for advice. Meanwhile, even though we did not have very much, we applied for a loan with the bank. At the time, Braco was still talking and dedicated some time to all who came.

We directly asked him about the credit loan to expand our business, and he told us it was not our time in December 2001. So as of 2002, we had received a call from the bank that they had approved our loan for $200,000 US. But as Braco said no, we turned down the credit line. We waited six or seven months and then decided to try again, applying for credit. Braco said it would be hard, but we would succeed and this happened.

Throughout this time we were compelled to continue, and we realized this force was Braco, the success he described. Braco was talking with me, and said I needed to buy this house. The next day the bank approved a $750,000 Euro loan, and we purchased the house because Braco had said so. The final loan could not have happened in my wildest dreams without him.

[Later Mate told me that the first loan had such a high interest rate that the interest payments would have crushed them. The second loan had a much lower rate that was manageable.]

When I came the first time to Braco, my wife said to him, I brought my husband, and Braco asked where is he, and that moment I knew that one day we would become friends. And after a couple of years I felt we were friends.

From the first moment, we constantly have a DVD or photo; DVDs are constantly in our reception – to honor Braco and to dispel any negativity that may harm us in any way. What became a part of my life, when any obstacle occurs, is to consult with Braco at Srebrnjak 1. And as a result it always has a positive outcome.

For thirty years Mate and Franka had their home and restaurant, but now they owned it all. Five years ago they opened the first rooms of their hotel, and one year ago they bought more rooms and now had sixteen. They were prosperous and content with what they had been able to create, and were lovingly proud of their beautiful hotel. But it was really the joy and peace in their eyes that told their whole story.

Dessert was soon to arrive and most of our group ordered espressos to finish our meal. Marina has been a good companion during the early courses, and now she retrieved a special box of organic tobacco cigarettes from her handbag, and offered me one. They were elegantly rolled in brightly colored paper with gold filters. Spontaneously, I wished to accept one, and she lit it for me. Braco looked at me surprised, and I inhaled with a playful glee. He then accepted one too from Marina, as did Ivan, and we all looked like we were holding party favors. Fortunately, the taste was very mild. Nikica and Damir's eyes were on me intently, and Nikica laughed loudly and I shrugged with a smile.

Braco gave me a questioning look still, and I told him I just had the wish to do it. Exhilaration filled me from our group; there was so much warmth and love that surrounded us. And now I was part of the Balkan ritual that most enjoyed and I enjoyed it thoroughly during those moments with everyone. With my pink cigarette in hand, I met Ivanka's eyes, and they held no judgment at all, no one's did. They only smiled and accepted that the unexpected happened here.

After dessert the night was late, and we thanked our hosts for the most splendid of evenings. Mate embraced me and told me when I returned, I would be his guest again, and I thanked him with deep respect for his accomplishments and generous nature. Damir and Ivan's son had left to get our cars at Ivan's house, and so we were able to leave Trogir and head directly back to Braco's seaside home. Nikica parted ways, since he lived in the other direction, but not before asking me to stay in Croatia with all of them. My heart was more than tempted, and I knew he could see that in me, but I had work to do in America, to clear a path for Braco's entry. I knew with a certainty I had to do this, my book, a conference event, and more before my path could bring me back to Braco's side. I had made my choice and commitment.

Chapter Nine

Day 12 – Friday, July 10, 2009

Adriatic Coast

During our first espresso at our favorite Café Rudina, Braco and I began our discussion about the locations in Hawaii he would visit. This was our first logistical meeting in which I told him details about possibilities on the different islands, and the contacts that I had to assist in the process. At this beginning stage, we were discussing Braco staying for three weeks in the islands, although this would in the end unfold naturally, and not by any set design. Now I only had to organize my conference, and another two weeks of touring for Braco through Hawaii afterwards. Everything in me wished to create wonderful surprises there for him, and many firsts for the work.

Then we continued over the bridge before 9 am, and stopped at our other preference, the Café Bar Light. We continued our talk and he suggested trying a gazing session outdoors. This was something he had done before for large crowds, and I could provide him with a special setting in nature. Whenever the gazing sessions took place, a specific instrumental music was always played. But in nature, we decided we could use a single person playing live traditional music. The next new idea to implement was allowing the people in Hawaii to come to more than one gazing session in a single day. Many people would travel a great distance, and most would be new, and Braco wished to help the people receive the energy more quickly, since his return could take some time.

Fortunately, the sacred environment would support people in having greater doses of the energy more quickly.

In Stuttgart, 1600 people had come through in a day, and twelve had been taken away on stretchers to the local hospital. All would later be fine; they were just overcome with the potency of the energy and particularly susceptible to its effects. This was why people were only allowed one session a day, but I had certainly demonstrated a different possibility and the natural settings on our island, along with the simplicity and respectful living of so many, would indeed support this experiment. Braco was always aware of how things would affect the people, and worked from an inner certainty that spontaneously led him to choose the best possibilities. And I loved trying new ideas and would set up our events accordingly.

After stopping next for croissants and pastries, we picked out enough for Dinka and Andelon, and joined them at the house for breakfast. Dinka had fresh-made yogurt for Braco and local honey, and I happily ate fruit. Nikica had gone home and only Damir joined us that morning. We would not see Ivanka until later when we embarked back to Zagreb, so only the five of us went to the seaside property, and had a peaceful day enjoying all the pleasures it provided. Braco played through the afternoon with his son in bocce ball, swimming and cards. I joined the card games that were competitive and entertaining.

Everyone took turns in the chaise lounge chairs under the olive trees, and because of all of the food of the previous day; we all wished a rest from such rich abundance. So Dinka made us a late lunch of pasta with olives and we all ate sparingly. Braco usually left a little food on his plate, and had explained to me that this was a good practice, because it honored the bounty of our world. It was something I did too, because I knew that our beliefs helped to shape all parts of our lives. If one overate to leave nothing on the plate, it was not only unhealthy for the body, but perpetuated a collective idea of eating up everything and having nothing left - of lack.

After some casual conversation, I told Braco I would walk back to town and spend a few hours at a local internet café to check my email before everyone else came back to prepare for our departure. Underestimating the sun, I perspired a lot, but still enjoyed the stroll through the rolling hills with a water view on either side. This walk took me about 50 minutes before I arrived at the house to retrieve my computer, and then hiked back down to the water and find the café. While I was busy with my email, Dinka prepared Coco, the cockatoo, their other pet parrot and a lovable squirrel for travel to Zagreb. Dinka would come back to the city for a day to attend the wedding of a cousin, and then return back to the seaside. Braco's mother, Ivanka, would also join us to visit her own home to water her indoor potted flower collection that I was told was quite impressive and extensive.

So once we were all back at the village house, everyone packed their bags and prepared for the move and three-hour drive. Dinka would chauffer all the animals, Andelon and Ivanka in one car, while Damir drove Braco and I in another car. Braco always liked to sit in the back seat. Along the way, we stopped at a gas station café and all regrouped to have ice cream and drinks. The temperature difference was noticeably cooler and we chose to sit indoor for once. Braco was animated as he told Dinka, Ivanka and Damir of the plans we had made that morning for Hawaii. Everyone expressed encouragement and support, including Andelon, who also genuinely supported his father's work.

On the later half of the drive, we spoke more of Ivica. Often he was a potent part of our conversations and his presence in people's lives and hearts was ever evident. Braco would watch Ivica, but the prophet never directly taught him. Only wanting to be close to Ivica, Braco had never thought he would be helping the people as his friend had. And of course, the fact that Braco never performed a healing while Ivica was alive displayed the true nature of their relationship; it was clearly not one of a student and teacher.

It was just passed sunset when we arrived to our destination and after Damir helped by bringing my suitcase and computer bag to my door, he departed with a amiable farewell. Shortly, Dinka pulled up too and we all parted company for the evening. It was time to repack once again, for the next day brought us happily back to the work of Braco's gazing, and we were off to Slovenia once again. My wake up time would be 4:30 am, so that night I was glad to go to bed early and have a good rest for a new day.

Day 13 – Saturday, July 11, 2009

Slovenia

After rising early, we both met a little earlier than usual, and were able to stop for a croissant and espresso after our 50-minute walk. During most strolls together, we would often spend long periods in peaceful silence. That morning in particular, we lapsed often into quiet as we breathed in the sweetness of nature. It not only refreshed us, it made us keenly aware of the forest and the serenity of our pleasant environment. Our walks would continually connect us to a shared joy in this way. Along the way I counted that it had been four days since Braco's last gazing session for the people. And I had missed them intensely. Every minute was enjoyable on the sea, but nothing could compare with standing in the presence of that indescribably sweet energy and feeling it's illuminating force active within.

Braco was also clearly happy to do the gazing again because he truly lived to do his work. He did not normally come in person on Saturdays to Srebrnjak 1, a recording of his voice was played instead for groups, but today we would be here until 1 pm and then leave for Ljubljana in Slovenia. We were actually at Braco's Center that morning because I had to gather pictures from Braco and Ivica for my conference, articles and book. It would also be one of my last opportunities to take my own photos of Braco in the bamboo garden, as well as to fulfill my need of shopping for a few items before heading back again to the coastal village. So with these chores, work could be done too, and Braco would not pass up an opportunity to offer gazing sessions in person for those who arrived today.

During the first session I took notice of the diverse array of faces in the room, and then I watched Braco walk to his gazing platform. His face was always so gentle and timeless for those minutes, and the effect of the energy was so immediately tangible. My heart and mind committed to an even deeper level to the mission for the people, to the energy itself, and I felt a joy of being able to achieve anything. A profoundly peaceful power was awakening so much within me, and I knew many in the group present would experience that power in different ways within themselves and their lives. I understood deeply why many came back whenever they could, because the energy could literally recharge an individual life in the very finest of ways.

Braco's selfless giving of his gift was another reason why so many people loved him like a family member, and came in huge numbers each year on his birthday to show their respect and affection. At Srebrnjak 1, there was no admission; it was always free to come to the sessions. Only organizers were allowed to charge people 4 Euros, that they themselves kept, to help cover their expenses for room rental, advertising and the many costs involved in setting up an event. And such people who took on this responsibility, with Braco's approval, were carefully educated so that the people coming for help would never get anything less than one hundred percent at all levels.

In between the two next sessions, we gathered in the kitchen with Stevo, our chef, who always placed good quality and delicious food out for everyone to partake in as they chose. While we conversed, the phone rang and Dinko answered a call from Austria. However, the caller asked for assistance in English and so he passed the phone to Braco, since no one else was in the kitchen that could speak that language. The person on the line was inquiring about Braco's schedule. She would travel the distance to Zagreb with family, and wanted to be sure to see him in person. It was amusing to hear this woman asking Braco if he was sure of the dates, and requesting that he ask Braco himself. How could she know that she had him already in person? Without revealing his identity, Braco reassured her about the schedule and said good-bye. Again, Braco amazed me with how amazingly clear he always was about his schedule for the work, despite its constant variance.

Another break had me picture hunting through computer files with the help of Ljiljana. Then it was time for another session and I asked Braco if a staff member could help me to acquire a couple of stories from visitors in the next group. I knew that the films about Braco were the best for this type of material. Words alone could not match watching the DVDs about Braco, in which people told their own stories of miracles, but today would be a final opportunity for any testimonials written with permission to share from Srebrnjak 1, and I decided that a few would be helpful. So after the session was complete, I was assisted with the translation and received the following two stories:

Slobodan Sikic – 43 years old

> I had a bad pain in my stomach and trouble going to the bathroom. I had arthroscopic surgery and the doctors found a bacterial infection. The doctors gave me many pills and medicines, but the pain was severe and I became weak. I went to psychotherapy; the doctors prescribed this to help me deal with the severe pain since no pills helped. I lost 30 kilos and was screaming in pain at night.
>
> My wife found out about Braco and she came with my picture to him. The next day the pain was completely gone and it did not return for two days. After this the pain came back and I personally came with my wife to see Braco. I came every two weeks, sometimes with pain, and sometimes without, but after one year of coming the pain was completely gone.
>
> My first time was in 2003. I think the best of Braco's work and I have no words to thank him. I support his work in all ways. I feel about Braco as if he were a part of my family – I feel about him as I do my own children. I wish all the love and best for this man.

Ljubica – 60 years old – Zagreb

I come when I feel like it, sometimes one time a week or one time a month.

I was living my whole life with illness, bad family relationships – for 8 years my daughter could not get pregnant and after seeing Braco, my daughter got pregnant and had a child. Her doctors said this was incredible, impossible, a miracle.

My sister had a pain through her whole body for over 8 years and was taking many pills. Doctors could give no specific diagnosis. A family member brought her picture to Braco and she lost the pain. Now she feels better and her doctors have stopped the medications.

What Braco is doing is like a gift from God and it makes life look much more beautiful. Braco's help to me is God sending energy through Braco, coming through his eyes – and it helps people not as people want, but as God wants to give to them, what God decides they deserve.

I feel very big and open love, complete heart and soul, for Braco. I do not know how to say this, so I bring flowers each time I visit to express my love. [Ljubica is crying now.] My tears are expressing my love. For me, Braco is one deep, incredible love that cannot be measured. He brings me a deep sense of safety, peace and love.

After this, I went back to the kitchen to Braco's side and the dance tunes of the American 1980's were playing on the radio. Ljiljana was there and I asked her next for her own story of coming to Srebrnjak 1, since I wished to know as much information as possible about family, friends and those working so devotedly at the Center. Yet once she began to tell me how she came to Srebrnjak 1, she became almost speechless, which was odd since she was a most eloquent speaker. So we decided to wait to do it another time, because I thought the potency of what she was feeling and all that it meant to her just needed a little more time to settle, so that she could find the right words. Later she would find those perfect words to convey what she dearly wished to share.

For the time being, since I had to leave in a few hours for Slovenia, we decided it was a good time to go shopping. But first I went with Braco to the bamboo garden and took dozens of pictures of him. I was always impressed how natural he was in general, in all circumstances, and before the camera was no exception. While alone again we began to talk on the topic of destiny. Braco perceived that everything had a destiny - a person, a family, and a country, even a house etc. and every situation had one too.

Ivica could often see such destinies. Braco could perceive them also, and back when he was still talking to the people, he used this information to help those who came to him. Consciousness in this age would rise only because it was the destiny of the age, and therefore, people would desire change due to the age. When I asked Braco about God, he would not talk in these terms. Braco would not talk about God because he had such deep respect and did not feel competent to talk of this – God was too sacred.

I then asked what would help the people be less fearful in practical terms. For Braco, information was a key. He perceived that there was too much information around us. New things were often seen as bad, and it was normal to be afraid. Braco did not watch television news. He did not want to get under the influence of the negative information. For everyone, it was important to think less of that type of information, filled with so many negative images and stories. Focusing on other things, such as spending more time in nature, was how he lived and dealt with this reality. In a general sense, if something were bad, it would go away, so it was better to focus on the good. Of course, some people had a destiny to expose evil or corruption too, and this was a natural balancer.

After I returned from shopping with Ljiljana, who patiently took me across town to find what I was looking for, it was time to leave Zagreb. Tedo arrived and would be our driver to Ljubljana, the biggest city in Slovenia, and one of the loveliest I would see. Branko joined Tedo in front and we were off to another new destination. As we drove, Braco and I would share how it felt like years had passed since my arrival, that it seemed as if we had known each other for a much longer duration. There was such comfort and ease in our time together, as if we entered into a spacious timelessness.

Once in Ljubljana, we drove directly to our hotel that was a modern building with an inner courtyard setting and glass everywhere. Our event the next day would take place here in a grand ballroom, and after dropping our luggage off at our spacious rooms, I met Braco to tour our event space. Then Marjana from Slovenian joined us again, and I was glad to see her after our triumph together in Rogaska Slatina in which she had acted as my interpreter on stage. She had assisted the organizer for this event for Braco too. Smartly dressed and with a sweet smile, she was ready to show us about town. We only waited a brief time more for two other staff members, Anja and Dragana, to arrive and show us their city.

Anja was a young, attractive blond who wished to build an event herself for Braco in the future, and Dragana was a pretty woman with a spark and determination in her smile and eyes. To Dragana, I felt an instant kinship, and regretted we were not able to spend more time together over the course of the two days. All of us would go together in two cars, Marjana driving Braco and I in one, and Tedo, Branko, Anja and Dragana in the other. Our first stop was a special castle that held a legend of a dragon, the great protector of the city of Ljubljana.

While driving, Marjana, now in a brilliant turquoise outfit, told me that her entire wardrobe used to be in black, for work, evening and all. Then Braco had told her she was done with this color, and now she only wore it twice a week. She used to plan her wardrobe for a whole week in advance, but now with colors, she would wait until she woke up to see what color she felt like for that day. The room for spontaneous inspiration had entered her life at a fundamental level.

Our castle stroll gave us beautiful views of the countryside and walls steeped in history. Yet our tour was cut short due to exhibit closures because we were passed regular viewing hours, so after a group chat at an outdoor café within the walls, we drove off separately to meet again soon in the downtown area. But first Marjana took Braco and I for a walk along a great riverbank. Here we stretched our legs until we could walk no further, since the path ended. At this point our choice was to turn back, or scale a plant covered stone wall eight feet up to another path that continued further onward.

Braco and Marjana were ready to turn back and I stopped them. I told them we could go up the wall, and Braco said he would after I did it first. So in a slim skirt with a fortunate slit in the back for movement, I took my shoes off and proceeded to climb up and over successfully. Braco remarked how Branko would kill us for doing this if he knew, but I chided them on with the point of his absence, and Braco soon followed. Then in truly impressive style, Marjana made the assent in high heals and we were on our way again. In the distance, we found a riverboat serving refreshments, and climbed aboard the rocking wood deck, enjoying the break from the summer heat.

We stayed a bit long, unaware of the time, and when we finally arrived at the downtown, Branko and Tedo had posted themselves at different ends of the street looking for us. Branko forgave Marjana for the delay, since he could not resist her pretty smile and expression of innocence, and we all sat down together at a outdoor restaurant on a exceedingly beautiful boulevard filled with stone architecture and century old buildings all kept in perfect restoration. Shops and café restaurants flowed endlessly in all directions, through manicured streets small and large. And off in the distance was the city's protector, a great dragon on display at the town center.

Seated around a long table, we had a lively time together, often teasing Branko, especially when he turned down all salad, bread and vegetables to stubbornly save himself for a hearty slab of meat. Most of us had wine and after dinner we all tried heaping deserts before calling our night complete. Finally, when we walked to Marjana's car, we found it had been towed and had to call the others to get us. Marjana had been a bit hasty in ignoring a parking ticket found earlier on her windshield after our river stroll, and now she would have to retrieve it in the morning with its fine. Tedo and Dragana soon came to our rescue, and we were back to the hotel in short order. Marjana would get her car back the next day intact, thinking nothing of it.

Chapter Ten

Day 14 – Sunday, July12, 2009

Ljubljana, Slovenia

Since we had to leave the hotel that day after the event, I came down with my suitcase packed at 6:30 am and met Braco in our break room next to the event hall. Here fruit, pastries, drinks and as always, an abundance of cookies and chocolates were set for us on tables with flowers. Braco told me that he came to this location each month, and they regularly had crowds of 3000-4000 in a single day. But again the holiday time could decrease the number. Everyone was bustling about setting up floral arrangements, displays and organizing the registration, so all was ready for the crowd, no matter the number, which would come that day. Rudi had arrived with others from Srebrnjak 1 to assist in the gazing room with the audience, and Rudi would later work as my translator on stage.

He, like Dinko and a few of the others, often worked entire days presenting to all the groups without a break. Their dedication and heartfelt caring was much to be admired. And that day, I would learn more about Rudi specifically in several ways. Marjana then joined us a short while later, and though she was pleasant and smiling, it seemed like she was a little distracted. At some point, Braco would ask me if I knew why he had invited her to translate for me, and I answered that I thought to groom another talented person for making events. But the reason he revealed made me think differently. Marjana had helped out some of the organizers in Slovenia, but he explained that it was not fair to allow her to join us all day in the break room without contributing.

There were people working with Braco for ten years who had not received as much of his time, and so he had invited her to translate onstage to put her to work. But she did not yet understand this, and I felt a subtle tinge of envy that day of my own time together with Braco. Marjana had a conflict between her wealthy material life-style and her call to things more spiritual. Braco would help keep her near the energy, to help her cross this divide, and because of a health problem. But she was fighting within herself and had to discover certain things on her own. Once I knew this side, I made a point of encouraging her to spend time with Braco when she could. The energy would do the work on its own to support what needed to unfold.

At our next tour stop of Macedonia, Marjana would join us once again, and we would reestablish the beautiful bond and support that had marked the beginning of our relationship. For now, we had big groups to see and my job, with Rudi and Dinko, was assisting them to open to the possibilities of the gazing energy. Marjana would also help this effort by not only translating, but also bringing her own warmth to some of the groups that morning before she had to leave. I was later delighted when reports would come back to me, that several people were remarking that my personal story of transformation through the energy inspired them. Individuals in wheel chairs came, on crutches, some crippled and many holding pictures of loved ones. So many were encouraged and they came to receive a gift toward a better life, better health or help for a loved one in need.

My strength was slowly building with each group, each gazing session, each day spending time with Braco in companionship, and I knew this opportunity had not been placed before me without a strong purpose from the energy itself. I had a new responsibility to honor, and an awe inspired happiness of fulfilling something vast within myself was immerging into bloom. Not for one moment did I take anything lightly or cavalierly, for I knew in my heart if I lost my way, exerted my own will to control or ignore this miracle, it would jettison out of my life as quickly as it had entered. Now I was swept up in a force immeasurable, and once I gained the power to move mountains, it was obvious to me I would have to move some.

After Marjana left, Rudi stepped in to translate. He had done so before at Zagreb on a few occasions, and generally knew the different stories I would tell. It did not matter that his English was still coming back to him, and that a few of my words were a mystery, he understood the feeling and ideas behind them. He would deliver the message with his own thoughtfulness, and I knew he did a good job. This I could see on people's faces as they reacted to what they heard. That day we began to bond through our close interaction. Rudi told me that he had actually lived in the United States in the mid-1980's, in Chicago and Minnesota. Liking America very much, he had not felt compelled to stay because that special calling was not there for him. This meant he also had a better knowledge of English than he originally revealed, but after so many years, he needed some time to become confident again with that knowledge still present.

Rudi was so supportive and grounded, ever bringing me stories from the audience members who stepped forward to share their triumphs and healings, and he would always give me feedback on my presentations in an insightful and kind way. He told me that there were many comments that people felt energy from my heart when I spoke, and this pleased both of us. He certainly felt the people deeply, and I could see how he warmed to me over the days as he saw my own commitment. Although the day was cool outside, and the air conditioning strong in our session room, by noon the room was hot with the transformative energy. This was always the case, and in places where we had no air conditioning, the gazing room became a vibrant sauna of energy during this summer season.

Braco and I spent all our spare time together over the entire day. We were always with our heads together when we were free from the stage; making plans, coming up with new ideas and discussing the different group sessions, the challenges of organizing events and other related issues. Our hostess would soon deliver a nice vegetarian lunch for Braco and I, and he continued to join me in my dietary ways. Before our meal, however, a woman named Connie from Italy joined us. She had brought a group of 80 people, in a bus from her hometown, to see Braco. Originally, Connie has been a huge disbeliever in this type of healing, until she came to experience a session herself. She had done it to prove her friends, who spoke highly of Braco, wrong.

Changing her mind completely after her first session, Connie told me she saw a large, white aura around Braco, and felt the energy tangibly. After this experience, she began to bring friends, and then more people called to join her assemblage. She had brought her first group in January of that year, and now she had a bus full. The owner of two boutiques, Braco asked her to leave them that August, to come to join his staff for an event in Austria. That month was her high season, but she was considering it, and she understood Braco wanted to help her to learn to present to groups herself. Connie was an elegant, confident and caring person, and she possessed all the necessary qualities to do well.

Braco then asked her to watch my next presentation and return, which she did. By now my confidence was strong and natural, so I was effortlessly able to stand in front of large groups and connect with them, no matter their diversity. Afterwards, Connie came back with praise, and when Braco asked her if she could do what I did, she was excited to try, enthusiastically stating, "Yes!" She understood what was required. Suddenly, she decided right then to help with the event in Austria despite her business demands, but asked not to speak yet, and all was agreed.

After she left, Braco opened a boxed cake on the table and took a slice. He offered me some as he always did, but I declined, thinking nothing of it. Again he asked that I taste a small bit, knowing that I had not sampled this type before, yet I was not interested and continued to reject his offer politely. Then a game began between us, for he continued to insist that I try it in a playful but resolute manner. I mistakenly took this as a challenge, and 1 was determined not to lose in the spirit of competition. Finally it became clear that I would not change my mind and he relented.

With his buoyant Croatian accent, Braco declared it okay, and told me I could now refuse anything, helping myself to what I liked as family. Then I had to leave for another presentation, but I felt as if I had just lost something instead of achieving a win. Quickly, I realized my error, and by the time I came back into the room, I was ready to fix it. I, in fact, liked trying all the new things Braco offered, which opened me to new possibilities at all levels. This simple refusal spoke to a common social pattern of staying within preferences and known comforts, and ignoring life's moment-by-moment variety. Even a small taste of something new offered an opportunity, and I no longer wished to casually dismiss even such modest things.

So I came back after his gazing was complete, and told him that I really liked, and appreciated the new things he offered and encouraged. He smiled brightly at me, and I could tell that he was honestly pleased. Once our lunch came, Braco served my plate from a dozen dishes and I tasted them all, often just a bite, but that was enough, and I felt in balance inside again. Somehow this took away a boundary that so easily could arise in any relationship.

At the start of the morning, lovely 26-year-old Anja had come to our break room to try her hand at a presentation at Braco's invitation. She had dressed smartly and felt sure of herself, and he gave her the choice of first watching me or taking the very first group herself. Choosing the later, she stepped onstage soon after. Braco had spoken with her at length about her responsibility to reach the people, and she said she was prepared. I was asked to watch her, and Braco listened behind the closed door. Contrary to Braco's instructions, she was not warm with a heartfelt personal story to touch people and open them to new ideas. Instead she was cool and professional, like a talk show hostess selling products.

Braco instantly saw that she had not offered anything of herself, nothing for the people to connect with her. He had asked me afterwards what I thought, and I answered that Anja needed time to be developed to bring out her potential. Yet he was not pleased because he wanted better for the people. Since she had given nothing, he was firm. Then I found out that she had been fighting with her boyfriend, who did not want her here or respect her choice of pursuing more spiritual work, and her mind was torn as to which path to take. Anja was not given another group.

Now in the late afternoon, she came back into our break room and I left for the stage, and another group. When I returned she was crying next to Braco and soon left. I saw that he did not want to bring pain into her life and so she was told to go back to her boyfriend, and to only come when she wished to attend gazing sessions. This solution removed her conflict, and in the end she was thankful for Braco's help to balance her world again. Clearly I was reminded that the demands of this service were not for everyone.

As with Ida in Stuttgart, Braco always put the people who came for help first, and would be directly honest with someone organizing or assisting. When they compromised, even in a small way, that which was offered to all who came for the energy, he would tell them immediately. Later I heard that Ida was in bed, crying everyday because of the events at her conference, and Braco's confrontation with her. Everyone was tested for his or her commitment, and Braco often remarked that this path was a difficult one with many demands, often pushing people to their limits. Yet when a break-through occurred, the person gained new strength each time. Before I left for home, I would hear again about Ida, and her evolving perspective.

Gazing sessions lasted between 7:30 am to 5 pm that day, and by the last session 3000 people had attended. This was good for a July, and we were all content with our jobs well done. Again it amazed me how quickly Braco and I could be in the car, speeding away only minutes after the last gazing session. I was totally spoiled in never having to carry or address my own luggage since Branko, Rudi or Miki always took it where it needed to go, or grabbed it from me if we were about to go in transit. With this logistic handled, Branko came to our sides and swept us out quickly, past all the crowds lined up outside, into a waiting van with Tedo ready to pull away. The crowds waved at Braco, and he smiled shyly as we drove away back to Zagreb.

As we traveled, I mentioned to Braco our different attire preferences and casual dress in Hawaii. Enthusiastically, he was ready to come with only the clothes he wore, and then throw even these into the ocean. Adopting the local styles, he would acquire a new wardrobe there on the islands and blend in perfectly. Inspired by the idea, I decide we could buy him new items to wear of a local nature, and then make a traditional Hawaiian-style ceremony of this liberation with the help of the water.

When Braco first came to Ivica, only three or four days after joining him, he was told to bring over all his shoes, which they took to a local stream. Ivica asked if Braco knew why they were getting rid of all his shoes? Braco responded that he trusted Ivica had a reason, and he could tell him or not as he wanted. The young man knew he would find out why, if he needed to know. Then Ivica told him the reason was because he could no longer wear shoes with laces, because when one tied their shoes it was like tying their lives. Of course Braco's parents were shocked by this action. And all of Braco's shoes went into the stream and Ivica bought him new ones that had no laces or ties. Later, Braco's clothes would end up in the stream too and be replaced. As many young men, Braco used to wear the color black a lot, but adopted the brighter colors that Ivica wore after that time.

Another story Braco shared was about a night in Zagreb, when the weather was very cold. He was staying at Ivica's home with his family, and had put on a few pairs of pajamas and more for bed because of the chill. When Ivica came by and saw him get into bed this way, he was very angry. Ivica demanded that Braco get up and strip off all his layers of clothes. Surprised, Braco got up and took off all his clothes, down to his briefs, in the cold winter night air. But Ivica demanded all clothes, and Braco looked down hesitating and unsure. Instantly, his friend stated plainly that he was 'not going to fuck him', and Braco did as he asked. Finally, Ivica said that now he was like a man, and this was how a man should sleep.

Braco slept that night and all nights since, winter or summer, without clothes or a blanket. The young man used to get colds and runny noses all the time, but after this experience with the knowing Ivica, he never again had such ailments. I had wondered about the sparse number of blankets in my apartment at his house, and pondered if this was the explanation, or if people in the Balkans just did not use blankets in the summer. I had gone to bed several nights wrapped in a heavy kimono to keep warm and satisfied, but I was intrigued by this idea and ability. Many yogis spent years in meditation to acquire this discipline of mind over matter, but Braco had achieved it spontaneously in a single night with Ivica's challenge. This was very impressive indeed.

Once we arrived back at the house, we had a beverage together. This was to be my last night at his home in Zagreb, and the next day we would fly to Macedonia for our grand finale of events, before retiring back into his yearly vacation time on the sea with his family. Shortly, Braco received a call that Rudi had been in a car accident. We waited two hours to hear word and hoped it was not serious. It was only after I left to finally go to sleep that Braco had another call that he was unharmed, but that the front of his car was badly smashed. As I lay in bed, I wished for the best for Rudi, and realized that the night ended a second week on my magical journey into awakening and new territories. And fortunately, the end of my stay still felt eons away, in a vast distance through a different time continuum.

Part Three

Wishes of Awakening

Braco & Angelika at Matka, Macedonia

Dr. Atanas Atanasov, daughter Bonjana & wife Danka at Matka

Branko, Dinko, Tedo & Miki, Matka boat trip

Braco & Tedo

*Angelika & Braco in break room
in between sessions, Macedonia*

*Sead finds a comfortable spot to nap after lunch at the
Pantelemon Restaurant, Mt. Vodno, Macedonia*

Skopja, Macedonia

Macedonian Singer Rebeka Jankovska Risteski & son with Braco

Chapter Eleven

Day 15 – Monday, July13, 2009

Zagreb

We left for our walk at 6:15 am, and it would be our very last one together from his home to Srebrnjak 1 through the sprawling park. My bags were packed for our later departure to Macedonia, and someone from the staff would pick them up. That morning we had many silent moments as we enjoyed the song of the birds, and the sunlight beaming through the overhead canopy. It was never hard to be in silence with Braco, it was natural, and it allowed us both to simply feel good without the interruption of words. This was an important factor, experiencing our feelings quietly thorough the myriad of events that paraded before us.

At some point he told me that all of the thirteen books written by Ivica had been completed in two to four hours. Ivica would just receive the information from a higher state of consciousness, and speak the information to someone who wrote it word for word. Nothing was ever changed, grammar was not even corrected; it had to stay as it was given. There was a power beyond the mere words in those books, and this was evident by the accounts I had heard from people who read them and felt better, or even placed the book itself on a pain to relieve it.

Once in the city proper, we headed toward a particular café to look for Branko, and others from the Center, since they often stopped there for early morning refreshments. Branko was there along with Miki, Tedo and a few others, and we gathered extra tables together. Braco had his milk and honey first, and then espresso with me. Then Branko ordered an amber beverage served in a small glass. I asked about it and was offered a taste; being told it was a morning fortifier. I almost spit it out because it turned out to be a strong alcohol, and I was informed it was Jaegger. Amazed, I asked if this was a normal routine and I was assured it was for health and vigor, so yes, one was normal on occasion. This drink reminded me too much of the dance club days of my youth, and I only laughed and declined ordering my own.

A technical upgrade was taking place at Srebrnjak 1, and we arrived to find Damir busy installing a video camera on the office computer. Braco had instructed him to buy it once he learned from me that it was possible to see each other when we spoke via a program called Skype. This program would allow us to not only call each other through the computer, but the video camera would enable us to view each other live. Braco did not even carry a cell phone, so this was news to him, and in time we would experiment with the gazing via this remote camera connection too. My knowledge of the more high-tech possibilities was slowly opening up some new options for times ahead.

Then word came of Rudi's accident, and I further learned that no one was injured, although both cars were severely damaged. Later Rudi would show me his vehicle, and the front end was a sorry sight. He would definitely need a new one. I was deeply relieved to know the accident had not inflicted physical harm to anyone and that he was well, if shaken. Later when I saw him, I told him of everyone's concern, and he bowed his head saying how much he was sorry to have caused worry. This attitude of heartfelt thoughtfulness for others made me appreciate him even more fully, and I told him only his safety was important to all.

Soon I went before a group, as Braco wished me to do, so I could speak more of Hawaii and his upcoming travel away from Europe. He was always thinking of preparing the people for the future, so that they would not be surprised or hurt once he left for longer durations, or even for good. He saw that the people had come to accept me as only wishing to share him with more of the world, and they understood in their hearts that Braco had a greater destiny to fulfill. Though they did not want to lose him, they still were able to now openly show affection. It seemed that I was no longer a stranger, and I was honored to receive their kindness.

Not Tedo or Ida in Germany, certainly not all those who worked and supported Srebrnjak 1, not Braco's family, nor the people of the Balkans wanted to face the looming possibility of such a dramatic change yet. But destiny was indeed unfolding, and somehow I found myself a direct part of this process. Never would I have dreamt this before boarding that fateful flight on my way to Croatia - my power, resources and inner strength would have been questioned by me in all ways possible. But now I too believed I could do something important that would open new doors. The energy had given me this gift, and Braco had ensured that I received that energy in an immense measure.

A special breakfast was next undertaken in that cheerful Center kitchen, and the morning's fare was crepes with fresh blueberries that had been left by someone to express their love for Braco. We all enjoyed the treat and our filmmaker Sead, who always had a healthy appetite, did himself proud. Braco and I ate with our fingers with pleasure, and I wondered if I would be able to remove the blue stains for Macedonia. Fortunately, a good scrub worked. But we looked like children before we cleaned our faces and hands.

During this time, Ljiljana came in and told me that she had written down her personal story of meeting Braco, and coming to work at the Center. She stated that the words she could not quite find the day of our talk had come to her, and she handed me two pages with them. I thank her for her love and care in expressing herself on a subject that meant everything to her.

Ljiljana Jurcevic – Spiritual Awakening with Braco

My first encounter with Braco was an encounter with something powerful, yet gentle . . . something untouchable, yet familiar . . . something unknown, yet recognizable. It was like getting to oneself. I think that day, back in 1999; I embarked on a journey to find myself.

Today, 10 years later, I am certain that I am on a journey that leads to a goal that is still miles away, but I am wishing, believing, moving towards the light, purity, unconditional love and absolute truth through which Braco moves me. Sometimes when Braco gazes, I feel it so strong that I wish the feeling would never go away ... sometimes my human imperfections cloud the 'view', diminish my experience, dull my senses. Sometimes they deceive my mind, which then becomes confused, seduced by the passing earthly delights.

Meeting Braco was my confirmation of what I've always felt truly exists, that there truly is something that guides us, something that knows, that 'sees', something we are all made of.

Seven or eight years ago Braco asked me if I would come work for him and fill the position of someone who would speak to the people about him in order to try and bring him, and that which wells up through him closer to them. He told me to think about it. I didn't. Would you think about accepting water when you are thirsty? Would you say no to air?

For me Braco is water . . . air . . . life. For me he is absolute truth.

Now, after seven or eight years that I have spent at his side, I can honestly say he is unique. He is made of a special 'thread', one that is different from the one 'regular people' are made of.

It is irrefutable that he is here with a mission.

Years ago, he told me of certain events regarding him and his work which he has 'seen' will happen in the future. He didn't know exactly at which time they will happen, but he knew they would. Most happened, and now when I speak to him about this he seems not to recall he predicted them.

Among these, he also spoke about leaving this country . . . about working by great water . . . and I think this time is now coming.

The world needs him - people and nature both.

I hope that he will bring peace and serenity to the people that are touched by his gaze.

I hope that he will move the dormant truths within us all, that he will melt the ice that holds our hearts captive, that he will clear the cobwebs from our souls and help humans be HUMAN. He will do this by letting us feel that we are all as one, connected, and that all we need we already have – purity, love and peace. Everything we need is to become aware of it and find ourselves. When Braco 'sees' me I feel as though his eyes are deep as the abyss, a passage, and a way that connects us with our true being which exists in a parallel universe. It is akin to that time of the day when our shadow unites with our body.

I also know that this is not an easy task, because it can be very hard to reach and move people. People doubt and fear. But when one believes, when one becomes brave enough to face the truth, to face change, to face oneself, everything is possible.

If we allow ourselves to be at peace, we allow Braco to help us achieve it.

That is what I would like to communicate to everyone who Braco's gaze will silently and softly reach ...

Many groups were seen that morning, and Braco was ever playful, peaceful and happy in between sessions. We could be rolling in laughter or in serious conversation, and then it would be time for him to make the gazing for a group, and he instantaneously changed. He did not need to prepare himself in any way. The energy would simply take him fully into that place from which it could offer itself through him. It was clear that his personality was not a part of the gazing itself, or he would not be able to so effortlessly turn on his miraculous ability.

Finally it came time to leave for the airport. Many from the Center would come to the event, because the first time Braco had appeared in Macedonia, nearly 10,000 people had shown up for the day. The organizers had planned for a few thousand, and were quite overwhelmed. So Miki, Rudi, Dinko, Sead and Branko would join us in our travel. Later Marjana would also meet up with everyone at the airport. Our entire luggage had already been collected, and we left directly from Srebrnjak 1. The ride was short and after we checked-in, we all gathered for coffee in the now familiar Zagreb airport at the outdoor café.

Dinko had a local paper with many advertisements in it, especially those for men seeking companionship of a short duration and a better sex life. Miki and Branko immediately recognized the paper, and began to tease him that he was reading these ads. Then Branko, laughing, explained that Croatian spirituality accepted all things and did not deny anything. So the joke soon became that Branko was interested in Dinko's newspaper because he was so spiritual. The men had a rollicking time with this tangent. When things quieted down, I asked Miki, who had been so supportive and caring towards me during presentations, if he could tell me about himself and meeting Braco. He was happy to do this and shared his story.

Miroslav Miki Skrbo – Braco's Test

On October 21, 1995 I heard about Braco from my neighbor. I had a bad pain in my spine, and so I went to visit him and Braco gave me a book. I was surprised that Braco was so young, 28 years old, with short hair and very strong words. Braco asked me my name and my problem. Then he handed me a book to read, and said if it helped, to come back in ten days. I was doubtful, but as soon as I left the pain decreased.

I read the book in one sitting, but Braco only came one time per month to Germany at that time. So I came each month and I really felt better. Then my family came and were also helped. The first time I came with my mother, and the second time with Tedo and others. I believed in this type of healing in general.

My mother and father had a restaurant they rented. Because the place that Braco was working at was too small to see all the people, and the police were making problems, my parents offered to let Braco work there and he did for five months. But the town did not like what Braco was doing so we all moved. My sister found a new restaurant in Kraichtal. This is the place Braco still comes to twice a month today. At that time, I would sometimes talk with Braco at dinner after the work was complete.

Braco at that time still talked with people and he always told the people he would try to help them, and if they felt better they could come back.

Once Braco asked me if I could learn a short introduction of text to present to the people, and I accepted. I tried the first time, but could not remember the words. The second time I was able to remember, and I spoke from time to time. I was very nervous about speaking in front of people, but I did it because I wanted to help.

One year and two months ago I came to work at Srebrnjak 1. Braco had called me at 6 am one morning, and asked if I would like to continue talking and work at his Center in Zagreb with him all the time. I said yes, and Braco told me to come at 8 am the next morning. The first day, my bus was three hours late.

That day, Braco took me walking for three hours. I had an operation on my leg three weeks before, and the doctors told me I could not walk on it for at least six weeks. Braco was testing me. He wanted to see if I believed him or the doctors more. After the walk, my leg was a little sore but OK. Then I began working at Srebrnjak 1 and traveling to other countries too.

Miki was not able to tell me more because we had to leave for our plane, but I smiled at the end of his story. Braco certainly tested people all the time, but he did so only with a purpose. As Ida and others had found out, this type of work required an incredible commitment and strength. One had to often push beyond self-created comfort zones to meet the challenges and situations, and one had to believe in something greater that the physical or mental. Such a foundation and stability would reap an immeasurable reward with hard work. And now I had learned that Miki and Tedo were related, and they certainly shared a common goodwill and giving spirit. They also both always looked after me in the most caring and thoughtful of ways.

Skopja, Macedonia

Our plane flight was easy and relatively short to Skopja airport. After taking off, Braco told me some information about Macedonia and the conference organizers. On November 8, 2008, a man named Dr. Atanas Atanasov, a psychotherapist, and his wife, a psychologist named Danka, organized an event for him. It was Braco's first time in Macedonia. The crowds came in unexpected numbers, and they saw almost 10,000 people in a single day. Politics were a tricky business in this country, and there was much corruption. Government leaders were uncomfortable with the fact that a single man could attract so many people without even speaking. Their small mindedness led them to seriously question the threat of Braco deciding to speak, for then he could lead the people against the government. This was a concern of certain officials.

For the current event, Dr. Atanasov had to go to extreme lengths, including bribes to get the proper permits to allow Braco to come once again for another event. Sixty people were under him in his organization. Even more, he and his wife had hired 30 police officers to act as security, and had Red Cross ready with beds for those overcome by the energy. And then the doctor and Danka had to deal with ticket sales, finding the right venue to handle a large crowd, advertising to let the people know of Braco's return, and much more. He was actually risking his professional license, home and everything he had to make this event possible. Later I would gather his story to see what had led him to take on such a tremendous undertaking and challenge.

Braco did not ever like to see people suffer, and it pained him that the Atanasovs were risking so much. Yet it was not his place to stop what he knew had to move forward. Instead he helped in all ways possible. He had a great respect for those like this couple; who would go so far to help the people despite all challenges. That was the nature of his life and his work. There was also a threat making him vulnerable; of being taken into custody, and imprisoned if the wrong government officials became too fearful. However, it only made Braco more determined. The people had shown their support on his first visit, and now he would not refuse to come back.

Braco was not ever easily detoured, and threats meant little to him. His vision on a greater goal drove him with a lion-hearted strength. When I heard all of this, I silently thanked the universe for letting me be at his side at such a questionable time. It also gave me a taste of future challenges ahead, for fear would always drive people of ignorance to do unfortunate things. This was a glimpse and a preparation for what was to come, and I appreciated Braco's stamina and determination even more. As Ivica had stated, Braco would never be afraid in the face of his challenges.

After our conversation concluded, I placed my head down on my giant handbag on the tray table in front of me, and closed my eyes. Sleep must have come, for I suddenly had an exhilarating dream-like experience of being swept up from the plane into a vortex of energy; which seemed to hold all qualities of energy, positive and negative in balance, and was dynamically vibrant. My whole body was filled with light and made alive by this force, and in the encounter I found it completely exciting. Afterwards, I had no idea if it meant anything, but I was sure I had slept for only 5 or 10 minutes. It turned out it was a full 45 minutes, and we were ready to land. Braco rested too during that flight, and we both were fortified for our new adventure.

On the ground I felt a wave of anticipation; there was a tangible feeling that was calling to memories long past that I could not quite touch fully. Something was going to happen here, I could feel it deep down and I was elated. Later, I would understand that my dream on the plane was a preparation by the energy itself, and connected to my expectancy of a mysterious forthcoming encounter. This would be my last chance at a wish I had made that was yet unfulfilled, and it was spurred by conversations with Braco, and words written by Ivica about Atlantis. I wanted to remember something locked away inside myself outside of time or this lifetime. It was not something I dwelled upon or even thought about now, but it lingered in the air for me.

During the morning gazing sessions at Zagreb, I had told Braco I felt like something unexpected would happen in Macedonia. The final gazing session there had brought a force of energy so big into my heart that it had felt like it would burst open in some magical way, and tears of joy had come with it. Because of my sense of responsibility to be composed to talk with the group afterward, I had stopped myself from fully going into that feeling, but it was still there inside of me growing into something that was an unknown, and would further connect here.

Our hosts met us at the airport with their two beautiful daughters. Fifteen-year-old Bojana had a grace, innocence, and a mature self-confidence that made me take note, while her younger sister was quiet and sweet spirited. They were all filled with light in their eyes, yet Danka had a noticeable weight of responsibility on her face too. I knew she was dealing with many factors that perhaps only her family could appreciate. Tedo would drive a van for us, and we all went first to the event conference hotel. Its name was the Hotel Aleksandar Palace, and it was beautiful inside like the mountains surrounding the city. Great Murals of castles were painted across a wall rising up many stories in an inner courtyard. It was modern, filled with sunlight, and very comfortable.

We were shown the conference rooms, which were massive, and opened up to each other with movable walls. Heavy crystal chandeliers hung high across their ceilings. The total space would be divided into two sections; one for Braco's gazing sessions, and the other for the groups to receive an introduction by a Center staff member before entering for Braco, and my own presentation. After viewing our workspace, we all sat in the courtyard café and had beverages. The doctor shared information about the Hotel Aleksandar Palace owner, who would be threatened later that day by a government office to close down Braco's event, or be subject to relentless health and safety inspections at his hotel.

Fortunately, the owner would tell the Atanasovs to move forward anyway. He had once owned four such spacious and upscale hotels in Macedonia, but the Balkans could be harsh on those who were successful, especially in this nation. His neighbors in government had worked against him in lawsuits, and would eventually close three of his properties. Coveting what others possessed was par here, almost ingrained in the psyche, and the American work ethic of bootstrapping oneself up was not a part of the local mentality. Instead, neighbors envied even the new car or small accomplishment that singled a person out, and would openly show their hostility.

The next day when I addressed the crowds, I would see something in the people that was a type of self-interest that made it clear to me that Braco had to leave for new lands. In the groups for the first time, I encountered a frame of mind that did not want to share Braco. It absolutely surprised me when I saw it in their faces, their attitudes and through their communications. Yet they deserved all he could give them, and any human flaws were overlooked; Braco would not be detoured from coming again when invited if government permission could be acquired once again.

Atanas and Danka Atanasov, along with all of us ordered refreshments, and the doctor began to talk with Braco in an animated fashion while his wife looked on, and nodded now and again. The conversation was incomprehensible for me, so I sat and felt the energy of our new location. Spontaneously, I had the clear impression that the real work would begin here. Again later, I would discover that I was prematurely picking up on something that would impact me personally in Macedonia. Now I noticed that invisible bubble once again, that field of Braco's energy and I was happy. I was dynamically in his world, in a more conscious reality; while the majority still captivated by a slumbering, material illusion existed side-by-side. Yet I also knew that Braco's energy and reality would spread in time, as others felt and chose this state of awareness to spirit too.

A new guest arrived at the invitation of our hosts, and it turned out to be Macedonia's most famous pop singer, Rebeka Jankovska Risteski. She was a young and beautiful woman with a flawless olive complexion, flowing golden hair and a large smile. Her eyes were expressive and completely turned to Braco, who had helped her son in his recovery from a severe case of epilepsy. Because of her prestige, she had been a key person in helping Dr. Atanasov to successfully gain his government permits for the event. She did not stay for long, but only came to meet Braco once again. We chatted briefly, and I found out that we would see her at dinner that evening.

Our organizers, wishing to entertain our group, next took us on a trip into the beautiful surrounding country to a river with a mighty dam. As we drove, and I watched the rapids of the river, it looked more than inviting on this very hot day, but I was told it was too shallow for swimming, and soon we would reach our destination. Once there, we walked and chatted until our host received a call. A health inspector was at the conference hotel, threatening to shut down the event because there was not proper paperwork. This seemed very odd, especially since this was a government agency that usually inspected restaurant kitchens and rest rooms, but they had the power to close all down. Therefore, Danka had to leave us immediately to go to the hotel to meet with him with all her permits.

Something had begun that would plague our event the entire time we were in Macedonia. There were people in power who did not want this work to continue there, and they would send various officials to try to stop it. Another facet of control by the government was the media. The major news and television stations were under certain controls, and we would experience the brunt of the tension here next. But for now we finished our walk early, and would head back to the hotel until we rejoined for a special dinner our hosts had planned. We would also spend the next day at leisure, because the Atanasovs wished to show Braco their love by showing him and his group a few special places.

At a nearby hotel, close to the event, our rooms awaited us. It was a small establishment, and my room was in the opposite wing to Braco's. Unfortunately, it turned out to be on the street side, above busy cafes that play loud music to the small hours of the night. During the day it is not very noticeable; I would discover more at bedtime. For now, we dropped off our bags, and gathered once more without Atanas, Danka and their daughters to take a long stroll; the

European tradition. None of us were familiar with the area, so we walked without real direction getting to know the surrounding area. Braco would talk more of Macedonia to me, and the challenges that were before us that could increase. None of this was unsettling; it only made me shake my head at the follies of people's fears.

Braco did not like any of this, but he moved forward without pause. So to change topics, I began to tell him that the surrounding area, which looked less than prosperous, reminded me of places I had visited in the Philippines and Mexico. That began a conversation of some of my travels, and Braco marveled at the places I had seen, and we spoke of him in time visiting countries beyond Europe as his work expanded. My experience was deeply rooted in treks and facts about various cultures, and I could fill in his own inexperience in the same way that he was filling in mine. His great knowledge of the spontaneity of spirit, and embodying a higher power, offered a level of integrity I had not before witnessed so fully in an individual.

Often it would seem that he was reading my mind, and we thought much alike on many things, sharing a joy of similar activities. I did not believe he could in fact actually hear my thoughts, but I knew he felt them, and that was more than enough for him to constantly surprise me with acute perceptions. Several times, he would encourage me to talk to him if ever something was wrong, so that nothing would come in our way. I did not understand at first the depth of importance here, but would later perceive that there were many subtle energies that could cause friction and misunderstandings. Our communication together would mean everything in ensuring that confusion did not occur because of outside factors.

Sightseeing was a bit lack luster, but enjoyable because of the company. Evening was approaching, and we would all take time to shower and change before our special dinner. Once at my room, I unpacked and freshened up. I also tried my computer for Internet access, but found none in my room, and was a little glad not to have the responsibility of answering emails temporarily. So I changed my clothes instead, and soon met everyone outside on the front balcony of our hotel. Our hosts were late to greet us due to more complications over the upcoming event, and once again we all admired their tenacity.

Dinner took place at a large, and traditional-style Macedonian restaurant with seating outside next to a wonderful fountain. Live musicians played through the night, offering delightful folk tunes. I sat to Braco's right and Marjana to his left, and later Rebeka arrived with her husband; a handsome, dark haired doctor, and she was placed on my other side at the table. We talked often through the night, and she was endearingly warm and spoke excellent English, as did her husband. She told me about her son, and her work, and I asked if she would tell me the story of meeting Braco and how he had helped her son. With a brilliant smile, she agreed.

Rebeka Jankovaka Risteski – Macedonian Singer & Pop Star

I was at T-mobile for an appointment regarding promotions for a new album. I went out from the building and a person stopped me and called my name. He asked politely to speak with me. The man was short, with one leg longer than the other, and he asked if I would come to support his organization for invalids. I told him I had a sick child, and we would have to align our schedules. He asked about my child, and then told me about a woman he knew with breast cancer who had been helped by Braco.

I did not remember Braco's name, but I took the man's number. The next day I was at a court judgment, and a friend told me of a man in Zagreb who could help my son - Braco. I was impressed that two people in two days told me of Braco. This man said he would give me a DVD of Braco the next day. Then I was out the next day with my son, and a girlfriend met me and told me of Braco. That was three times in three days.

My son has epilepsy and seizures. I called the first man, and got the number for Zagreb and Braco. Then I joined a group going on a bus to see him. The next day, a friend who is a doctor, and who works at a clinic mentioned that Braco would be in Macedonia in November (2008), so I waited for Braco to come to town.

I cried during the gazing session, and had the feeling that Braco was looking only at me. I felt guilty and told this to a friend who was there, and she had experienced the same thing. One month later I had a dream that my son would be okay. There was no immediate change, but then I had this dream. After the dream, my son was seizure free after five months. Now he only has occasional mild seizures, and doctors in many countries now say my child will be in the 30% group who recover. This will be a miracle.

Epilepsy that begins by age one is always devastating, with no chances of recovery.

Now Rebeka would bring a picture of her son to Braco again with the heartfelt wish for him to be completely cured. She was a truly spiritual person, and complimented by her husband. He was doing research work in all forms of cancer except leukemia. Having breast fed her son for 22 months, she was always aware of sending him her loving thoughts while doing so to help him. For three years, she had set her popular singing career on hold to be solely with her son. Her husband too was equally broadminded, and believed strongly in energy medicine and holistic healing. They were a delight to converse with, and we touched upon many subjects of a spiritual nature.

She told me of difficulties with the press in her country. It seemed that the press would print complete libel, and engaged often in this practice. One event that was painful for Rebeka was a time that a dog darted in front of her car, and she could not stop in time, and struck it. The next day, several papers ran stories of her intentionally running down a dog on the road, and they labeled her heartless. Her love of animals made this even more cutting, but she had learned to ignore such stories. Fighting them only produced more ugliness. A sensation seeking media would use the opportunity to launch even more vicious attacks.

Rebeka had personally discovered a newfound strength through her son, and now spoke to parent groups as a mother with a child with epilepsy. She would find that others came to her in thanks for her courage, and the strength she inspired in others with her talks. Never had she imagined that she would possess such fortitude, and could talk about a subject so heartbreaking to her in public. Yet when her son was in the hospital for attacks, she would always sing happy songs to him. Her own mother was very sad over her grandson's condition, and would tell Rebeka how strong she was to sing these songs with joy. Rebeka said she firmly knew that she had to do it to give good energy to her son.

Later she would sing for us Macedonian folk songs of love, and her voice was honey sweet, and rich with the emotions that transported our whole group to new levels of happiness. When I was not talking with Rebeka, I was laughing or smiling with Braco. It was a magical night as healthy, well-fed cats came out from behind the fountain, onto a lawn next to our table. The doctor's daughters were busy taking meat off a large platter, which was piled in abundance, and feeding it to the many felines who would come bravely for a meal. The whole family expressed their love of animals, and especially cats; and since I had two Siamese at home, my affection was with them. The girls were doing what I myself wished to do with all that extra meat.

Good wine and food flowed across our table in abundance and sublime variety. We wanted for nothing and had everything. After Rebeka sang her songs, Braco told me how he would like the whole world to experience the happiness and joy that filled us all that night, even the daughters. Our host, Atanas, was glowing with this delight. He was risking everything to make this event happen, and this night he shed any weight to join with us in the grace of life.

After dinner, Braco even reached for my wine glass, and finished the last large sip. And I reached for one of his cigarettes, and smoked with him in an abandon to the spirit of togetherness. It was our mutual wish of that moment to share in the enjoyments of the other. Of course Branko, Rudi and Miki all nodded to me mischievously as I smoked, knowing that it was an activity that bonded us Balkan's style. Braco would teach me that I could eat anything; that my delicate stomach was from years of cutting away foods, and a product of my own denials of life. Now I poured olive oil liberally over many dishes, as he did, no longer rejecting natural foods; in this case due to my social programming about fat calories.

That night when we returned to the hotel, I stepped into my shower only to find the shower knob broken and no hot water. So I dressed back again, and went to the front desk. Fortunately Marjana had not been able to sleep, and was having an espresso with the desk clerk, who spoke no English. She was able to convey my problems, and we had them addressed, but next the noise from the street below would make sleep a bit difficult at first. Only the pleasant feelings still alive from our wonderful dinner helped me to ignore these things, and drift off to sleep.

Chapter Twelve

Day 16 – Tuesday, July 14, 2009

Skopja, Macedonia

This was a day to play in Skopja before our big event tomorrow, and Braco had told me he would meet me for a walk between 6:30 and 7:00 am. I waited patiently but when he had not shown up at the front of the hotel by 7:15 am, I decide he had slept in, and went for a walk by myself. I had a slight headache from the heat indoors, so I knew movement would make me feel better. Stepping down the front stairs to the street level, I found the morning was warm but pleasant, and I headed out in a new direction from our group walk the day before.

Somehow I managed to stroll perfectly through streets that brought me to the banks of a great river, with walkways on either side. The river had rapids, small waterfalls, and led in one direction towards a natural setting with trees, and only a few homes upon its banks. Absolutely delighted to have found water, I climbed the long stairway down to the river's edge, and began to walk briskly. While doing so, I could not help thinking how much Braco would enjoy this place, and I kept my walk short; hoping to meet him now so that I could share my pleasant find.

With headache gone, I came back to the hotel and still did not see him, so I ordered water and an espresso at a bar in the front lobby. It seemed odd to me the Braco would still be asleep by this time, so on an impulse I again went outside, and saw him standing at the stairwell looking out to the distance. Happily, I called to him, and we gave each other a good morning hug. He had indeed slept in, but had been walking around for some time looking for me. He asked why I had not knocked on his door to wake him. Yet I had not known his room number, and the front desk person could not help since he did not speak English. Then he asked if I would like to walk, so I came back inside the hotel, quickly finished my espresso, and we were off with Branko along too.

Eagerly, I told him of the wonderful pathway I had discovered, and we first stopped at a bakery for long bread rolls, the only choice. Walking and eating, I went a little ahead as they chatted in Croatian, and once at the river, Braco was delighted at seeing it. We were all grateful for the good fortune of my find. Along the waterway, I scooped up a feather and put it in my hair without thought. Braco then told me that he loved Indians, and had always played the game of being an Indian when he was a child; he never wanted to be the cowboy. So I told them both that this morning, they were Lewis and Clark, the great explorers, and I was Sacagawea, their Indian guide. They did not know who these people were from American history, so I explained their significance and roles. With confidence, I assured them of their survival on our journey of exploring the Macedonian river trail with my ready assistance.

Branko finally told me a few detail of his own story of meeting Ivica, and devoting his life now to the work. He was a strong, yet kind man, of deep character, loyalty and integrity. His watchful eyes were ever taking in details, and looking towards Braco's well being. The authority of a police chief was ever evident in him, and he worked without compromise. There was an obvious love between them, and I saw that Branko would do anything for Braco, and he had displayed this quality with Ivica too. Almost guardedly, he agreed to later tell me on tape his whole story. It was something I would not have left Croatia without.

Our trek lasted a glorious hour before we felt we had to return to the others. At the hotel, we all gathered for espresso in a café below our rooms, and everyone came. Braco would remark that many of those present did not think I would return home to Hawaii. Again my heart was tempted, but I knew they did not understand that for me to stay would only be self-serving. Clearly, Braco had taught me that to serve the energy, one could not willfully do as one pleased. Only opportunities to serve the work, wherever that guided me, would be appropriate and right. Yet I knew and felt I would return, sooner perhaps, than my mind could arrange.

To serve Braco and the greater mission, I had to go home to Hawaii, and not only make my conference and introduction of Braco there a success, but also open new doorways for him. It was more work than I wanted to think about, but I knew if I paid attention, help would come in many unexpected ways to support my efforts. That American principle of hard work to rise up was at my doorstep, and I accepted it. The day before at the conference hotel, Miki had told me that Braco was sad because of all the work I faced once I went home. Yet I told Miki I did not think in these terms, but only contemplated the starting point, and would work until all was done.

Braco was in many ways a regular man, he could hurt and feel pain inside too, but he was somehow more too. His goodness, peace and selflessness unlocked all situations in time, and would clear the path of all obstacles. He faced his feelings, and would always trust his deeper knowing, and his spontaneity was his guide. Present and connected to a greater spirit in each moment, he did not live on the roller coaster of emotions that plagued most individuals. His foundation was unshakable, mysteriously familiar to those who watched him, and with this he rose above all challenges with a grace that was truly inspiring.

Others talked together at the café, and I told Braco of a property on the Hawaiian island of Maui that I had seen advertised a few months back for sale. In previous conversations, we had discussed the possibility of him relocating to create a new Center on one of the islands. So off the top of my head I suggested this property as a potential. It was acreage on the water next to the Hana coast, a rural portion of Maui, and it had a natural waterfall and bamboo forest. As I described its charms, Braco, in another moment of child-like spontaneity interrupted me to declare he would buy it. He could hardly believe how good it sounded, set in nature yet an easy drive from a major airport so people could access it.

Surprised at such enthusiasm, I offered that I would first have to inquire if it was still on the market, and gather more details since it was at least three months since I had come across this real estate listing. He agreed to my plan, but would ask me several times about it before I left, and I of course did an Internet search as soon as I was able, but I could not find the same parcel. Eventually I would have to admit to him that it was probably sold or off the market, and this made him noticeably sad. But I told him once he came, we could look together to see if in fact Hawaii matched his earlier visions about a place on a great water that would become his new home. I was more cautious than he was.

Soon after our hosts arrived to escort us for a day of adventure, and everyone loaded into Tedo's van, except for Braco and I, who were invited to drive with the doctor. Today we would explore a treasure of the country, a place called Matka. After driving toward one of the many mountains surrounding the city, and off into the country, we came to a road with many military men dressed in uniform, and passed them on our way to the sacred lake gorge that was our destination. Here our host's fifteen-year-old daughter, Bojana, nicknamed Bonnie, would tell me this wonder of the natural world.

Lake Matka

Our breaths were absolutely taken away by the sight that met us. A valley with pristine forest rising up both banks of a lagoon style lake invoked a mystical quality of a land time forgot. At the entrance to this valley, an outdoor café and restaurant welcomed us, while a boat dock launched old wooden skiffs for the tourists to float up the lake and partake in an even more spectacular view. The mountainsides were of large grey rock, mighty and strong, and a path wound along the lake on one side, cut into the stone.

In the noon heat, I wanted nothing more than to dive into the clean water, but I was informed it was too cold. I was not detoured and would keep asking, encouraging Braco to join me, but Branko was absolutely firm that Braco could not go in the water. He was head of security, and he saw this as a breach, he would protect Braco even from his own calling to play. For the time being I accepted a delay, and sat with everyone under a canopy at the lake's edge at the café. We ordered refreshments as our hosts shared the latest challenges to the next day.

They had gone to the Ministry of Culture to get their permits for Braco, but it seemed that even though this was the proper agency to authorize such documents, other agencies could work at cross-purposes and cause chaos. Yesterday, Danka had to leave us to deal with the Health Department Inspector. This inspector had threatened the hotel owner and Danka with closing down the event due to inadequate paperwork. She was able to show him her documents, and convince him she had gone through proper channels, but he gave her a very difficult time before consenting not to close the event.

Next Atanas pulled out a newspaper that had published a very negative story about Braco that morning. The newspaper also claimed that the proper authorization had not been acquired from the government, and further stated that Braco did not have the proper credentials to help the people because he was not a licensed doctor. This argument would plague us through our event, via the media. There was a very archaic mindset in this land, and the government corruption and media control fueled the fires to try to break the bond Braco had naturally with the people.

Finally, enough was said and discussed on this subject that now had a life of its own. So Sead asked to film Braco in this glorious setting, walking in nature, for an upcoming film. Unexpectedly, Braco announced to the group that for the first time, he would put someone else with him in a video. Then he turned to me, and invited me to come with him. At that moment, I did not think about what this meant or his reasoning behind it. I simply accepted his choice. My mind was quiet, something was happening inside of me that was taking place so naturally that I did not notice at first. Yet a substantial stillness, and acceptance was awakened within, and I felt anchored and trustful of my abilities to meet the moment, and any requirements without hesitation.

No one looked surprised or made a comment, and then Sead asked us to walk along the stone cut path that was lined with trees in part, and open to the lake further down. Braco walked first, and I followed behind with our cameraman positioned behind for the first shot. I emulated what Braco did and naturally walked, enjoying my surroundings - this was simple. Next we were positioned atop a rock outcropping, and asked to quietly sit. This was more challenging at first; to position myself on the steep rock in a way that I could relax, but once I found the spot, we sat without words for perhaps five or six minutes communing with the glories around us.

It was magical to sit in that special place, and my heart easily opened to the nature around us. For Braco, this was like an effortless form of meditation, and his love of the natural world took him into a very special place merging outer with inner magnificence. Large birds flew on the air currents above, and the water sang a song of movement with the wind. The inspiration that only earth's beauty conveyed enfolded the moments and us; we merged into a splendid peace. Afterward, Sead would remark that he thought he had captured something very remarkable on film, and he said quietly that magic had happened. To him, we became like brother and sister during those moments.

My mind was still quiet without questioning, and we took one more shot of both of us walking on the trail towards him. Creative ideas came, and Sead spoke of making this particular film or one soon to come without any words, but only images of us in nature. Later, I would learn they planned to finish the film in Hawaii after my conference. Our group members had also come with us on the path, but stayed at a distance. Now all together, we walked back to the café, and I practically bounced my way back in the joy of the experience. Braco was pleased too, and next we would all go on an old wooden skiff to explore the long lake, and visit a cave further down on the other side of the water. I was ready for that plunge into the cold water, but Sead advised me to wait because he wanted more film of us.

A long bench lined each side of the boat, and there was plenty of room for all of our group and the captain. Slowly, we made our way from the launch into a lagoon paradise of solitude. The water was green with algae at the banks and the bright sun illuminated the water in shimmers. Braco stood at the front of the boat, with me at his side, and we remained quiet, appreciating the waterway and steep mountains before us. Passing a small wooden house built on stilts on the lake bank, Braco became animated seeing it. He loved its simple charm, and I told him many houses in the islands looked similar.

In Europe and especially Croatia, most houses were built out of heavy, enduring materials, and so it surprised him when I described our houses out of wood or bamboo; many on stilts because of the slopes of the mountains that comprised the many islands. Our residences were simpler in character than homes in his country. Again he brought up the property on Maui. He spoke long and lovingly about Hawaii to everyone, and I could tell by the look on some faces that they were happy, and alarmed at the same time by his zeal that would take him away.

Soon we stopped the boat at a wooden stairway up the steep bank, and disembarked. The stairs were long, and led to Vrelo Cave, known in the area for its impressive formations achieved by dripping water on rock. Once inside, someone found a light switch, and a massive cavern was illuminated before us. The air was instantly cold, and it was a welcome relief from the heat outside. Braco darted off, and I tried to keep up, but my flat sandals gave me little traction on the slimy walkway of rock. Deeper we descended until a destination spot was reached, which boasted a colony of bats high above.

Miki stepped forward to offer a helping hand, and Branko kept his watchful eye on Braco, in case his exploration led him too close to a plummeting edge. Sead followed up behind, and found a camera position, and we were instructed to climb up on a larger rock formation in front of the bat colony. This was not easy, because the formation was covered with slime and bat droppings. The smell of ammonia from our winged friends was distinctive too, but I slowly managed to make my way next to Braco. Then we relaxed ourselves in the earth's womb, and allowed the cave atmosphere to fill us. Sead achieved the footage and viewpoint that he desired, and soon we were done.

Coming back into daylight, I saw that I needed the help of the water desperately, as slime was smeared across my feet and hands. Soil and dirt did not bother me, but in this case, I wanted to wash them as soon as possible. Braco fared better without noticeable markings, and I was impressed how easily he had climbed around in the unstable footing. He was certainly in his element, and Sead later told me Braco had often been filmed in highly dangerous settings because he liked a view or a special spot. He was willing to dare the obstacles, and inherent dangers to get to them. Because of his adventurous spirit, Braco was a man who touched my heart with his intrepid nature.

Finally, we were filmed together standing at the bough of the boat coming back down the lake, and once done, we sat for a final few quiet minutes before arriving at our dock and disembarking. Bonnie, a teenager radiant with life, walked by my side on the way back to our vehicles, and told me history about the area, and the special activities for young people growing up in Macedonia. She was delightful company, her English was exceptional, and I was glad for her presence with us. We had worked up an appetite, and were off to a late lunch at a special mountain restaurant named Pantelemon, which held a spectacular view of the city.

While driving, I told Braco how much I appreciated what we had witnessed. To me this was far superior to any town or city with its many attractions. Braco felt the same, and he spoke of our hosts love in sharing these things with us, creating a special holiday for our group. Then Atanas expressed that he felt I was a woman of charisma, and invited me to come again as his guest for Braco's next return visit. Grateful and happy at the thought, I thanked him for his kind generosity, and said I hoped I would be able to accept his offer for the future. To my surprise, Braco did not translate my full response, and told me the timing would be off. Unfortunately, he was correct because if another event happened in Macedonia, it would take place in November, and this would be too near too my own conference to leave for the required time.

Pantelemon Restaurant

After driving up a mountainside, we wound through country roads and came to a large parking area. Here was sprawling a restaurant of old stone architecture, built with outdoor seating, and large open windows displaying a splendid view down to the city below. We first walked the grounds together, and then sat down at a table big enough for all of us. As soon as we situated ourselves, Danka received a call, and a difficult conversation ensued. There were more problems with authorities at the conference hotel, and both Atanas and his wife had to leave immediately to put thing right. They would leave Bonnie as our hostess, and promised to return as soon as possible.

Braco appeared very concerned for this family, and highlighted again that they could loose everything. In a moment of mild anger, Braco told why he would not come back to this country, but later would reverse that declaration, and state that he must return. It was a sorry business, but it was clear to see that the doctor was not deflated by the challenge, he was determined, and ready to fight to see things through to completion. He was not in the least bit thwarted to give up, and his wife faithfully joined him.

We all had to let our situation, beyond our control at the moment, go and we quickly changed moods. Especially since both daughters were present, there was no need to dwell on misfortune. Bright Bonnie acted as the perfect hostess and ordered our meal served, which was to offer traditional Macedonian dishes. Even by U.S. standards, the portions were absolutely huge, and the appetizers alone were enough to make a complete meal once again. Fresh tomatoes, cooked peppers and a mild white cheese was accompanied by freshly baked country bread, and olives for a starter, and Bonnie made sure my vegetarian plate was full. The kitchen then made a special vegetarian soup only for me, and though the first wave of food had already filled me, I ate it too, and then rested.

That nourishing energy was ever feeding me, and my appetite for food was still small. At this meal Braco would make a foray into the meat dishes because our hosts had specially ordered certain dishes for him, and they wanted everyone to enjoy

Macedonia country cuisine. Braco was in a spirit of play, and as the main courses arrived, he took plates from Miki and Rudi and piled them alarmingly high with food. This was a sort of Balkan's humor, and as a part of the joke, they would try to finish all that food. I was grateful not to be included in this play, and Braco would only give me tastes of dishes he knew were meat free. He was so kind to me in this way. Without chauvinism, the men treated women with a respect in general, and I appreciated this thoughtfulness.

After the main courses, Sead immediately found a place for a nap across the courtyard on a pile of stacked chairs. We laughed as he made a bed out of a row that he lined up neatly, and we lost his company for the next couple of hours. Braco thought of playing a joke on him too, but it never materialized as desert and espresso was served. Bonnie told us about Macedonian traditions and culture, including our desert cake called Treska, a type of honey and raisin baklava, only much lighter and more flavorful.

Once all was complete, people drifted off in different directions, and Braco and I walked around the restaurant complex together. We constantly discovered new things to talk about, and I do not think either of us ever had a moment of boredom. He just did not live that way, each moment meant something, and was used to its full advantage. After a while we returned to the table and found Branko. It was time to get him to talk, and so we all decided to go for a long walk along the country road and digest our meal, while I asked questions and recorded his answers with Braco translating for me.

Branko Belak – Interview with the Former Police Chief of Zagreb

A. How did you meet Ivica?

B. In the spring of 1990, I visited my neighbor and we had coffee together. He explained that he had visited this man named Ivica who was dealing in alternative medicine and energy, and since he had a problem with his son, he began bringing him to Ivica.

A. Were you interested after hearing this story?

B. I was very interested because my wife, Marija, had a problem with her eyesight, and she was beginning to loose her sight. And then I went with her to meet Ivica. My wife had been in the hospital before and was getting medical treatment for her eye condition. In this time Ivica was not yet working at Srebrnjak 1, and he would only see one person at a time, not like later when he saw groups. And he used to touch people with the energy. After this first visit, my wife felt better. Soon after we were walking in Zagreb, and there was a sculpture very far away, and she saw it. Marija had never seen it before because of its distance, but then, after visiting Ivica she could see it.

After that I began to be more interested in Ivica, and at this time I was the police chief for one district in Zagreb, one of ten districts. Ivica did not know who I was, and the second time I went alone to see him because I was interested to know what he would tell me about my future. At this time Ivica was not only doing the healing work, but he would tell people's futures and past. What Ivica told me was absolutely incredible because no one in the world could have known what he told me. Even my wife did not know this information from my past. I was absolutely curious how he could know such things.

After that first session alone with Ivica, that same night I dreamt of him, and that Ivica was not his real name. I dreamt his name was Toplica, and that he was not born in Croatia, but in Serbia. The next day I went with my neighbor, who had told me of Ivica, to visit him again. But Ivica was not in his office, and I had come to tell him my dream. So we waited outside for about 90 minutes, and then Ivica came. He came by the bus and he was dressed in jeans. When he saw me he just said, "Hi". I wondered why Ivica had not come over those 90 minutes, and I thought he had found out that I was a policeman and had become afraid, and decided not to come.

What I thought turned out not to be true, Ivica just came a little late. Ivica took me and my friend first in the room, and I told him my dream. Ivica simply said that my dream was true, and he said he would tell me his first name the next time, and when I came back he told me his real name was Toplica. After two days, I was at home and my second in command called me, and said that they had taken a man into custody who was telling the future. The police had come to Ivica's office, and taken him and a few others into custody. What Ivica was doing, healing and telling the future, at that time was illegal in all of Yugoslavia. It was communist so anything like this was forbidden in the whole country by law.

In this moment, I told my sergeant that I knew this man and he was innocent, and so the police let him and the others go from the police station home. I was willing to put my own career on the line for Ivica by doing this, and at that time I was Croatian and Ivica was a Serbian man – and the war had begun between Serbia and Croatia.

A. You did this after knowing Ivica only for such a short time?

B. Yes, after only two times, I gave the order to let this man out. The next time I went to visit Ivica; when Ivica saw me come he was chewing gum and said from now on I feel that you are my brother, and for me you are my best friend in everything. Ivica told me, "God sent you, you must be here, you have to be here, the chief of police, because you must protect this mission."

A. What did you think about this statement?

B. For me at that moment it was a little funny because I had a completely different life. I was living under normal conditioning; school, university, you understand?

A. Very conventional?

B. But on the other hand, as a man and not a professional, I liked Ivica so much because he was so open, he was so friendly. Ivica was so true that I just liked him. And my wife very much believed in Ivica's power, and abilities to help people with past and future. And also, it was 1991 when the war really started between Croatia and Serbia, but Marija went to visit Serbia and the place where Ivica was born. And also, Ivica had abilities to put sometimes visions into a person. He just did this to some people, and people could relax, and then he put his hand out, and people would start to have a vision. They would start to speak because they could see something with their eyes. At this time I was very surprised, because he made my wife have a vision.

While I was standing next to her, Marija saw at this moment everything about Ivica. The place where Ivica was born, living as a small boy, later about school, about his coming to Zagreb. She could see everything. But before this neither of us knew this story, so she was just telling what she saw, like a film on television. Next she saw the future, how there would be one house similar to Srebrnjak 1, and there would be some beautiful wooden table and chairs, like for a king - you know the table and chairs at Srebrnjak 1 now. So at this time Marija was seeing a future picture of today. So he probably put her 15 years into the future, it was 15 years ago.

And then Ivica started to ask some questions of Marija, for example he asked if she could tell him who would be the next President of the country? She tried to explain the man, one who would have a beard - and really our President had a beard. Ivica asked who would be the next Pope? Marija told him that someone would try to kill the Pope - and it would really happen several years later. And also Ivica asked her if I would have some changes in my job? And she exactly explained the time in the future that I would soon change positions, I would be promoted. Marija also explained about the people around me, and it really happened, everything about my future. And after my wife's visions were finished, we were talking like friends, Ivica and I.

He used to say many times there would come a time when a young man will come to me, and when this man comes many new ways will be open for this mission. He was thinking about Braco. The next time he put my wife into another vision, Ivica also put his son, Alan into a vision. So there were two having a vision, and they were telling the same things. They were telling exactly the same vision. What one saw, the other also saw. After that time Ivica and I became very good friends. After his workday, Ivica would come very often to my home to have coffee. Then he would tell to me many visions he had about the future.

Listening to these things seemed funny because they seemed impossible, but I liked Ivica, though I didn't believe. Ivica said maybe now it looks funny but one day in the future you will come here and work here. Ivica said to me that one day I would come to work at Srebrnjak 1. Once in this time, when Ivica was coming to my apartment, he told me that my building with many apartments was not a good place. Because this place, many, many year ago was a cemetery. And there will come a time when you will get from your police station a new flat. After two months, I suddenly got a much bigger and beautiful flat, exactly like Ivica explained.

At the same time, during the war, I became the main Chief of Police in Croatia for contact with Serbia and America. I was the top-level person for communications in the war with other country's police. At this time when I was in this top-level position, I really believed and loved Ivica as a man, because everything he said in this short period became true - like getting a better position in my job, and changing the apartment. These many visions became true. And more and more, day-by-day, everyday I believed more and more that Ivica had an incredible power, the vision of the future and past, a touch for helping the people. Now it was not a funny story, it was rational and now I really believed what he said.

A. How often were you coming to visit Ivica at that time? Were you seeing him every day?

B. A minimum of three times a week we would see each other. Ivica would come to see me at 11:00 or 12:00 o'clock during the night, and we would stay together until 3 am although I had to get up at 5 am to go to my job. I asked him why he came at midnight? He told me he just had to come because he got the message, and he had to come and see me. That was Ivica's answer.

In 1993, one evening Ivica visited me and he was so excited. He said, "He came, it happened." And I asked what? Ivica said that the young man had come; he was born in Zagreb, he was 27 years old, he came from quite a rich family, he finished university, he has a master's degree in economics. This man had come, and Ivica said he was like his right side, and this man would be his helper. Ivica said that this man who came, that it was incredible, that he even slept at his home during the night. Ivica said that he took care of him more than to his own son, and he didn't see the end to that.

He used to tell me that this new man also sometime surprised him because this new man sometimes asked such crazy, but good questions, which Ivica didn't know how to give a good answer. Also this young man had such beautiful ideas for the future, which sometimes surprised Ivica. Most confusing was when this man came to Ivica's office, and gave him a present of a large golden sun and a gold watch. It was the most surprising thing for Ivica, that this new man gave him such presents. At that time Ivica called Braco young man.

One time when Ivica came to me, he said he would take me very soon to see this young man, and I would meet him. And one day, Ivica came with Braco for the first time to visit my home. I was watching Braco very carefully, and he looked like a real boy, not his age, and I didn't believe Braco could become what Ivica was predicting for the future. It was completely a story for me, what Braco would become and is now.

A. What was the story that Ivica predicted to you that you had trouble believing?

B. In this time Ivica explained that Braco had a master of economics degree, that he had big energy, power in himself that he was not aware of yet. I expected to see a stronger man, stronger character, not with this baby face. I was sitting there ashamed at the table. And also I was surprised because when Ivica was planning to do something, he always asked Braco what he thought about it. For me this was a shock. I thought why does Ivica ask this young man Braco, what does he know, nothing? Ivica was always asking Braco for his opinion because he knew something.

A. Did Ivica ever explain to you why he asked Braco for his opinion?

B. No, he never explained. But I saw that he really believed in Braco, and I could see a few situations that things really became true when Braco said yes or no. And also I was thankful to Ivica because once when my daughter had completed her university studies, and a student holiday trip was planned, I didn't have enough money to send her. Ivica ask Braco what he thought, if he should give me money to help, and Braco said yes, they had to give the money to me. At that moment, I said I didn't want this money. But despite me saying no, Braco got up and went to the car and brought in the money. It was a very beautiful thing when Ivica gave me that money so my daughter could go on her trip.

A. How many years did you know Ivica before the accident in Africa?

B. I knew him for five years before this tragic accident.

A. And are there any other prophecies or visions about the future of the mission?

B. I just remember one special moment about this house, which is now Srebrnjak 1 ... that in front of this place would be thousands and thousands of people. Ivica won't touch them or explain, but there will just be thousand and thousands of people at Srebrnjak 1. This was incredible 15 years ago; since first there was no house, and second there were no people. So how could thousands of people be there? And also it was true what he said about Braco continuing his work, and this really happened, that Braco would have a lot of energy to continue the mission, this is the second . . . and also one thing that is true, when Ivica said many years ago that I would come to Srebrnjak 1 to work there, and this is true. And also Ivica told that there would come the time when I would travel to many, many different kinds of countries. At that time it was impossible, because I was working for the police in Yugoslavia, and people couldn't go out of the country.

A. What year did you come to Srebrnjak 1 to start the work?

B. After Ivica died, Braco used to come and visit me because there were not many places Ivica and Braco used to go together when he was alive. Braco didn't have many friends or a girlfriend, and was completely alone. So very often he used to come and visit me. Then people started to come more and more to Braco, and then 2005 came, and I was sitting one evening with Braco. We were eating something, drinking coffee, and then Braco explained to me that there were more and more people, and he needed new people to help him. He asked me if I could come, and I thought why not. I don't know why I said yes, I don't remember what Braco did, I only remember it was 10 pm in the evening. At 8 am the next day I was at Srebrnjak 1. I don't know how Braco succeeded in convincing me that evening to be there the next morning at Srebrnjak 1.

When I came to Srebrnjak 1, I came for the very first time to attend a gazing session with Braco. Because Braco and I were friends, we came to visit each other, but I had never come to Srebrnjak 1 to a group session like other people. This day I came like the others and stood watching Braco. So I was standing in front of Braco, and Braco started gazing. This first time I was a little nervous, but after a few seconds, I started to feel much more calm. And what was incredible for me was that I saw Braco coming closer to me and moving farther away from me. I saw Braco like that, and I wasn't feeling nervous at all, I felt so free, so light, not nervous or anything anymore.

I explained the same story to my wife and my son, who afterwards also came to feel the energy. After some time, Braco came to visit Marija and I, and he put my wife into a vision just like Ivica did. It was really strong for Marija because she got this picture of the moment when Ivica was dying in the ocean. She was crying, and everything she said was exactly what happened. While Marija had this vision of Ivica dying, she was crying at the same time, and I was a little afraid for her, and asked Braco to please stop her vision. And then Braco stopped it. Marija opened her eyes but didn't remember anything. And of all the questions I asked, like with Ivica before, she was also giving many answers. I remember being told someone very important from the Army would be coming soon, and after a few months a general came. Now we are very good friends, me and this general. He is now in America, in Washington D.C. He came to Srebrnjak 1 just like Marija saw. She also saw that one very important person from the government would come. And a few years ago our Foreign Prime Minister came to visit us at the gazing session.

One very tearful moment, which I felt after I came to Srebrnjak 1 a few years ago, was when buses from Macedonia started to come to visit Braco. One particular bus from this group was very old, and caught on fire after the group had their session. And these people who were poor could not get another bus, so they stayed in the garden of Srebrnjak 1. They didn't have food or anything to drink, and Braco immediately ordered food, cigarettes and water. Then Braco ordered a bus from Zagreb, paid for it himself, and got the people back home.

Also when Braco was in Basel, Switzerland for a big congress, many people came in wheelchairs, many who couldn't get to Braco's room for his session. This was a technical problem that made it impossible. They were in front of the door outside, and then suddenly I saw that Braco saw them through the window. In no time, he just went out and began to hug the people. It was an important moment for me what Braco did.

Another special moment that I saw during these years was with one woman who came from Canada who couldn't speak, she was born like this, and she came to see Braco. Braco couldn't take her with the group so he decided to make a special case for the woman, and for a whole session he watched only her. These are short stories I can tell about Ivica and Braco.

A. I'd like to know your opinion on Braco's world mission?

B. I remember that Ivica told me that a time would come when Braco would continue this mission, he will see thousands and thousands of people from all the countries, Braco will go to other continents, not just Europe, that people from America will come and offer to make events for Braco, and I believe in this mission, and that is why I am here to help. There is no reason I can doubt this, everything that Ivica said and Braco said - and I see all these people traveling around like Angelika - everything that was said has become true. So I completely believe that the mission will spread all over the world.

A. Did Ivica tell you how much this mission will change the world?

B. Ivica said thousands and thousands of people, then hundreds of thousand of people, will come from around the world. Braco will then not even speak, not even watch, but hundreds of thousands will come. And he said the same to Braco's father, Viktor - that it would not be easy for Braco, and that he would not like to be in Braco's position when this time comes. These are the words he told to me and Viktor. At the time it was funny to me, but now it's not funny because everything is true.

A. What do you see your particular role as at Braco's side?

B. Briefly I feel like Braco is my son. I have decided to stay with this work until the end of my life.

A. Did Ivica ever say anything about Braco and a connection with Atlantis?

B. Yes, Ivica told me many things about Atlantis, but I didn't know anything about this subject, and so I didn't give it any attention, it seemed like fairy tales and I don't remember anymore. I just remember that once Ivica said that long ago there was this continent that people lived.

A. Anything with America that he can remember? Any visions?

B. I remember that he said for America that one day a black man would become president. Also there would be bad period for America, Ivica saw many places burned, and this makes me think of the war in Kuwait. But I didn't ask questions because many of these things were strange for me.

A. Do you have any final memories you would like to share?

B. One moment I will always remember was when Ivica told me that he would have to put me in his book. He said he knew it wasn't the time because I worked for the police, and I could have many problems if he put me in his my book.

When Ivica wrote his twelfth book, he just mentioned my initials, B.B., and told of a time when someone helped him with the police and said 'thank you'. Ivica told me the time would come when somebody else would write about my story and it would not be in his books. It is probably now your [Angelika's] book, and this is why I decided to give you this story. Ivica said in his life he would write only thirteen books – and he did.

The same evening Braco's father came to visit me and Ivica came. What I will never forget is that usually Ivica always said before leaving goodbye - till tomorrow or next time. This time he said a goodbye, which meant forever. He did the same with Braco's father. There were so many things that happened, but this is what I think is the most important that I can remember.

Branko has been four years at Srebrnjak 1, and he traveled everywhere, including many countries with Braco, showing his love and care in so many ways. Braco knew that without him, he could not succeed at the level he was at because Branko helps him in so many ways. He came just at the moment when Braco needed someone like a gift. Our walk and interview lasted over an hour, and as all three of us engaged in the past, we lost our way back, and had to turn around to find our restaurant again.

The air was cooling up high, and was a relief from the earlier heat. Once back, we found our hosts had returned, and the doctor talked for some time in a lively fashion, informing Braco of the latest challenges. As of that early evening, everything was still moving forward. Danka look worried and concerned, but she too was determined. They both had a meal brought, and then had the Treska cake and espresso, and continued to tell of a new newspaper article published that afternoon. It was a paper that had favorably covered Braco's first visit to Macedonia, but now gave the same negative story as the newspaper that morning. Braco did not appear affected by this, he brushed it off, and they discussed strategies for the next day.

When this conversation was complete, I asked Atanas if I could interview him. I wanted to know what had led him to take on this great responsibility and risk. He agreed and called over Bonnie to translate. Interestingly, her accent was American, not British, and perhaps this was from the popularity of American pop music here, as in all the Balkan countries. She was studying English in school so she would have the chance to go to university abroad, and she had visited England. The doctor then answered my questions, and Bonnie would elaborate at times to lend her own perspective about her father.

Dr. Atanas Atanasov – Psychotherapist

A. What is your background Dr. Atanasov?

DR. When I was a younger doctor – maybe 30 years ago, I had an open-minded view. I was often reading books about alternative medicine, books on energy, bio-energy, acupuncture, homeopathy, etc. I was interested in improving the health. In Russia many years ago there were some people like Braco, who did something similar, many were famous. Also in India, for example, people like Sai Baba, the Dalai Lama, etc. There was one professor who used to live in the United States; she was a doctor in three different specialties very similar to modalities in Chinese medicine. At Congresses, she stated that we must let the people believe in what they want. I believe if people want to go to Sai Baba, the Dali Lama, Braco or a doctor, they should have the choice.

I am a doctor, a psychologist, a psychotherapist, and I like working with meditation, with relaxation, and similar things. I understand that people are a microcosm in one big macrocosm. Everything I understand I share with the people, and I help them and after many years I became interested in minerals and vitamins. I am not the type of doctor who practices only conventional methods, I believe in alternative medicine - but not only alternative medicine, but also complementary medicine. And when I found out without any symptoms that I had lung cancer two years ago, I had surgery, chemotherapy, radiation, and everything that medicine provided.

But I heard about Braco, and with an open mind, I went one year ago to Zagreb. I was impressed with what Braco did. So I read books by him, and watched DVDs of what people with very serious problems thought about him. After the first meeting with Braco, he called us and asked if we wanted to help the people in Skopje, because many people from Skopje, Macedonia were coming to see Braco. And they had to travel all day long to have a 15-minute meeting with him. That's why Braco wanted to come here, and help all the people in Macedonia. He is active with my wife, a psychologist, Danka, and they started to prepare for him to come. Before the New Year in December, we had an event with Braco. We also went to Slovenia and Zagreb to see how groups were organized.

A. How many people came to your event in Skopje?

DR. It was a great success, and there were about 10,000 people.

A. Were you prepared for that?

DR. No, we prepared for 2000, but there were 10,000. This was a problem, because the restaurant venue where we had the meeting with Braco was too small for 10,000 people. Today we have problems because some people in Macedonia don't understand what Braco does. They think Braco is a doctor or something similar, and that he took money from the people, and gave them nothing. They think Braco practiced medicine.

A. Who thinks this?

DR. Not the 10,000 people who came, but maybe one hundred people who did not come. About a 100 people don't like Braco. They don't have open minds - they only know conservative ways. They have a big problem with Braco coming here, and do not want to see him, because they think he is an ignorant man, a phony doctor. And they don't understand what Braco actually does. If they would only open the website that explains everything about Braco, if they would read only one book, watch one DVD, they would understand what Braco really does. Today was very difficult for us because we had all the documents of permission, all the permits, but some people are not giving up, and they want to stop the meetings with Braco tomorrow.

Now is July 14 at 9 pm, and tomorrow the meetings with Braco take place, and all we hope for is that it be a great day with no problems. Very, very much we hope Braco will come again in September, November, many times in Skopje because there are thousands of people who like Braco. I hope tomorrow will be a very good day, and he will come again. So my last words about this is that I am very happy about Braco, because he works in many different European countries, in America, and I hope he works in Japan and Australia also soon. He is very well accepted in other countries, and let's hope that some day in Macedonia things will change, because the Macedonia people love Braco very much. There are only those few that don't like him. And they will do everything they can to stop Braco from coming back.

A. You had lung cancer and you had surgery, and after your surgery, chemotherapy and radiation. About a year passed and then you went to see Braco?

DR. Yes.

A. What was the condition of your cancer when you went to see Braco?

DR. [15 year old daughter Bojana (Bonnie) answers this question.] He didn't have cancer when he went to see Braco; he had severe depression as a result of the illness and treatment. He wasn't happy, he was sad all the time. But when he saw Braco, he became happy, he had energy, he had the power to survive, to look after me and my sister, to look after his job. And now he is very happy. Two years ago he was a different person, sad, angry, no energy - but now he is a new man. That's why he now wants to help Braco to come here and help all the people in Macedonia.

A. I want to know why you have put your career on the line to bring Braco here? I understand the sacrifice that you and your family are making.

DR. Yes, I agree. I have a feeling that alternative medicine, not only medicine, but the power with Braco, the energy he gives is important in many different uses. Not only in meditation, in health, in love, money. Braco helps everyone in all areas in life. One very large Center, run by Vladimir Pudin, he is a head psychologist, professor of psychiatry, he says that he hopes that patients want to believe in doctors, like people believe in Braco. It is that people *believe* . . . and this is the most important thing.

A. Did you experience anything when you went to your first session with Braco? Did you feel anything?

DR. I had many feelings, perhaps energy, something I can't explain with words. [Bonnie adds that her mother was crying.] Especially at Srebrnjak 1 in the onyx room where Braco works, there is a very special feeling. I just can't explain.

A. Thank you so much doctor for sharing your story

Shortly after our interview was complete we would leave our mountaintop. It was now late evening, and we would go back to our hotel. Braco had agreed to visit with Rebeka and her son a little later that night at the café below our hotel. This was something he never did, but he would do so because this woman has worked so hard to help the doctor get his government permits for our event. Rebeka only wanted her son to meet Braco, with the hope that it would aid his recovery. Children were not allowed at gazing sessions until they turned eighteen, because of the intensity of the energy. In this case, Braco would not make an exception; he would only meet them as he did with some special friends.

I was a bit tired after our day and took a short time to relax and freshen up before heading downstairs again. Once I arrived at the café, everyone was already gathered, and Braco had the singer's son in his lap. Rebeka had brought her mother along, who was a newspaper reporter who was writing about alternative medicine and spirituality back in the 1980s, when people thought she was crazy. Now she said all her colleagues told her she was right all along. A strong woman, I could see where Rebeka had inherited a certain determination from her. The son, Markiyan, played on Braco's lap, but mostly he just looked at him with a wide-eyed wonder. Clearly the boy was captivated.

This was not his normal behavior with a stranger, Rebeka told me politely, and said he was usually quite shy. I knew it encouraged her to see this relationship develop between Braco and her son, and Braco held the boy in a fatherly way, patient and loving. I had a glass of red wine and began to chat with Marjana beside me.

Music was playing in our café, including MTV style videos projected on a screen in back of Braco. Finally close to midnight, Braco rose and everyone said goodnight. Rebeka would be back one last time for a gazing session the next day. It would be an early morning, and so I gave my hugs to all and left for my room.

Chapter Thirteen

Day 17 – Wednesday, July15, 2009

Skopja, Macedonia

Challenges in the noise levels from the cafés and bars below my hotel room window, and the heat from the hot day made my sleep uncomfortable that night. Then when I woke up at 5 am, I realized I had misunderstood the time we would gather to leave for the event. I had thirty minutes to quickly ready myself for the big day, and although I was only five minutes late, my mood was somewhat compromised. But as soon as I saw Braco and the others it quickly improved, and my tiredness left me in their cheerful greetings.

At the conference hotel our event rooms were set, and everyone swung into action to set up flower arrangements, registration, DVDs and more. We walked through the rooms, and Sead helped perfect the lighting so that Braco's face would be well illuminated for all to see that day. Ever changing our routine, Braco decided I would present to the groups after, instead of before he came on stage to gaze at the people. His thought was that he wanted people to leave with my words, and that day he would continually give me new instructions to change elements of my presentation to highlight different ideas he wanted emphasized.

I loved the variety, and would have become bored making exactly the same speech day after day. This gave me the opportunity to be creative, and his directions were enjoyable challenges to meet. A transformation had taken place so completely in me that I no longer had the need to prepare, or control all the factors I could think of in advance. It was as if I no longer needed to know the end of the story first, I was ready to enjoy the journey as it came. My mind had a new won peace, and I trusted my ability to flow with new circumstances. Braco and the energy had given me this peace.

People had begun lining up outside the event hall while still dark, and this was a very positive beginning. After all was well underway for receiving the first group, Braco and I retired to the special break room, which was always filled with interesting conversations, playful antics, planning and a fascinating visitor now and again. It was a portal into the backstage world of Braco, and I loved the time in this sheltered haven at all events.

Marjana was not translating that day, and she graciously stepped into the position of ensuring we were well taken care of throughout the long day, attentively bringing us espressos, beverages and snacks as we needed. I was grateful for her care and service. Today we would have the time to reach a new level of understanding and appreciation together. Before the first group, Braco asked me to leave the people with a solid understanding that he would be leaving to Hawaii, and new destinations soon. Again, I played the role of preparing the people, and I had to take special care to present it in a way that conveyed the importance of this change so people could support it.

Branko would come each time a group was ready, and he would escort Braco, and I would have Miki as my chaperone. After each of us was done with our job for a group, they would each immediately sweep in at our sides, and escort us back to the break room. During Braco's first gazing session, I noticed quite clearly how much the Macedonian people who had come loved him, and as always, there was so much hope on people's faces. I would stand during the day with each group for the gazing, and sometimes I would recognize a face from another event, and be greeted with a familiar smile.

After Braco finished, I stepped from the side of the crowd, and Rudi handed me a microphone, and together we walked before the group. I had been instructed to be clear about Braco's leaving, and so I delivered me speech accentuating this point at the end. It was always important to me that they felt me through my words. Yet as I delivered my first speech of the day, I felt I was not able to really reach them. My words were similar to other presentations, but I saw that the people did not like the part about Braco leaving for new lands. When I was done there was silence, and I left the stage, and Miki was quickly at my side to walk me out of the room.

Rudi had told me early on in the first week that people of the Balkans would only applaud if they liked the person on stage. I had always received the crowd's approval, but for the first time that morning there was no response. Miki, ever supportive, told me my speech was very good, but I told him I was not satisfied because I had not felt the people nor reached them. Now I was determined to make changes to fix this situation while still giving the message I was instructed to deliver.

Back in our sanctuary space, Braco immediately asked how things had gone and Miki answered very well, and I was thankful for his kindness, but I countered that I had failed to reach the people. They were of a different emotional nature than all the other people I had met in other countries, and I stated that I would try different ways to make that connection that was so important with them. Braco understood and spoke of the psyche of the country, and the dynamics of its people. I had delivered the message he requested, and many times later new points would be added that I knew the people would not openly embrace either, because they represented a change at all levels.

Marjana was helpful in suggesting I give the people something more to comfort them, and so in the next group, I changed tactics and added that Braco, a son of the Balkans, would always come back to his homeland no matter where he was called in the world. This was enough to make a difference with the second group, and all thereafter. I felt the people again, and I could feel them connect with my words. And finally the applause came of their support of the message, and I was happy. It would serve nothing to have the audience angry or frustrated with myself for taking Braco away, or at him for leaving, and now the right wording created the proper bridge for understanding and acceptance.

Now as I left groups, people would sometimes walk over to me to hold my hand or express words of thanks, and I enjoyed meeting them. I felt I needed to sometimes share that special energy now flowing through me more personally. But Miki would jokingly tell me afterwards to just run for the door. He was so diligent at protecting Braco himself from all who would crowd instantly around him, and he wished do the same for me; I felt well looked after. Braco appreciated deeply the expressions of love from the people, but he did not speak in public and this was important to keep all focus upon the work of the gaze alone. A healthy flow was established so that all the groups could be moved in a judicious manner out of the room, as a new group was ready to enter. The first priority was for everyone to see Braco in as timely and well organized a fashion as possible.

Braco would ask me each group to talk about America, alternative and energy medicine, the views of the media of such practices and more. He would never tell me specifically what to say, only raise a subject, and tell me to speak what I felt to be true. And I did, but sometimes I had to frame ideas; such as the openness in the United States with its awakening consciousness to alternative healing modalities, and the idea of taking responsibility for personal transformation, that was contrary to their own country's conservative views. But I did so with a special care and delicacy. Sometimes afterwards though, I would apologize to Rudi because I knew most people did not really want to hear these things, but they had too. He was so kind in always letting me know that he understood.

Many groups had now gone, and I came to the break room with a new observation for Braco. Of all the countries we had visited, this one was different because the people did not seem to be as open to sharing Braco with the world. Then it occurred to me that many of these people were crushed by their circumstances, and did not believe tomorrow held any rewards, why would they? Their country was poorer than most of the other European Nations, there were fewer opportunities, the Orthodox Church was strict, new ideas were criticized and the corrupt government worked against its own people to control them, sometimes ruthlessly. So all they knew was to hold on tightly to any goodness they possessed.

Braco listened to my observations, and as if on cue, our host entered to inform us of another negative story in one of the papers that morning. Again they said exactly as before; that Braco's lack of a medical qualification made him a fraud, and he did not have the proper government authorization to be here this day. All morning, Atanas and Danka had to deal with new inspectors. Danka could be seen running to and fro with papers in hand to convince each new official of the legality of the event. All day, she looked like she had a great weight on her shoulders, and Braco was deeply sorry for her difficulties.

Both the doctor and his wife had worked tirelessly for many months to plan this event, and they had gone to great expense; tens of thousands of dollars to hire police, acquire permits, hire the hotel, run advertisements and more. Now another wave of challenge had come as new inspectors arrived to threaten to shut all down. They even had an official from the Department of Finance watching every sale, and scrutinizing all bookkeeping until the event ended that day. Braco gave them his full attention and encouragement, but I could see he was not happy over these developments. Yet he remained ever strong, and would adopt a stoic attitude about these things.

At noon, the manager sent us a tray of chocolates, and it made me laugh. A table was set in our break room with an abundance of cookies, chocolates, pastries with sweet fillings and other sugary confections. Braco had explained that people of the Balkans expressed their love by giving sweets, so we were well loved with abundance. I was entirely grateful for a plate of fruit amongst the deserts, and I ate most of the grapes to sustain myself along with an occasional espresso. Yet I watched Braco and his staff eat everything without comment, and they all were vibrantly healthy and in good shape, which again spoke of the power of the energy in them all. Braco had told me before that it was our own judgments that made these things unhealthy for us or not.

By 1:30 pm, Danka informed us that 1631 people have passed through the door so far, and this was sad news. The bad publicity was obviously taking a toll, and Braco and I both were calculating if the doctor and his family would cover their costs. Then

Atanas came in and spoke with Braco, and I was informed that a young reporter was present that could speak English, and wanted an interview. She worked for one of the papers that had already printed the false statements that declared that Braco did not have permission to do his work in this country. I did not want to do the interview because I knew fairness would not be shown. But Braco was clear that we had to show love to everyone, even those who worked against us, and so I went. I was only instructed to be strong and to say what I felt.

As the reporter pulled out a recording device, she stated that she had never heard of energy healing, that she was raised very agnostic in a socialist mentality, and found this all difficult to believe. So I did my best to give her a brief education, but in the end I could well see how closed she remained and biased, so I knew there was nothing more I could do. I did not regret or feel deflated by the experience, but more determined to touch and connect with the people who had made the effort to come. And Braco only showed confidence after I gave my opinion of the interview, and told me that he could eat that negative energy. He could eat more than they had! And this is why I felt a complete devotion to him and his work, because it was the truth.

All day the press came, television, newspapers and magazines. And the question for us was how they would report the event in the end. So far, two papers printed outright lies, and Atanas asked Braco's permission to file a lawsuit for libel. At first Braco expressed that he would not sue himself, but would respect the doctor's wish to do so. Later, they talked, and Braco asked him not to move forward. For Braco, it was no one's fault; people had a right to believe what they chose. Atanas agreed that such a lawsuit could cause a financial settlement that would destroy the newspaper, and he did not want such a thing.

Atanas stated that bribes and corruption controlled his government, and that people who did well were automatically viewed as criminals. The jealousy here was so extreme that everyone worked to pull down someone who succeeded. If he could, the doctor said that he would leave the country because of the economy, the government, bribes, the need to renew the conference licenses each month and more. Braco was sad that the life of Atanas was now so filled with problems because of him. He spoke of this, and Bonnie, who was in a corner of the room, immediately came over with great enthusiasm.

She reassured us that Braco had cured her father's severe depression. I myself saw that Atanas was sailing through these challenges with great stamina and resolve, he was in no way crushed with stress, and in fact he was handling everything admirably. Alive with life, light and unfailing strength, he was showing no sign of weakness. He was a man pushing forward without looking back. In Bonnie's eyes was the pride she felt for her father and mother. Expressing without reserve her appreciation of her parent's work, and love for them, she also talked of the importance of the work of Braco. She was phenomenal in her maturity and grace.

Our best group that morning was almost 500 people, but at 2:00 pm the group was perhaps 100. No matter the size though, we treated each group equally, and gave our all. Sead did some filming at different times that day, and he remarked during the next break to Braco that I was different on stage than only a few days ago, and he liked the change. Valuing his opinion, I was pleased because I felt different too. Of all the people I was working close with that day, only Dinko, who was doing all the opening introductions was not able to spend much time with us. I was sorry that over the weeks I never had a chance to really speak with him, though the language barrier was partly responsible.

At this point, most people exited the break room, and Braco got up and began to shake his body like a child with an excess of energy. It was amusing to watch, and I joined him to try this unique activity, but he was much better at it that I. So instead, I sat back down to enjoy his fun vicariously. Shortly, Branko, Miki and Sead came into the room, and Sead began a game of soccer with a taped up wad of paper. I was up to this challenge, and with shoes off, Sead and I had a match. He was skilled, but I was determined, and it was a good game. Then Branko and Miki joined in while I rested, and the ball hit a glass wall with a resounding clunk.

Braco merely watched, but once I sat down he told me that he enjoyed viewing our match. It was a fair exchange from my earlier entertainment of watching him shake around. I remembered my first meeting with Braco, and how I thought he rarely spoke even in private life, that he was probably always in nature meditating, that he was like the many spiritual people who remove themselves from life; partaking in few pleasures because they were so elevated, and he was none of these things. His playful, animated, sometimes serious sides were all vibrantly engaged with life and he even had of forceful side that could show anger. My fairytale proved to be inferior to the real story.

It was time for another group and Branko led Braco, and Miki took my arm, and began calling me his beautiful blond playfully. We smiled at each other in camaraderie. The gazing sessions were continuing to awaken new levels in me, and I felt the energy each time. Often I saw Braco's form waiver on the platform, though he did not actually move. His aura also expanded in white, and sometimes it even looked as if there were two or more of him standing together. His face changed before my eyes, and my body grew hot with energy waves. So many people shared seeing these same phenomenons and it was uniquely mysterious. Many people cried that day and my big experience was coming.

Back at our haven, Marjana entered and told us people were asking what to do with the flowers they received, especially in a few days after they wilted. The people did not want to make a mistake; they viewed the flowers as special, and connected to Braco. They wanted to honor the energy, and the flowers were a part of this expression. Then Atanas came back in, and stated bravely that it was an important thing that no one had stopped them, that the inspectors could not find anything wrong. The loss of money was a small issue to him compared with these things. I also thought it was an important opportunity for him to spend time closely with Braco, and I knew only an intensification of the light, and strength in him would come of this.

Next the doctor was called away; a television film crew had arrived with a particular reporter who had given highly prejudiced coverage about Braco after his last visit. During the previous event she had shown up, and arrogantly demanded to interview Braco. She wanted be the first in the world to do so. Of course she was denied this, since Braco firmly refused interviews, and had never given one to press or media. After being turned down, she ran a very harsh story about him, filled with inaccuracies and slander. So Atanas went to meet her to tell her that she was not welcome since she had misrepresented the truth before.

A very heated talk ensued, and the hotel manager finally came over; he informed the reporter and her crew that they were on private property and had to leave. One of the cameramen picked up his camera to film, and security came and told him to stop or his camera would be broken. Then the crew was finally escorted out. Bonnie informed me that this reporter was very popular, and ran regular stories with a very negative perspective. It was sensationalism, incendiary-style reporting that had nothing to do with the unbiased disclosure of facts. The reporter ended up threatening the doctor during the exchange; if he refused an interview again, she would ruin his career, and run a story about Braco's lack of proper permits to hold this event. Undaunted, Atanas fearlessly stood his ground, and Bonnie was beaming with pride once again.

Finally, we came to the very last group of the day. No one showed weariness in our crew, in fact just the opposite, especially after all of the challenges that were conquered. This last group felt special to me, different than the others, perhaps because there were a large number of adults in their early twenties and thirties, especially young women, who displayed on their faces not only respect, but an open heartedness. It was special to stand with them as Braco took his place on the stage.

That gazing session was to become the most important moment of my entire trip. I had a final wish that had not even occurred to me that day, but the energy held it, and delivered it to me with a power beyond measure. As Braco lovingly shared his gift, I was utterly transported. My wish was to remember something inside of myself long forgotten, mysterious, but alive with a spark. In essence, I wanted to remember everything in the greatest sense of beingness, but what that meant I did not know. My wish was a feeling even unclear to me.

Yet this wish was based upon an experience I had years previous in a dream, which was more real to me than anything else in my life. I was in my mid to late twenties when I had this incredible encounter, but it was timeless and clear inside of me. In it, I found the consciousness of my waking self-looking upon a mountain top plateau with pristine, snow covered cliff tops surrounding in all directions. On that plateau, I saw an ancient, or perhaps higher dimensional version of myself sitting, cross-legged and in meditation. This other me looked exactly as I did, and I knew it to be myself, but somehow separate or unknown to my waking self. Dressed in a simple white tunic and pants, she opened her eyes on the plateau, and looked directly at me as the waking consciousness that was viewing this episode, and she smiled. I felt her knowledge of my presence.

Next, she rose and walked to the edge of the plateau, which held a dramatically plunging cliff side. Without hesitation, she leaned over and placed her hands at the cliff's edge, and rose into a handstand. She achieved an immediate and perfect balance at the edge of the precipice, and as she did, the brilliant yellow sun in the sky exploded in size. It turned into a vibrant mandarin orange color as it enveloped her, and all of creation, including my own watching consciousness. Suddenly, I experienced oneness with the universe, and all of creation, and this dissolved all my false perceptions into pure love. This transcendental moment lasted an eternity in a few mere seconds, and then I woke up absolutely awestruck.

Since this experience, I had been searching my entire life to regain that feeling and connection, and in Braco and the energy I saw this potential. He was living as the embodiment of the merging of that higher dimensional, ancient self in the material world. Miraculously Braco, through the purity of his heart, had been able to receive this energy of Source and all of creation through himself, and was able to offer it to the people who came to him. What he was doing had absolutely no limits, and had the potential to change the human condition back to its true state of spiritual expression. He was the template that embodied evolution itself for humanity, as a gift directly and divinely given.

Then the gazing session began and the energy came. I experienced immediately inside myself a greater reality, and then I was in that exquisite vastness of the energy itself. Feeling like I was set free of all boundaries, it showed me the pathways of all the truths of my spirit. I was in a divinely bound union with something so ineffable, and its shear glory filled me, and all of the pains, sorrows, degradations and evils that I had ever experienced were dissolved as inconsequential, illusions. I felt myself filled with the vision of truth, a truth that came from beyond the material. I was in service to that which was completely indescribable, but I would have done anything for it because any service to it was nothing less than a joy unimaginable and without end.

Nothing in my life had ever been pointless, worthless or harsh. It all flowed from the love of this All and it was unlimited grace and beauty in motion. In a single moment, every question I had ever had, everything I had ever endured was dissolved and delivered back to me in a perfection of unfolding truths that had purpose, illumination and unbounded love. A pathway from the time of Atlantis to now was present, and a greater service to a mission for life itself unfolding. I remembered everything in a way no mind could create or hold onto; I felt everything bathed in a loving joy so complete that nothing could ever be the same in my life, because I had remembered the feeling.

I had not thought it possible to feel so much so completely. As Braco finished, I knew what I served, and a vast purpose across time and reality. My heart was erupting in a love so immense that tears of joy flowed freely down my face, and I stood breathless out of time. A feeling was now anchored inside of me indestructible, untouchable, and it would illuminate my path forward not by mind, but by something more direct. I could not speak, and I could not move as Braco stepped from the stage, I was in an expansiveness of the eternal that now flowed through my veins.

My first experience with this ineffable oneness had been through a dream experience, at that time it had been the only way I could access it. Now, in a fully waking state, Braco had brought it forth for me again through the energy, in a more magnified and direct encounter, and I was eternally grateful to him. All I could wonder was if this was something near to what he felt when he opened himself to the energy, to do the gazing for the people. I knew that during the sessions, he embodied a potential that each one of us could rise to meet and become, and so I now knew he was even more of a miracle than I had ever imagined. And he was able to step into this feeling, an unnamable state of consciousness at will for the people.

All had been revealed, I had remembered everything, and it happened in seven precious minutes suspended in a feeling that lasted without end. Now it was time for my presentation, and I walked forward ever so slowly, I knew that my greatest challenge was before me. Now I had to learn how to merge what I had felt into my conscious, material reality. Only opening to this energy with continued resolve would solve all the seeming contradictions of a corporal existence, and allow spirit to prevail and fully enter the material world itself.

On stage, I somehow composed myself and saw almost all of the young women crying, and many holding friends they had come with in loving support. Arms were entwined across the audience. Something unexpected and immense had filled this room, this group; I could see it in the faces, the tears and embraces.

My heart opened to that group like none other, and something came through me that was so much more than I could personally offer. Rudi, so gracefully, delivered my final words to those people. Before leaving, I stopped to embrace those who came toward me, to hold my hand or express their feelings with warmth and love. Minutes later in the break room, all I could say quietly to Braco was that he had given me something in that session that was immeasurable. Now my love was a thousand times stronger for the energy, and for him and his work. My path was beginning, I had felt this beginning upon arrival to Macedonia, but did not understand yet its context. But now I understood my earlier anticipation, and the preparation of my dream experience on the airplane.

Still awestruck, I could not think. I did not want to frame any of it with words, ideas or concepts. I only wished to feel its residue, and so as the others chatted and packed up, I sat silently in my own inner world. Our event was complete, and everyone gathered in the inner hotel courtyard for refreshments to discuss the day. I came out too, but felt tears welling up uncontrollably, so I quickly excused myself, and went back into our sanctuary room alone to just sit. Perhaps ten minutes passed before I felt I could function again normally, behave again normally, but nothing was normal inside of me. Sitting back down with our entire group, I felt Miki and Rudi look at me intently, yet they only smiled kindly without questions, perhaps intuitively knowing all was well.

Atanas and his family would stay behind to make a final accounting, gather their things and settle all accounts. Tedo drove us back in the van, and once there; Braco and I made plans to take a walk by the river, and soon met again. Marjana and Miki joined us. To relax, stretch our bodies, and for the serenade of the roaring river, we welcomed the ritual of the long stroll. Laughing and joking, we had a lively time. I picked plume-like grass to adorn my hair, and Miki sang for me love ballads in a sweet, tender voice, revealing his professional musician status. So engrossed in our conversations as we traded off partners to walk side-by-side, we missed our street turn off, and saw more of the area than expected.

Dinner was scheduled for 9:30 pm at a nearby restaurant, but Atanas and his family were a bit delayed, and we arrived for our meal at 10 o'clock. Once again, our restaurant had a sprawling outdoor patio, and it was adorned with huge white umbrellas over our table. Beverages and wine were served, and Atanas began to tell Braco that all of the reporters at the event so far had given negative coverage. The doctor could not understand this, since several reporters had interviewed people in the crowd that day, and all had given positive, heart-felt statements. He finally had to attribute it to the government's manipulation of the media, and the fact that they did not want to lose control.

Despite all that had taken place, the doctor was still determined to bring Braco back again that October. He declared that he was willing to forego taking a vacation to do so. By this point, Rebeka and her husband, Milan, had joined us for this final meal together. Milan remarked that Macedonia was undergoing changes regarding questions, denials and solutions. To him, Braco's next visit would not be a problem, but I saw the open hostility displayed for Braco as a warning to take seriously. More than ever, Braco was a treasure beyond all value that had to be protected, as Branko so conscientiously did, even sometimes from his own daring ways to proceed with a vigilant prudence.

At dinner was the first time I saw Danka relax and smile. It was so good to see her relieved of her burdens, and watch her happily converse with Rebeka and Milan. I spent time telling Braco about the remarkable experience I had in the last session, but could not find words to really describe it. Instead I told him of the love I would always hold for him, the energy and the work. Because of his courage, and capacity to hold the energy as he did, he gave people something that could not be measured by shifting science, mind or material values.

Later Braco talked of his son, Andelon, who had sent me his regards; awaiting me to play soccer, bocce ball and cards. It was important to Braco that I bond with his son so that he would feel better when his father had to leave to be in Hawaii. I understood, and in the days ahead on the coast with his family, I came to enjoy his son's spirited company in play with great affection. Our dinner was superb, abundant as always, and afterwards I joined Braco for a few cigarettes as I finished my wine. Joy filled our table again, and many jokes with Branko captured center stage. At midnight we finished, and because of the energy of the work, Braco and I still wanted more action, so we suggested going to a disco, which he had not done since his youth.

Here Branko put his foot down, telling Braco that he could not go. Branko was concerned after all that had happened with the negative publicity on television, as well as in the newspapers, and I understood his concern. Yet I was so filled with joy I could have danced all night, even if night ended at 4:20 am, which was the time we would once again meet in the hotel lobby for the airport. Instead, we were all safely taken back to our hotel to call it a night. Skopja had been an experience much greater than I could have imagined. Once again, I was reminded that in the face of this energy, absolutely anything was possible.

Chapter 14

Day 18 – Thursday, July 16, 2009

Skopja, Macedonia

We all had to be up at 3:30 am to be ready, and packed for the flight back to Zagreb. Everyone had been tired after our dinner, but I was completely energized from my experience; and had ordered a cup of cappuccino at the hotel lobby desk, then gone to the breakfast room, which had a wireless Internet connection, to work. With exactly thirty minutes of sleep that night, I met our group that early morning. Now I knew with complete certainty my life was governed by something so mysterious and unfathomable, yet loving beyond all comprehension, that I would do anything for this magnificence that I had encountered. And I would do anything Braco requested of me to help.

After such an occurrence of feeling the true home of consciousness, it was an odd thing to come back into the everyday world. For me there was still a strong separation between the true reality of the Source of all of creation, and the material plane of our existence, but I knew now that they could be integrated. Braco was the living embodiment of this very synthesis, and being in his presence was a comfort beyond words. I believed that his strength grew as he integrated these two facets together. Slowly, and at a pace set by my own spirit, I was rediscovering what people had sought through the ages, and because of Braco, I now saw the assurance of the Golden Age Ivica had prophesied emerging now for humanity. A gentle, kind man with a youthful spontaneity and enormous spiritual presence, my loving host, the young man from Zagreb, was forging the path.

The doctor and his wife greeted us at the airport, and after we checked in, we sat to talk. He told us of a television report the night before that called Braco a Jesus figure, and the Hotel Aleksandar Palace similar to his church. None of the reports from the media, none, would offer any kind of favorable reporting. All were biased in the extreme with the same falsehoods told over and again. So our Macedonia chapter was closed until another day, and we all knew that the tides could turn, and they would turn quickly here if Braco were accepted in a country like the United States. Then he would return a hero, and even gain the media's respect; it was simply a game.

Braco would refuse to accept any royalties on the films and books Atanas sold at his event. He knew the doctor and his family had lost money, and so he gave to them as a gift over $5000. Further, Braco told the doctor that if he attempted to send one penny to his organization, he would never come to Macedonia ever again. So the family finally agreed, knowing full well Braco would not change his mind, and accepted his support and kindness. I was impressed that Atanas and Danka had come to meet us so early after all the rigors of their last days, but their own generosity of heart was immense. Plans were now in the works by them for Braco's return.

Our flight back was comfortable, and several from our group would return home to begin their own holidays over this vacation season in Europe. Srebrnjak 1 would remain open and fully operational as staff took turns with time off; but the people would come for groups now to hear a recording of Braco's voice, something I had not experienced yet. I was not startled when I heard that people still came in large numbers for this, and had experienced similar effects to when Braco was present himself. How could this surprise me since the energy carried through people's photographs, the sun symbol and films about Braco? Of course hearing his voice would work too.

Adriatic Coast

Back at Zagreb airport, Damir had not arrived yet to pick up some of the group, so we all once again entered the outdoor café while Braco stopped for a purchase. He came back with jumbo-sized bars of chocolate of different types, and laid them out on our row of tables pushed together. The philosophy of this group was that one always would bring enough for all; the concept of each man for himself was foreign to them. It was an inclusive and unifying viewpoint, and I respected this value that spoke of taking care of everyone. Thus, all were treated equally as Braco always displayed through his own actions.

Once Damir arrived, Dinko, Rudi, Miki and Branko left with him, while Tedo took Braco and I in his van for the three hour ride to the coastal village. Now Braco would begin his true yearly vacation, and spend quality time most of all with his son. At eight years old, he needed his father's love and attention in all ways. We drove directly to Braco's property seaside, and were met by Dinka's warm smile, and Andelon's youthful exuberance. Immediately, his son happily led Braco off, and I took the time to locate a swimsuit in my bag and changed. In no time, I was in the wonderfully warm and clear Adriatic, and making my way down the coastline for an hour. When I returned, I was refreshed and felt good as new, despite my sleep deficit.

To Andelon's amusement, I pulled out some wheatgrass powder out of my handbag, my curative for sugar or wine indulgences, like that at the airport with Braco's chosen breakfast. It instantly balanced my body back to normal, since I had not yet acquired Braco's ability to be completely unaffected by food or drink. Braco's son had never seen anything like it, and the bright green color in the water made him step back. Finally, smelling it was enough to send him running off, until he came back for a game of soccer. Fortunately, my wheatgrass fortified me for this intense play. In a long dress, I managed a good game.

It amused Braco no end our match together. Andelon was accomplished, and fast, so one game was enough to leave me breathless and in need of rest. Fortunately, Tedo was ready to take over for me, and we were all as pleased as children together enjoying the sun and fresh air. Now I was making friends with this sweet child, and it made my heart glad that he had requested my company. That afternoon, Andelon encouraged all of us to join him in bocce ball, which I had ignored as beyond comprehension my first visit. Now I would learn. Braco and I teamed against Tedo and Andelon, and though they won, I improved quickly. Braco was naturally athletic, and good at this game, as were all the men who came to visit. It was a popular sport here that could entertain for hours.

I amused Braco some more by showing my knowledge of card games, and taught them five-card draw and seven-card stub poker. The question came of how I knew these things, and I admitted I had been to Nevada's Lake Tahoe casinos a few times in my youth. But black jack had been my game of choice, and Braco revealed that he had visited a casino too in his younger days, but had only played black jack. So we teased each other about our commonality, and played with rocks as our poker chips. Andelon displayed by far the fiercest determination to win.

Then off to the water next, where I had a splash fight with my young playmate, until I was truly tuckered out, and needed a nap under an olive tree. Braco and Tedo would make their way here too at different times, so we all passed the time in wholesome fun and lounging. Dinka took care of all of our needs with snacks and refreshments, and she enjoyed the sun and conversation with a female friend who stopped by for the afternoon.

Braco and I had been filled to capacity with food in Macedonia, thanks to the generosity of our hosts, so we both asked for a light dinner. Thoughtfully, Dinka made us pasta with olives, and wholesome olive oil from the trees of the land. At dark, we packed up, and drove back into the village to the summer home. Here we waited for Detlev, who was visiting from Germany and had assisted me in the sessions with translation; and Stevo, who would cook for us here, to arrive. They called several times with car troubles, and by 10:30 pm they were still working to get to us. Braco had hired an apartment for them and Tedo, so we did not see them that night.

At the village house, we all lounged together on the large marble balcony, and spoke of our latest exploits, while Andelon took center stage. Braco had given his son Zagor comic books as a gift, which was Andelon's favorite hero. I had not heard of Zagor, but I was educated in the fact that he was a long time super hero, who Braco too loved in his childhood. Then Andelon brought out his collection of metal cavalry men on horses that Braco had collected as a boy, and given to his son. This was a special gift that Andelon would one day pass on to his own children.

It finally came time to call the night complete, and I bid my farewells, making the short journey to my flat below. It was Friday night, and the ever-popular 1980's music filled the air as a band played at a café-bar below. The acoustics in the village, banked by hills on both sides of the straights of the sea, brought that music into everyone's homes. It was an accepted part of the culture of the area. Now I was used to it, and I finally went to sleep in its dynamic sound waves.

Day 19 – Friday, July 17, 2009

Adriatic Coast

Braco would now only return to Zagreb during his time at the sea for Ivica's birthday celebration on August 4th. On this day thousands of people would come, and Srebrnjak 1 would provide food and drink for them all, along with gazing sessions for everyone throughout the day. This job required extensive planning, and the support of all who worked at the Center. But for now, life slowed down for everyone, and Braco was able to spend time with his family, and best friends.

Early as planned, Braco came to my door for our morning walk and café stops. Happily, we strolled through the streets, and headed for our waterside path. Our instant friendship had grown into something so special that I valued it beyond measure. Every action he took spoke of caring, and thoughtfulness; and his courage and commitment was unstoppable. I could not separate the man from the energy he shared, to me now they were one, or he could not do what he did so effortlessly.

Tedo, ever the gentleman, brought over extra chairs when Braco and I entered the second café to join him. And our new arrivals, Detlev and Stevo had finally turned up quite late the night before. Detlev told us about an upcoming business trip to China, and the etiquette he had to learn for his corporate meeting. He had left Braco's organization to take an executive position with a German company, and his upcoming travel was described as quite rigorous. Then a phone call came for Braco, and as he spoke, we all watched him become quite animated.

He made a very strong statement unlike anything I had heard from him before. It turned out that he was talking to Ida, his Stuttgart organizer, who was still insisting that one could not push like the Balkans in a western European country. But Braco was schooling Ida that individual feelings, and comfort zones did not matter here, because all had to be done for and given to the people. Marjana, Ida and others were being shown by Braco to rid themselves of their airs, and this was a challenging process. Braco had high hopes for Ida, he trusted and believed in her. She only needed to make a breakthrough in her social conditioning. It was obvious he was using strong language with her intentionally; he wanted to wake her up to new possibilities. This conversation would later prove to be the final straw to a very positive outcome.

We then left to go to the seaside property, and Braco, Detlev and I decided to walk from the village. Warm sunshine heated our journey along the water's edge, and as we came to the last pier before turning inland to get to Braco's seaside property, I stopped my companions. It was time for a swim, and Braco boyishly told me he would go in if I did. Detlev had some valuables with him, and was at first reluctant, but I made a pile of everything with my dress wrapped around neatly, and then dove in. Braco followed, and Detlev too decide he could not resist. The water felt like an absolutely necessary preparation for the hot walk ahead, and we chatted, and swam a short time before climbing up the docking ramp.

Opportunity quickly presented itself as Braco walked passed our pile of clothes, and stood looking out over the water. In an instant I lunged, pushing him in with delight at my success, but Detlev saw the same opportunity with me, and I found myself flying into the water too. Giving an impish smile to Braco, I quickly swam to the ramp before he could extol any reprisal. But he only laughed taking all in good spirit, and soon we were on our way once again.

At the property, we meet up with Dinka, Andelon, Tedo and Stevo, and once more needed to cool off in the inviting Adriatic. Braco and I had a conversation about people who had worked for him in the past, who began with the best of intentions, but were eventually warped by monetary greed. To Braco, I was still that baby bird on such matters. He would teach me to better see the dark sides of people's characters, not to judge but to be aware. I in exchange would teach him about my dolphin friends, and the creatures of the sea he had yet to meet. It was a desirable education for both of us.

Tedo, our transplanted Yugoslavian living now in Germany many years, was of firm interest to me next. He faithfully embodied the trustworthy qualities often rare these days in business and friendship. At our refreshment tables under prime olive trees, I found him, and asked if he would share his story of discovering Braco, and how he came to now play such a key role in Germany for the work of service. With little hesitation, he bashfully agreed, and I listened carefully, writing down all his words.

Tedo Brankovic – A Miraculous Healing

On the morning of Saturday, October 1995, my parents-in-law and Miki left to go somewhere, and were gone two or three hours. When they came back, they told me they had gone to see Braco, and I was not interested but I did not disbelieve. In April 1996, I just had a spontaneous idea, and asked my mother if she would go again, my idea was to try it. So we drove to see Braco without even knowing his schedule, and we found him and the people coming with flowers.

I had no idea why I had come. When I was called in, I first watched the people talk with Braco. [Braco was still talking to people individually at this time.] Finally, it was my turn, and I was standing in front of Braco but I did not know what to ask. Braco looked at me, and after a few minutes he began to talk. Braco said that he knew I had been working very hard my entire life, but everything kept slipping away.

I was still silent, and then I had the wish to take some of the books. Braco stopped me, chose one and gave it to me as a gift. It was his first book. I took it, and thanked him and left. And I still did not know why I was there. Then I thought about what Braco had said, and I knew it was absolutely true.

After that I came for years to all of his gazing events in Germany, accept for one time when I was far away.

My parents-in-law were running a restaurant and hosted Braco. I was always there because I always helped my parents-in-law, but I was not a part of Braco's inner circle. The first time when Braco asked me to join his team was in November 2006 for the Basel PSI World Healing Conference. Everything was organized for the Basel conference, and we arrived on a Thursday for the three-day event. On Monday, three days before, my father had passed away. I attended the funeral in Bosnia, and when it was finished on that Wednesday, I drove twelve hours back to Germany for the Basel conference.

[Tedo was Orthodox and such funerals go on for weeks, but he left because he felt he could really help people now. And this was the first time Braco had asked him for his help.]

Braco came to Kraichtal at Christmas, and again I left celebrations, my family and work for him. I had achieved everything materially, and now I only wished to serve.

During the days when Braco was still talking around 1999, I had a slipped disk between the third and forth vertebrae due to hard labor. The doctor told me that I had to have an operation, that there was no way around this. But it was very dangerous, and I was told I would not be able to do physical work anymore.

When Braco was at the restaurant at that time, I could no longer help due to this problem. So I just came to be there, and attended his sessions. Braco asked me my problem and I told him. And Braco replied that I should not worry, it would be okay. The doctors said that in ten days I must be ready for my appointment for surgery. But after several days, I began to slowly walk, and slowly got better.

I did not go to my appointment, and instead I went to my boss to ask for a job that was a little less hard labor than I did before, and I forgot about my injury. Eventually, I even took my old job back. Two years later, I had an x-ray with my doctor. The doctor compared the new x-ray with the old one of my injury. He said it was unexplainable, that my disks were perfect. My doctor asked me why I had come, and I told him it was two years since my scheduled surgery, and I wanted to see how I was. All was perfect.

[I asked Tedo how he felt about Braco and his work, and Tedo showed me that he immediately had goose bumps up and down his arms.]

What Braco is doing … it is nothing one can put into words, because there is nothing to compare it too. It is something so big and so special, what Braco is doing for the people … nothing else exists for me. I feel so indescribably honored to even be a part of this work.

After Tedo finished telling me his story, he further explained that his spine had been curved, and the healing to his spine and the disks were incomprehensible to his doctor. The doctor even stated that the x-rays should have been reversed, that it was impossible to see a spine fixed in this way, and the new x-ray should have been before his injury, not afterwards. With sincere humility, Tedo spoke more of his love of Braco, and his respect for all that was being brought to humanity through the gift of this exceptional man. I could see clearly that Tedo would do anything to help Braco, no matter the challenge or hardship.

In the afternoon, Braco's mother, Ivanka, arrived and joined us for more sun, while we played cards and bocce ball games with Andelon for hours. Stevo was our chef for the evening meal, and he spoiled us with a wide array of local flavors. Dinka, Ivanka and I partook in a nice glass of red wine, and Tedo and Detlev joined us. Pleasant conversations and some innocent joking ensued. After the dinner, to help digest our big meal, Braco, his son and mother, Detlev and I walked back to town on our 40-minute hike. Braco translated so I could talk with his mother, who was always so gentle, soft-spoken and kind, and she told me about the things she loved most, including of course swimming for hours, flowers and her son.

On one of my previous walks on this gravel road alone, I had seen three big foxes on the path in front of me, and so Andelon was on the look out with the hope of seeing them too. Not ever tiring of each other's company, and with an ever-steady flow of light and sometimes deeply thoughtful conversations, we decided to gather one last time in the late evening at another outdoor café below Braco's home. So Ivanka departed for her own home a few blocks away to change. Detlev too went to his apartment. Braco, his son and I headed up the steep alleyway of stairs to his house to shower and change before our last stop for espresso and kugels of ice cream.

At 11 pm, everyone looked fresh and bright from the relaxing and nourishing day, and we all took seats around several small tables that we joined together. Andelon never seemed to tire, and could keep up with the adults in the late hours. He was vibrant and happy, and even more so when Dinko showed up with his own son, only a few years older. Dinko was now on his vacation time, and he also owned a summerhouse nearby, and was here with his family. Not only did everyone work together, but they also embodied a harmony and brotherhood that was stable and true. Everyone was so present in life and expressed their love in countless ways. Only after much more festive and effortless conversation, and with our sweet tooth satisfied, did we finally bring our evening to a close.

Chapter 15

Day 20 – Saturday, July18, 2009

Adriatic Coast

Our morning walk was peaceful and contemplative, and after Braco and I had our first café stop alone together, we joined the others at the Café Light. Detlev's short foray into our idyllic world would end after today, since he had to leave in the early morning hours of the next day. I could see that he clearly would have liked to stay with us in our special circle with Braco, but his business responsibilities were calling him back to work, and soon to China. At the café, the man who built all of the beautiful stonewalls around Braco's seaside property joined us. He was a physically strong and robust man, and yet watching him, I could see that he was actually very empathic, and talked with deep feeling in his words.

It was his time in life to relax now on the Adriatic, but he had worked extremely hard for thirty years. On Braco's land, he had worked for over a year, for ten hours straight a day, to finish all the walls he created. For him, the stones were alive and like a true artisan, he felt the stone. His work was absolutely exquisite, and so carefully crafted with love and a sense of pride in his work. Here was a man who knew he had proven himself in life; and now he was offering to take Braco and I into the rocky hills, to find those plants that were wild crafted and deliciously edible. A meal of such plants sounded completely inspired, and I was ready to agree until Braco reminded me there would be no time. So we decided to plan such an excursion for my next visit.

Stevo quietly sat and watched our exchange. I dearly liked Stevo because he had such a simple grace, and kindness to him. He really cared about people, and he had often done little things over the weeks to make me more comfortable in all ways. He also felt deeply and fully; it was a common trait in all the men who worked closely with Braco. When our stone master left, I encouraged Stevo to tell me about coming to be the chef at Srebrnjak 1, and he shared his short story as I wrote away in my red notebook.

Stevo Pernjek – Cooking for Braco

My younger sister told me of Braco in 2001. She explained to me briefly what Braco did, and showed me a picture of him. I was a little surprised that my 19 year old sister would visit a healer – what kind of problems could she have? Seven or eight months later I decided to see Braco. I do not remember what I asked or what Braco told me, I only remember a beautiful feeling like I could fly. I did not have a special problem. I continued to come only because of this special feeling, and I would usually come two times a month - once to Slovenia and once to Zagreb, or at least once a month.

One day Braco was talking with Branko, and expressed a desire to have a professional cook. Braco knew me, and told Branko to call me to come to work for him. I recognized the phone number from Srebrnjak 1 on my phone, and I was scared to answer at first. But I did, and Branko told me to come over and I did. Braco then spoke with me, and invited me to come and work for him in January 2007.

At the time, I was living in Porec, and I told him that I had a wife and two daughters, and I had to think about it. Braco told me there was nothing to think about, he would pay me the same salary as at the hotel I was working at, and he said I could sell my flat and move to Zagreb. Without thinking, I said 'yes', and one year ago I sold my old flat, and now have a beautiful apartment in Zagreb.

[Braco remarked at this point that Stevo knew exactly what people liked, and took care of everything quietly, as if he was not there. He was there now 2 ½ years, and Braco loved how he tranquilly took care of everything, always making the right amount.]

I heard of many stories of healings from people in my town through the years. I think it is beautiful that Braco can help the people step more easily through life. I appreciate the simple beauties. Braco is a very simple man compared with the doctors and lawyers and others who came to the restaurant I used to work at, and this appeals to me. At first, I went crazy when Braco would ask for such simple things as milk and honey, or boiled chicken. I wanted to show my talent. But now I am happy to make Braco happy, and I cook special dishes for the others there.

Now my family comes regularly, and supports the work in every way. They feel that same happiness. If problems appear, they come, but they usually just come because of the energy and the beautiful experience.

Island of Murter

On that day, Braco had made special plans to take me to a new beach and town on another nearby island. So we left our morning café, and headed back to his house to prepare. Tedo, Detlev and Stevo joined Braco, his family and I on this special excursion. We packed our beach and swim gear, and were off along the coast. All the Italian-style white villa homes rose from the banks of the sea, and the scenes flowed one beauty into another against the turquoise water. After perhaps fifteen minutes, we turned into a town and pulled up to a popular beach area. Here a water slide, and vendor stands abounded, with outdoor restaurants, and loud music playing from sound systems. We walked to a sand beach absolutely covered with people enjoying the sun and atmosphere.

After the quiet of the coastal village and Braco's secluded property, this area overwhelmed my senses. Unexpectedly, I felt a strong disappointment inside that I could not explain, and did not understand. The beach was very commercial, and although we were able to walk on a path along the sea to a less crowded place on the large stone boulders that comprised that side of the beach, a myriad of campers, cars and people ever present made me feel terribly unhappy inside. It was as if I would lose my precious haven for a day in this cacophony of noise and bustle, and all sense of pleasure left me.

What I did not recognize yet was that the conflict in me was between my exquisite experience in Macedonia, during the last gazing session, and my encounter with a facet of reality that embodied the humanly contrived material world. That spiritual grace was clashing with the course constructs of this pretty, but highly commercial beach area. Yet because I did not grasp my inner battle, I was left blindly looking for the source of my disquiet, and I attempted to intellectually attribute it to the crowds and noise. This further led me into irrational thought, and I grew angry at being brought to this place.

Oddly, I just could not connect with the loveliness all around us through the artisanship of nature. Even my joy of adventures in new surroundings was not stirred. Alarmed, I watched myself become withdrawn, and I felt helpless to stop it. Awkwardly enduring something that was meant to be a fun-filled change of scenery specially planned by Braco, I kept searching to resolve the point of my distress, which I knew was an overreaction. After distancing myself from everyone, I finally made myself get into the water for a swim, yet was back in twenty minutes completely unimpressed with the magnificent stone seascape beneath me.

Then I had a finale to my inner war. While I was swimming, Braco had gone with Andelon to retrieve some food, and while everyone was eating savory type fillings wrapped in flat bread, on my towel was a type of flat bread covered with powdered sugar and chocolate sauce. Everyone looked at me expectantly and I ignored it at first, but then a swell of anger rose in me, and I took it and flung it into the ocean. Unreasonably, it represented to me everything that disturbed me about this place.

Everyone looked shocked; Braco looked almost hurt, and Dinka asked me why I had thrown it into the ocean. I merely answered that the fish could have it, and I went for a walk to find something without sugar to eat. Still angry, I could not understand my chaos of emotions. Only later would I recognize it as the ultimate challenge within between the spiritual and the seemingly artificial. Braco had led me home again through the energy, and everything within me was crying to be with that again fully. But this environment made me feel a million miles away from it. Somehow, that magic bubble had burst, and I was catapulted from one end of the spectrum to the opposite end, at least in my senses temporarily. This experience then turned into a great gift, because only the recognition of this could help me heal this wound of perception.

Separation was the great illusion, because the Source of all things was ever present in *all things*. It was only a perspective away, and Braco was actually weaving the spiritual and material together without denying any facet in life, even the contrived and man-made; he simply did not judge, all was equal. This afternoon excursion was revealing to me my own judgment of life, which was the viewpoint of slumbering consciousness, and it in fact was keeping me from the very thing I wished. Braco knew the energy was everywhere, was everything, and now I had to know this much deeper than intellectually too in order to move forward to fulfill my wish. I had to feel it honestly, not merely think it and in doing so, a door would open for the energy to be present in any situation or any environment. This was the synthesis of the material world with spirit.

We stayed several hours sunning and swimming before we packed up, and I was so glad to leave since I still did not understand my turmoil yet. Tedo, Detlev and Stevo drove in the van, while I took the back seat of Braco's car with Andelon. Once we approached our village, all traffic stopped and I found out that the drawbridge was up for 25 more minutes, and we all had to wait. The heat was still intense from the day, and so I stepped out and Braco did too, and walked with Andelon to watch fish along the water's edge. Without thinking that pedestrians, as well as cars, could not get to the other side of town, I began to walk toward the bridge.

I walked past Braco, and he finally stopped me and asked what was wrong. But I could not answer; I did not understand and tears came to my eyes. I instead asked why he had brought me to such a place and he should have known I would not enjoy it. Then he told me that Andelon had not wished to go, he wanted to stay at the property seaside. But Braco had told him it was for me, so I would have something new to experience, and not be bored in the same place again. He also explained that he had spent considerable time finding a cafe that could make the special dessert for me with a nut filling, and the same chocolate sauce I liked to order to top my cappuccinos. All of these things had been done in love for me and I was speechless. I felt absolutely stupid inside.

Tears rolled down my face as I told him that I did not understand myself what was wrong. Yet he did not get hurt or angry, he only encouraged me to communicate right away if ever something upset me. He wanted to make sure that nothing would come between us, and now I understood completely why he had stated this same thing once before. Gently, Braco hugged me, and I hugged him back with gratitude. My day had been arranged in love, and now I saw that love flowed through all things if we could see underneath our sleeping illusion. This was why all my pains and sorrows had simply dissolved in the presence of that ultimate experience of union in Macedonia. In those moments, the feeling of pure joy and oneness was complete. But the next leg of the journey was to learn to reawaken this feeling at will, much like Braco did for the gazing. It was to find a mastery of self that could transform the pains and sorrows of the moment back into light, to their *real* value, without getting caught on the surface level of appearances.

My job ahead was no less than learning to *see* again, to see the love and light present everywhere, within everyone, to truly see the equality of all things. Braco had used the simply analogy of the baby bird that first must breath, then see, then touch. What I had taken initially to be whimsical was proving to be magnificently profound. So my journey now embodied that first phase, but I knew after I completed my twenty-one days and left, my next return to Braco's side would begin the second phase, the real *seeing* of life, and the penetration below the surface world that I would only later describe and share in another book.

No one judged me for my mood or behavior that day, no one mentioned it at any time. They only smiled with me when I was smiling once again, and back to my real self. Braco informed me that we would have a special meal that night in a small town near the city of Split. Once again, it was planned with love. So, I walked back to the house, since the bridge was now rising, and this gave me an opportunity to clear my senses. Braco had informed me that we would leave in a little while, and I had time to shower and change. Quickly I found my inner clarity again, and by the time the water hit me, I was fully revived.

I enjoyed taking special care to look pretty that evening, and was the first to appear, so I sat on a porch swing and waited for the others. Braco came out next and we smiled at each other, and my heart was joyous again. He wondered why, since I had something so pleasant in Hawaii, that I would want to join this work? Perhaps like with Atanas and his family, he questioned if he would only bring me sweet pain. But for me, there was no turning back no matter what was to come, and I plainly emphasized this fact. I did not explain the depth from which my answer came, I only insisted I would proceed forward. It was enough, and he sincerely looked happy at my answer. And I knew when barriers came, so would breakthroughs.

That evening, Braco would get another call from Ida. She had finally had her leap forward; the great breakthrough, and she recognized the truth of Braco's words about strength and leadership. Now she expressed her great enthusiasm to build more events to bring Braco to more people in Germany. Braco was absolutely delighted at the change in the tides, and Ida's new won confidence. He would support her in all way in the times ahead to achieve success, and I think he now saw her as one of his strongest organizers. Ida was a woman of determination and courage, and she would work as hard as was required to accomplish a job well done. At dinner, all of us joined in the new joy of a worthy advance.

Near Split, we came to an exquisite town of elegant charm, palm trees and a great courtyard filled with people and tourist shops. Local seashells, pearls and sea sponges abounded at outdoor vendors. We all strolled along the water before finding a restaurant that appealed to everyone, and when we were seated I was told that tourism here in this town was so diminished that now we could sit immediately, when in the past we would have had to wait at least an hour. All along the Adriatic, businesses were suffering because tourism was down everywhere as people decided to save money, and vacation closer to home.

Andelon was in ever-high spirits, as was our whole group as we ordered our meals. Many at our table had a local fresh caught squid, including Braco. After he finished his plate, I offered him the remaining half of my serving of gnocchi in a Gorgonzola sauce, since he had told me I had picked his favorite. Although he refused at first, he later appropriated the plate and finished it off. After our meal was complete, we were standing in front of the restaurant awaiting everyone to leave the table.

With Tedo, Stevo, Detlev and I present, Braco unbuttoned the top button of his pants and smiled at how much he had eaten, stating that he never had so much, and jokingly inferred it was I who had brought out this behavior. He was in the process of undoing another button, with his hands under his shirt, when a couple in their 50's stopped in front of him. They recognized Braco and reached to shake his hand, glowing with happiness as they expressed their love before departing. We all burst into laughter after they left, and Braco made fun of himself, lifting his shirt for our whole group to show the undone buttons, while making an exclamation, and remarking what they must think. He did this with a straight face, and it only encouraged us to laugh more.

After that, we walked for an hour to prepare ourselves for ice cream later, and ended up in an outdoor arcade playing rounds of pool, foosball and air hockey with Andelon. It was an excellent hour spent, and by the end we were ready for our ice cream kugels. Once we were all provided for, we finished walking the boulevard, and headed home. Our evening was as pleasant, and relaxing as any vacation could be and I was glad to wish Detlev a good trip to China after we had all been so well nourished.

Day 21 – Sunday, July 19, 2009

Adriatic Coast

Today would be our last morning walk along that rocky shore of the vibrant blue-green waters of the Croatian Adriatic coastline together, and Braco's strong presence surrounded me. We spoke together like life long friends, and I knew our bond was one of unfolding meaning in the future ahead. The time was arriving for Braco's departure from Europe to embark on new levels with his mission, and I had been given a glimpse of my own role. We stopped to buy fresh bananas and croissants before sitting down at our favorite café, and he began to talk about how all people must come to treat each other as they did naturally initially, the very first time meeting; with respect, openness and kindness. It was important that people would not change that initial open attitude, even as those around them changed. We all could come to learn to see other's flaws without judging them, or feeling personally offended by such things. I duly noted that the song, *Living on a Prayer* by Bon Jovi, filled the air loudly during our discussion of this topic, and smiled to myself.

We also embarked on the topic of destinies and roles in life once again, and Braco illustrated a point with his own wife, Dinka, whose role in this life was to take care of their son. He could often not be present because of his demanding work schedule and time on the road, but she naturally and joyfully fulfilled this clear responsibility. For Braco's destiny, he himself would not have developed the power of the gaze without having met Ivica. In fact, he would have quit the mission many times due to the difficulties and demands of this service, but because of his dear friend, he had made his pledge. In this he honored Ivica; and he knew if he stopped all Ivica had done, the foundation he built, would be lost.

Braco would never allow that to happen, and I felt that he would freely give his life itself to ensure the continuation of the work.

On my second day with Braco, he had given me my radiant gold sun necklace. It vibrantly embodied the energy he brought fourth, and it was extremely important to me for many obvious reasons. I expressed my concern about wearing it swimming in the ocean, since the waters had claimed many of my prize necklaces, but he encouraged me to always wear it and not to worry. He would replace it if ever it was lost, and that was the nature of his ever-generous spirit.

After all the many private conversations we had, I understood that Braco could see far beyond what others saw, especially in people. Even those things that people tried to hide were obvious to him, and yet Braco was always kind and tolerant. He would allow them to stay near despite their flaws, and this was another endowment he passed onto me. I realized that I had only accepted flaws in people up to a certain point before distancing myself, but his example demonstrated the path to a greater loving way that would allow everyone, despite their shortcomings, to still be treated equally.

Unexpectedly, Viktor came over to our table and greeted us. He had been in Zagreb for over a week tending his gardens there. Thoughtfully, he presented me with a bag of pears he picked from his own orchard, and he told me they were for Andelon and myself. I took one and ate it, and I could feel the love that filled the fruit from his care. Anyone was capable of bringing their love to the land, and to their gardens, and my affection and admiration for him allowed me to value his loving energy in that pear even more. After a short visit, Braco's father took his leave and would join us again that evening for dinner. I was so happy I would see him one more time, and have an opportunity to have a proper good-bye with him and Ivanka.

That morning, I had wished with all my heart not to be sad today, and the universe had answered me in kindness by filling me with a sense of inspired purpose, which delivered the bright happiness of determination through it. The deepest sense of loss; of the companionship of a man who exemplified the integration of the spiritual and material so effortlessly, who mysteriously brought forth the great energy of miracles; and who had created such a loving spiritual family around himself, this loss did hover before me. Yet my new won strength did not allow me to be crushed or helpless. I would leave to create for the mission, and return with the satisfactions of a greater progress. Gladly, I would follow the spontaneity of the energy to show me my own destiny, which Braco had set free to fly.

Stevo and Tedo met us at the Café Light and more plans were discussed for Hawaii. It was decided that a film would be made of Braco in the islands, and I promised breathtaking backdrops to make the film burst with the beauties of nature. Shortly, Stevo received a phone call from Dinko; he had the bad news that his car had major problems, and he could not make his scheduled shifts at Srebrnjak 1 for two days. Because of the vacation season, this would leave all the presentations on the shoulders of Rudi alone, and this made Braco unhappy. If Rudi were to have something unexpected happen, there would be no one else, and this situation was not acceptable to him. He would drive people when needed to overcome their problems to meet the demands of the work, no matter the situation. I did not know how this was resolved, but Braco's concern about the people who came to him was again brought center stage.

That morning we also decided to try something new with Braco, since now he had a video camera set up on his computer at Srebrnjak 1, to speak to me live via Skype. We had tossed around the idea of performing a remote gazing session with Braco in Zagreb, and myself in Hawaii. I would try it first, and if I felt the energy this way, I would invite some local people to try the experience and gather their input. So we set a date for our first trial on the night before Ivica's birthday celebration on August 4th. This was a wonderful prospect, because now I would get to experience Braco's energy again in the long months ahead, and so already the blow of our parting was benevolently softened.

Next I left our group to go to a local Internet café to put more of our plans of the morning into motion. Quickly and efficiently, I sent off emails to friends in Hong Kong, Japan, Canada and Australia who could possibly help with the work of bringing Braco to new countries. Hopeful ideas set new creations in flight, and I was so excited to tell friends far and wide of potentials and possibilities with Braco. Once done, I closed my computer and set off to walk to the seaside property with a bounce in my step.

Ivan, Nikica and a woman named Miranda, a bright young dentist I met in Trogir, were newly arrived; and we all partook in the fine cheeses Nikica once again brought, along with grapes and homemade bread. From this came a request from Andelon for cards, and the next hour was spent in competitive play as we were given ten rocks each to make our poker bets. Yet it was not long before Nikica and Tedo ran out of betting rocks, so they used cigarettes in the stakes pot. Soon others, including myself ran out for the kitty, but having no cigarettes my sunglasses became my wager. Andelon in the end lost his shirt, shorts and shoes to Nikica, while my only sunglasses went as spoils to Ivan. It was convenient that some clouds loomed overhead at that time, because Ivan and Nikica would not sneak each of us back our lost prizes until the end of that day.

Afterwards, Braco and I talked about the recording of him speaking, played for groups when he was away on tour, or in this case on vacation. People simply referred to this type of Braco session as *the Voice*. I expressed my regret that I had not experienced this important aspect of the work, and Braco immediately had an idea. He had booked an air ticket for me from a local airport, flying me into Zagreb for tomorrow, to connect me to my afternoon flight to Barcelona. Now he decided he would cancel this flight, and instead have Tedo drive me to Srebrnjak 1 early the next morning at 4:15 am, so that I could experience *the Voice* with three groups before departing for my afternoon flight out of Zagreb.

I knew that this was an experience I could not miss, and all was spontaneously agreed upon between us. Braco immediately was on the phone to Damir to cancel my flight, which brought my departure from the coast a half day earlier. That was the only moment that day that a pain of separation filled me, and I momentarily froze in its intensity. Yet gratefully, I was able to pull myself back swiftly, and turn my attention to Miranda. She was a friend of Braco's for many years, and spoke so highly of *the Voice* experience that I decided to make her my final interview. As a person, Miranda was sincere and open, and as a doctor her assessments would make a valuable contribution. I directed her to a private spot and we began.

Miranda – The importance of Wishes

A. Miranda, could you start by telling me what first brought you to Braco?

M. It was January 31, 2000; I was nearly finished with my university, and for a long time I was looking for something to fill me up, fill up my soul. I was looking for something that would bring meaning to my life. I had everything you know, while studying there were no problems, but while I was mature in my head as a person, I was looking for something to help me to become myself. A person told me about Braco and I said okay, I would go and see. I came to him one morning - it was Monday. It was very strange to me.

A. Was this at Srebrnjak 1 that you came to see him?

M. Yes, it was at Srebrnjak 1 at six o'clock in the morning, and I was so excited to meet him. And when I came to him I had no specific problem, you know. He told me some things and I said to him, okay, so we will meet again. I will visit you. And then I started my life. I needed to finish my university, I needed to find a job, and it was very difficult to start a new life. When you finish something, then you need to take one step to go into life. And he helped me to find a job.

A. When you met him for the first time at Srebrnjak 1, you came to him and you didn't have a specific problem like so many people, you were looking for something spiritual …

M. Yes, I was looking. But the first thing I asked him about is love, because I thought that this is what I'm missing in my life.

A. And did he tell you something … [Braco was still talking with people individually until 2003.]

M. He said I don't see you here, I see you in a big city, you will live in a big city. And that was it. Then I went again in April, and when I read his first book everything opened for me. It was the book, *The Awakening*. And during one period, I was coming every seven days, during another every fourteen days. I was getting a book and reading. It was filling me up.

A. What is your age at this point? You are just finishing university …

M. I was 23 years old.

A. That is really young for someone on a spiritual quest.

M. I was trying to find something in my religion, you know. But I didn't find it, and then I was maturing myself; problems in my family, relationships, my mother's health, everything was going bad. Challenging.

A. So you started coming to Braco even once a week.

M. Yes, once a week on a regular basis. I went to his wedding. He helped me to find a job. Whenever I finished one year with a job, he helped me to find another job, and I found myself going to Srebrnjak 1. I think I am becoming a better person. It's been my way of life.

A. Do you feel that since the time you met Braco that he changed your outlook in ways to help you in life?

M. Yes, yes, I wouldn't be the person that I am now if I hadn't met him.

A. What kind of person did he help you to become?

M. I became open. I didn't measure people by money, by look, by religion. He taught me how to look at every person as equal. But I'm choosing which person I will be with. He was teaching the basic needs that everyone requires, what must be met. When I look at you; I don't care if you are from America, some place in Hawaii or some village. He taught me to do this and I am grateful for it.

A. So now you have known him for almost nine years. And you still come here to Srebrnjak 1 now and again?

M. Now I don't live in Zagreb anymore, I live in Split, so I come once a month. The longest period I haven't gone is three months. I try to go once a month, and I'm going to sessions with *the Voice*. When I have some problems, when I want to let my business go, I go there and listen and everything opens up. I think that I am richer spiritually, in material as a person.

A. Have you noticed anything about other people that you know who go to Braco, who changed in some way?

M. Yes, my mother, my brother, my sister, they have come with health problems, in relationships with their partners, everything was going bad. My mother had some pain in her shoulder, and I didn't think about it. I said she was an old lady and it would go away. But it was a cold pain all the time, and doctors didn't know what it was. And one Saturday I was in Srebrnjak 1, I don't know why I thought about my mother and about that pain. And in a few days, I was back in Split and my mother told me that there was no pain, and it never came back. Before she couldn't walk, you know everyday there was this cold pain, and doctors didn't know what it was. After that, the pain never came back.

A. That's a beautiful story. You were just thinking of her?

M. I was just thinking of her during a session with *the Voice*. I didn't think the way most people think - it must be, it must be. I was just thinking, okay, I wish that my mother doesn't have that pain anymore and it goes away.

A. I've noticed Miranda that people around Braco wish for things. It's not as aggressive as when you really want to try and make something happen. It's much lighter. Like when we wish as children. I see so many stories of people who say I just wished it and it happened.

M. Yes, yes, yes, when we try to take it aggressively, it doesn't come because it's not natural. But I think Braco brings us to basic feelings in ourselves so we don't have to be aggressive - I must this, I must that, I must that! When we are basic in ourselves about feelings, about everything, then it flows. We let it go. When you let it go, it will just come out. That's why I'm happy in my life that I met Braco, and that I know that feeling. And that feeling I was looking for in my life.

A. People I've interviewed who go to Braco regularly; I've noticed with many of them there is this light inside their eyes. There is this strength and I can see it so clearly, and it's a strength that

*looks like it does not diminish, it doesn't lessen. Do you feel
something like that inside yourself?*

M. Yes, I have a lot of people around me who don't know
about Braco. And when I'm returning from Srebrnjak 1, and
my friends don't know that I visited, you know what they say
to me? Oh Miranda, you look very beautiful, what has
happened to you? You know there is something in your eyes.
Every time when I go to Srebrnjak 1, lately it's on Saturday,
and I go to drink coffee afterwards, and they say to me you
look very beautiful. I think that something, that light - I can
bring it to other people. Something in myself, I'm not
trying, you know. I tell people with problems of Braco and I
tell them about Srebrnjak 1. They come away very satisfied,
and they are very happy. Everyone who listens to his *Voice*;
one can feel a release, that something when we are like
children that happens.

*A. Now I've noticed that some people think that if you go to
Braco, he will take all your problems away. And of course in life
you never will be without problems, or challenges. It's just life, but
what I see is that this light that he brings out in people, however
that happens, it gives people a greater strength so that when they
face problems they are different.*

M. I am a doctor and I think that every problem, especially
medical problems - I don't have a medical problem - but I
think he can solve them. That's my confession and I think
that nothing can change my confession.

*A. Besides your mother with her shoulder pain, have you heard of
other stories of people who had physical illnesses?*

M. Yes, my sister had some spots on her legs, and the doctor
didn't know the cause. The doctor told her to remove the
amalgam fillings from her teeth; maybe it was the amalgam

in her mouth. It was very strange, and I was studying in Zagreb and I said, okay, you must go to Braco because your health is not good; your husband is also not good in health. And the first time she went to Braco, it went away. Just like that. She was living with her husband's mother and father, and she didn't have her own place, but everything worked out - she bought a place, an apartment. Then children came. Her situation in life changed. She is very satisfied now with her life.

A. What do you see as Braco's role in the world? Right now he is visiting and accepted in parts of Europe. There are several countries that he travels to regularly, but do you think he has a bigger role to play?

M. Yes, he must have a bigger role, Europe is a local thing. More must be prepared for him because he has so much strength, and I want all people to meet him, because only meeting or hearing him - I think something will improve. People then will know when they have a problem or something, they will know that they can go to Srebrnjak 1, to Austria, to Hawaii, I know these people will have a place to go at some particular place.

A. So you'd like to see Braco traveling more, and the Voice set up in more locations?

M. Yes, yes, yes I would like this because *the Voice* is something beautiful, and it gives so much strength in people, and it's intimate because I think every person must hear Braco, and his voice is something spiritual. You know just listening, your mind is changing, and I want that people in Hawaii and Japan to hear about Braco. Because I think he has so much strength within himself that he can bring it to all the people. I think that he is number one in my opinion.

A. I would agree with you. With everything I've seen, from all the people I've met, I would put him at number one too.

M. Yes, I didn't have a physical need before I met Braco; I had a need to see those who were giving people something spiritual. Now that I met Braco, I respect everyone, but Braco is number one. You know, okay, I respect everyone - *you are great* - but I think that Braco is number one. I think that when he goes to the world, to other continents, that he will have more and more strength. That he will give more to people, that is what I think.

A. I think that's the way it works too.

M. He must because I think he needs to have a bigger stage for all people. I think it's a new evolution that we must have. Ok, in the world there are lots of material things that have limits - money, destruction, in everything. Now is the time for people to take care of their soul, and to seek a little bit and to say, okay, I have found something; and I'm good and I'm satisfied. I think people need to be satisfied now, that they we are not running for money, or something like that.

A. He in a way is delivering that very thing you were looking for, that more spiritual life integrated into this more regular life that we live.

M. Yes, you must live, you must work, you must travel; he takes us inside ourselves and into what we are based. That's what I'm thinking about him, you know. I didn't have many problems when I came to Braco at first, but he helped me when the problems came, while I was becoming a person. I was a person, okay, I was studying ... but I needed to take in life. He helped me at a very good moment, helped me to become what I am now. I'm not completed, but he helps me every time I go to Srebrnjak 1. I see an evolution taking place inside myself and everyday working. I work with a lot of patients, and my patients say to me that I am so calm, and they feel so relaxed with me. But I'm a dentist you know, people are not relaxed with dentists. So I think he helped me in that.

A. That's beautiful because I've seen that so many people come, not just with the severe illnesses, but I've seen so many people say they just come because they feel better from the energy. They don't have a specific problem. They feel better in life after they leave Srebrnjak 1 or wherever they've seen Braco.

M. And I'm very happy when I see a lot of young people. You know, I think that *that* is the mission for people, and the children of those people are coming, so the generations will be better. Some problems will go away for that generation, so this world will be better.

A. When we went to Macedonia, the very last group was of about 250 people, and I would say that half were in their twenties and thirties. It was amazing to see girls, these young woman hugging each other, and really feeling the energy. And you just knew looking at their faces that they were going to take that energy out into the world and do something with it.

M. I told you, when I go to Srebrnjak 1, people see changes in me, they see it changes me! So I need just that - changing myself every day. In life, some days I'm better, some days I'm not so good, but I'm trying to be better in the ways that I can. So that's it.

A. Thank you so much Miranda.

After the interview with Miranda was complete, it was more apparent than ever that the universe had delivered the perfect ending for my trip with my own upcoming experience of *the Voice* of Braco expressing loving words about life, our inner spark and the energy. Once Braco left Europe, travel demands would escalate to their natural limits, and so *the Voice* could become his legacy here to help the people without limitations. A divine hand was unfolding the path here in the most unexpected of ways.

Braco's parents joined us for dinner that night, and I was so joyous because their graciousness and sweetness made me feel a part of a new family. Here I watched too Braco's son raised with such nourishment and wholesomeness, and his carefree play reminded me the days of long ago when the world was simpler and more innocent. Here there were no computers or television to baby-sit or entertain, instead there was a father who fully lived his precious time with his son; swimming, playing bocce ball, soccer and so many games while they talked together meaningfully.

The bond between father and son was deep, as it was with Dinka too who exhibited all the patience and care of a mother at peace with herself, and with a bounty of love to share. I cherished the intimacy I was so generously allowed to experience, of a reality very foreign to me in so many ways. Braco was a complete man, balanced and sincere in his appreciation of the simple joys of life. He was not a man to lecture and promote unobtainable ideals, but a man who demonstrated a path of integrity and a great awareness. Without veils and illusions, he saw things as they were, and accepted them with patience and kindness, and with strength and boldness when the work called out its demands.

Penetratingly, Braco would see people's shortcomings and goodness better than they realized it in themselves, and yet he would treat people with an enduring equality. Through his own relationships, he forged the path forward to display a tangible and accessible way – one that everyone could benefit from by emulating. That dinner was filled with good will, camaraderie and love. Stevo's cooking even reflected this care too, as he fed us marvelous dishes meant to please us. I sat next to Ivanka, and we exchanged smiles often that spoke the feelings in our hearts, no words were necessary.

Our dinner came to its natural finish, and we went back to town for a final gathering at the café below Braco's home. The seaside village was filled with hospitable charm, and we drank espressos and wine in the music filled air. Ivanka was feeling the pain of my leaving, and asked me, through Braco, if I was feeling the same. I looked at her and expressed that if I gave into my sadness, I would never stop crying. Here Braco teased me by communicating my heartfelt words to his mother, yet telling me that he told her I was unaffected. I strongly wagged my finger at him for his antics, and he delighted in a merry game of keeping me guessing on the accuracy of his translation. But I knew him well enough to know that he understood and honored our feelings, and was lightening the atmosphere to help us.

Finally we all rose from our tables, and Ivanka began to cry as she embraced me. It was difficult for me not to join her, and I hugged her dearly. Viktor then shyly bid me his kindhearted farewell. Tedo too called it a night, since he would be up at 3:30 am to prepare to take me to Zagreb. The rest of us decided to take a final stroll together through the town, and along the water's edge, as Braco told me of his nights as a child under the stars. At some point then, I saw the biggest shooting star imaginable, like a comet streaking across the horizon. It was my parting sign of confirmation of things to come.

Once again at the house, it was now the early morning hours, and I said my farewell to Dinka and Andelon. To Dinka I expressed my gratitude for her thoughtfulness and generous hospitality that made me feel like a part of this special family. To Andelon, who was bashful with partings, I thanked for all the good games and fun with a handshake. I wanted to express so much to Braco, but there were no words really to say what I felt. It would be a final gift from him that he woke up at my 4:15 am departure. With Tedo at our sides, we hugged our last goodbye, and it was enough. I was happy for this last kindness. My twenty-one days were complete, and now only Srebrnjak 1 and *the Voice* of Braco would place the finishing touch on my journey.

EPILOGUE

The Voice

At Srebrnjak 1, Branko, Rudi, Sead, Stevo, Pero and the others working that day happily greeted Tedo and I. Branko and Rudi were first to see me, and their genuine smiles and warm hugs displayed the kindred spirit within the relationship we had built over the 21 days together. Without delay, I was brought into that vitally alive kitchen on the second floor with music playing, where Stevo was already serving European-style crepes for breakfast. As soon as I sat down, he thoughtfully offered me a cup of my favorite green tea, and one of Braco's cigarettes. I was charmed by this simple act of care; and though I at first refused the cigarette, he would offer again and I accepted for nostalgia sake. Since Sead and Rudi spoke English, they each assisted me that morning with communications. Shortly after I finished off several crepes filled with local honey or jam, it was already time for the first group I would join.

Branko was my escort and he led me to the great wooden doors at the front of the Center, where a group was ready to go into the onyx room. The size of the group was similar to the previous days I had witnessed with Braco present, so I immediately took note that people honored and respected this form of the work without reserve. I found this exceptional that so many people were able to overcome the limited value of the five senses alone, and be open to the idea that a recording of Braco's voice was in fact a powerful conduit for the Source energy too. For a Western mind, this was a mystery unfathomable, but yet people here in great number trusted and believed despite this mystery and benefited immensely as a consequence. As always, some carried pictures of loved ones, along with the flowers they would take home from this experience. Once the doors were open, those of the staff of Srebrnjak 1 led the people as they filed in to stand in rows, and then took their places on each side of the group. Attentively, they watched in case anyone needed assistance since the energy could sometimes overwhelm individuals.

So far, everything was the same as when Braco himself would walk out on stage, and Rudi stepped in front of the group to make a very brief introduction. I did not really have any expectations, and I did not know what my experience would be. Miranda's account of the importance, and impact of *the Voice* recording of Braco speaking in Croatian loving words certainly made me excited and curious at all levels. Of course I could not understand the Croatian words, a language I still found mystifying, but I had been directed by Detlev that this would not matter, the importance in all sessions with Braco was to hold an open heart and to simply feel.

Then that special music that was always played during Braco's gazing sessions began, and his familiar, grounded voice spoke to the people. As I stood amongst the others, I slowly began to feel a quietness come over me, and gentle energy flowing all around my body. That morning I was feeling a tangible nervousness about leaving, about the loss of that bubble of energy that I experienced around me because of Braco's consciousness. But now my mind stilled, and found rest as I was brought into a space of gentle and natural expansion.

This first time was completely soothing and relaxing, and it brought the comfort I dearly needed inside, for I was about to fly away from the man who had not only given me back my dreams and strength, and reconnected me with the Source of oneness I had searched for my whole life, but one whose company I treasured beyond words. It was clear to me that the gift of Braco's energy carried through his words, his voice even as a recording, could affect the body and more. I had come in with a preference for Braco's physical presence, but I left knowing it was not actually necessary to help and reach the people. And this was an important direct validation.

A second group would follow within the hour, and once again Branko guided me down at the appropriate time and I took my place with the people. As Braco's voice began, I had an image in my mind's eye of standing before all of the work ahead of me, uncertainties of the future, changes that would take place in my life upon my return and more. Mentally, this seemed like such a great mountain, but the energy flowed across everything before me, delivering again a peace that connected all the appropriate possibilities. Spontaneously, I felt an intimate trust arise in me for all that would come. It was wonderful and uplifting, and I bounced out of that second session with the sense of being able to fly.

It was another direct experience of confirmation that the energy was vitally alive, and active through this means. This meant that Braco in time could reach vast numbers of people with the gift of the energy, and it was potent enough that it would benefit the many. Finally, for the third session, once it began, I felt warm energy going through me, especially in my midsection, and I felt a wish rise out of me for robust digestion again. During those minutes that Braco's voice played, I felt certain this gift was granted, and it no longer mattered what had led to my condition of delicacy in this area, I only knew a healing was taking place within me, of that I was certain.

After the music and words ended, Rudi introduced me to the group, and I received more well wishes for my journey home. As the group exited, a woman approached me and spoke in English with a thick Balkans accent. Currently living in New York City, she told me that this was her fourth time to *the Voice* session, and it had changed her life. She had never met Braco in person, but she stated that she could clearly feel him through his voice. Her problem had been an extreme fear of being alone, and she had been unable to sleep alone in her apartment at night. Then she heard of Braco and came, and when she arrived *the Voice* was playing for groups.

Now, because of Braco, she happily told me that she was so strong, and unafraid that she could sleep in a graveyard at night alone without problems. Braco had done this and more in her life, and she wanted me to know that she felt she owed her new confidence and more to him, her life had improved in so many numerous ways. Currently, she had stopped in at Srebrnjak 1 once again, since she was visiting family, just to feel the joy of the energy through Braco, and to carry this home with her back to America. Her love and gratitude was filled with the grace of a woman who had found something shining within herself. I thanked her for sharing her story, and knew it would help others to understand even this was enough, nothing more was needed.

Rudi would tell me after the woman left that many people shared such stories with him on the days that only *the Voice* played. This gave me a stronger glimpse into the future, of Braco's legacy that would soon expand across Europe to be offered at more locations to groups. It would support the people through their lives, and the trials of our challenging times. Then it was time for me to leave for the airport, and I was able to express my love to Branko, Rudi, Stevo and everyone else that had shown me such kindness and warmth during my stay. They had truly made me feel like a part of their special family, and I told them we would meet again, perhaps sooner than we thought possible, for the energy could do absolutely anything.

Braco and Gazing into the Future

Awakening is upon humankind, it is the destiny of our age, and it is the prerequisite for that prophesied Golden Age that is the next chapter in the history of our world. Perfect balance is the key, and it begins with a balance between body and spirit. Once this is achieved, then the mind next can be strengthened so that it is no longer susceptible to the negative thoughts and influences of the collective slumbering contrivances of a world based only upon surface appearances. Braco lives in this perfect balance, and the energy he is able to offer because of his stable foundation is the tool to spark the spirit back into harmony with the body and mind, to realign our lives back to our natural state of purity and equilibrium. This is our birthright.

The proof of this next evolutionary stage on the planet is Braco himself, for he embodies the template for what is possible for all of us. His mysterious gift can awaken and transform those who would come to him, to help people rise up toward his level of consciousness, and when enough have done so, all will change. Therefore, he himself becomes a key to this golden future that is now at our door. Through his work, light can again govern hearts and lives, enabling those who open to it to move briskly forward with a determination and focus that cannot be stopped or detoured. It is the will of the Source of All itself to bring this to us home, to bring home spirit to our natural world to govern again.

Professor Schneider of Switzerland aptly stated that the doctor is our first level of treatment for the body and general health. When the doctor is not able to help, or at least not to a person's satisfaction, then the healer is next to be consulted as the second level of treatment. Braco represents a third level that embodies whole life transformation and awakening, and at this level, not only the body, but also the life ills and challenges are overcome, and the individual regains an awareness of personal inner strength and the answers within. The ability to fly and soar through life is restored.

Consciousness is changing on our planet, and it requires people's hard work, and devotion to right the wrongs we have inflicted upon each other and our natural world. Braco is living a life devoted to an energy unlimited in its scope, and power to transform consciousness and any of us. His way of living is simple, and one to be emulated in its respect and love of nature, of living consciously in the present moment, of becoming childlike once again, open to spontaneity and inspirations of the spirit, and treating all people equally despite their flaws and shortcomings, thus acting with kindness to all.

Our destiny is calling for all of us to open our hearts now, and it is no coincidence that the power behind Braco's gaze acts most potently with the wishes of the heart. For the heart is the direct channel to spirit, and it holds our individual perfection that once heard, fulfills our lives and our finest dreams. More and more people are having spiritual encounters, an expansion of their hearts in precious moments, experiencing a love for all people, nature and the planet. In time, nothing less than an experience of unity, achieved through a natural balance of mind, body and spirit will touch the majority of people in this world, as our inheritance of the remembrance of who we really are, and why we are here.

Braco's power and strength is developing, perhaps in direct tangent to the power and strength of people's awakening consciousness ready to be guided to a next step, and as he grows, so will we. That is the way of the divine; there is a natural unfolding and process at work, and people are not offered more than they can truly handle. With the beginning of 2010, Braco will begin his journey out of Europe, first to the United States, and soon after to new destinations. He has not done so before because the timing was not right. Ivica prophesized with great insight that Braco would not come to America until a shift in the consciousness within the nation had taken place, and now it has and we are ready.

Help always comes once we are ready to accept it, and open the door to allow it to enter. Braco has never given an interview to the media and has never advertised himself, he has allowed his work to flow and evolve naturally, and ten years ago he told his staff that someone from America would come to bring him out of Europe. Now that future prediction becomes the present, and so opportunity comes before us. Drago Plecko, the Croatian scientist, called Braco's gaze similar to a phenomenon in India known as Shaktipat, the conferring of the divine grace by someone who has achieved an elevated state of union with the divine energy him or herself.

Many will try to understand the great mystery of Braco's gaze, placing labels; those spiritually minded as well as the scientists will use our latest understandings to explain, but this is not only unnecessary, but a hindrance. Scientific explanations create boundaries, as do spiritual labels; they do not help us to open our hearts to the innate beauty, wisdom and magnificence of the mysterious gift at hand. Such things only distracts from the experience of the feelings invoked. Feelings are too big to be explained by mere words and our limited concepts, which only offer a mere shadow of the whole. When and if the answer is needed, it will be made perfectly clear, but until such a time it is best not to categorize or decipher that which is one of the glorious unknowns of the universe at work.

Ivica specifically called Braco a child of Atlantis. He also said that during this time period, the children of Atlantis would awaken and set things right in the world, and that a Golden Age was dawning. Ivica lamented that people had no idea what was really lost in that time period in our ancient history, our real history. Braco would give me two books by Ivica that had been translated into English. The prophet wrote in one that humanity fell asleep due to dramatic events, and would begin to reawaken now. This transformation in consciousness is being experienced globally.

Interestingly, a modern sage from Russia named Anastasia, written about by Vladimir Megre in a book series over the last ten years entitled, *The Ringing Cedars*, tells a similar account of humanity falling asleep to its true spiritual nature. It too speaks of our current awakening, and the absolute need for people to love and live off the land again, to live more simply and to embrace nature. Braco is coming out to the world to help us all reestablish, and awaken that inner spark within so that we are not wreathing with the burdens of our lives, so we can care more about each other and all things. And this in turn will change values and priorities away from a focus on material acquisition, back to those pursuits and activities that feed our souls, and lead to a lasting wellbeing and happiness.

In the future, the work of his mission to help the people will grow, not only through his own travels, but through modern technology that can broadcast Braco live, or through a recording of his voice into countless countries, and communities that value and perceive the opportunity offered. My own first session with Braco restored the strength of my dearest dreams and brought them back to life inside of me. No one had ever given me such a gift before. And now it is my dearest wish to see the energy that made this possible accessible to all those who would seek and embrace it too. It is a gift that is absolutely free, and it is the gift that spans all possibilities.

Destiny is calling, and it is offering us an opportunity, the gift to have back our happiness and strength, and it has come in the most unexpected of ways.

TRANSCRIPT OF 'THE VOICE'

You have come to me, to Braco, to my gaze or to my voice, not knowing if you will see me or listen to my voice. But that is not important because you can't see it or hear it, you can only experience and feel it. Me, Braco, or rather my power is here for those who want it, and for those who hope to get or to feel what thousands of people have already experienced.

I am here to embrace you with the same love and warmness, with the same thoughts and wishes, and to ensure that you really get what you came for. Perhaps some will get it this time, some another time, you are the ones who decide when you will come, or rather your spiritual guide who will make you meet me. You come to me spontaneously, when you wish to come, depending on your feelings, possibilities or needs. You have found what you are looking for, you will get what you desire, depending on the Source; which will decide whose wish and how the wish will be fulfilled, whose problems will be relieved or sometimes even made to disappear. Today you are listening to my voice, some other time you will see me, and then I will try to give you through my gaze what you deserve by affecting you the same way, at the same moment, with the same love! It is not important if you are listening to me or looking at me, because you always get the same, and what you shall get is right here!

Some feel warmth, a flow ... some feel their tears. Then you will unite with me, with part of the Source, which carries help. This inexhaustible source of energy, which is flowing through your beings, will try to make you and your dearest, whose photographs you have brought along, happier, more fortunate, more sensitive, healthier. In the same way as I am touching you now through my voice with this invisible energy; respect one another, boundlessly, because you must know that the human bodies, in which our souls are living are not singular. Singular is what unifies us, what we feel.

People believe rather in what they see – in the body, and therefore respect one another depending on criteria like color of skin, appearance, gender, religion or belief. And often we forget what's in it. We forget this invisible spark, which makes us happy or sad, tired or rested. And I'm trying to help your sparks blaze more and more, and to become a flame that will warm you! Let's unify our sparks, our flames, and let us be a big sun, which will diffuse inaccessible brightness and flare, no matter where we are or with whom we are together. Let's inflame these little sparks so that they shine brightly, and that the flame of yours reaches others. Let's begin to think of ourselves; not only of our body, but also of that spark which exists in it.

Let it recover without burdening it with needless information, without thinking only of oneself, of one's appearance, without wishing only to help your own neighbor. Let's rather pass a hand of help to everyone and think positively. Don't allow yourselves to be captured in darkness and hate, because then our sparks will disappear.

Remember my beginning, Ivica's beginning. Remember how you were helped once, and how you are helped today. In the past, my spark was much less intense, and I was not able to help you on a big scale. Touches, conversations, advice and signatures were necessary, and now only one look or the voice.

Look around you; turn to your neighbor next to you. Why is he here and does he get what he came for? Exchange your experiences, talk to one another and be pleased. Why? Because your souls derive from the same place, from the same Creator who decides what, how, and how long something exists on this planet. We are all living in the same world, and that's why you shall make the first move right here, in this room, in which you also hear my voice. Take the first step and step up to the other, so that you can later, when you have left this room, talk to another, meet the challenges of life.

Respect your spark, which is your SOUL and which carries life! Me, Braco, will be here for you, whenever you want it, and I will try to light up the path you are treading, by having the wish to get you to know yourselves! Come again when you feel the wish, or need for it in order to affiliate to this source, to get food for your body, which will affect your healing, to inflame the spark and to feel happiness, satisfaction and pleasure!

That is what I can offer you. The possibility to get to something through me, and it's up to you to decide, when, how much, and to what degree you will get it! I wish that you go on to carry in you what you get through my voice for a long, a very long time…and that this flame goes from your spark to others. Perhaps next time, you will look at a face of a person beside you that was brought right here by your spark! Let's become sparks that light up the darkness, and that makes it possible to take firm steps in life.

If we respect ourselves, our body, our spirit, we will understand how easy life is, and we will understand the values that were not so important to us. It will do to meet my voice or my gaze. Later on, you will tell what has happened to you. Besides, you are those who will be my judges because you are also fruits of that source, which is growing bigger and stronger.

The surface level of the life of Braco has been revealed, but there is much, much more to be told . . .

Index

ABOUT THE AUTHOR

Angelika Whitecliff is a multi-disciplinary researcher involved in the study of consciousness, energy healing, telepathic communications, anomalous archeology and humanity's ancient origin. Her radio interviews and lectures at conferences in the United States and foreign countries dynamically offer an education to the public on the topics of human evolution through transformative consciousness, the arrival of a new golden age and extraterrestrial contact.

Over the last twenty years she has worked with healers, shamans and spiritual leaders around the world to promote the work of global transformation through awakening consciousness. Angelika is on the Board of Directors for the Exopolitics Institute, writes a popular news column for the Examiner.com, is co-founder of the annual Earth Transformation Conference in Hawaii, and has a professional intuitive counseling practice.

In the past five years, Angelika has been called by the cetaceans of Hawaii and the humpback whales of the Caribbean to actively swim and forge a relationship of interspecies communication, DNA activation and mutually beneficial interactions regarding the Earth's and humanity's shifting galactic consciousness. She currently lives on the Big Island of Hawaii, U.S.A.

Websites: www.Braco.net, www.AwakeningWithin.us, www.EarthTransformation.com & GalacticDiplomacy.com

Made in the USA
Charleston, SC
26 May 2011